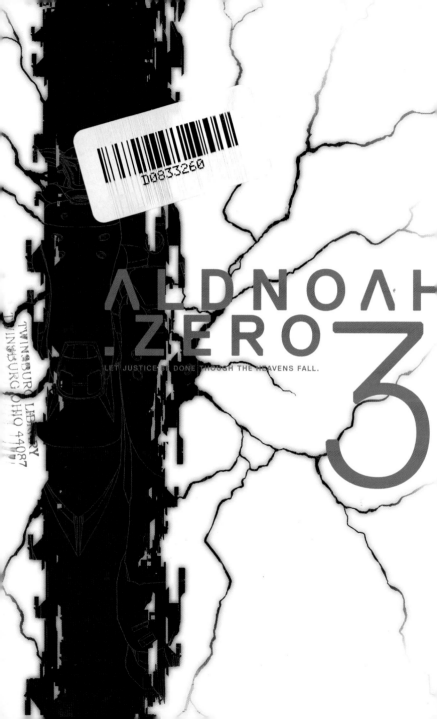

# ΛLDNOΛH ZERO 3

LET JUSTICE BE DONE THOUGH THE HEAVENS FALL.

# 3

ALDNOAH.ZERO 3
CONTENTS

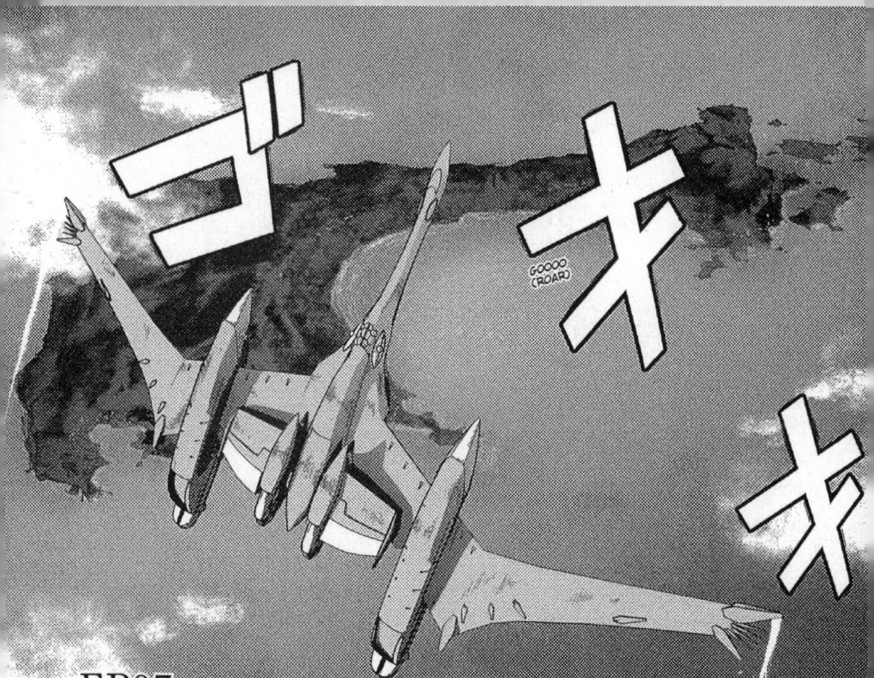
ゴォォ
GOOOO (ROAR)

# EP07 Their Chance Meeting —The Boys of Earth—

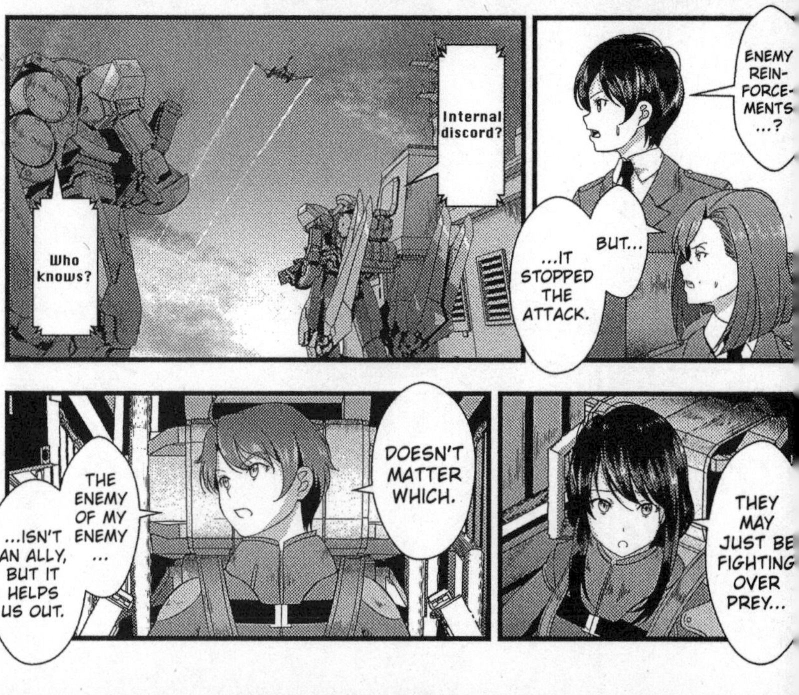
ENEMY REIN-FORCE-MENTS ...?
BUT...
...IT STOPPED THE ATTACK.
Internal discord?
Who knows?
THEY MAY JUST BE FIGHTING OVER PREY...
DOESN'T MATTER WHICH.
THE ENEMY OF MY ENEMY ...
...ISN'T AN ALLY, BUT IT HELPS US OUT.

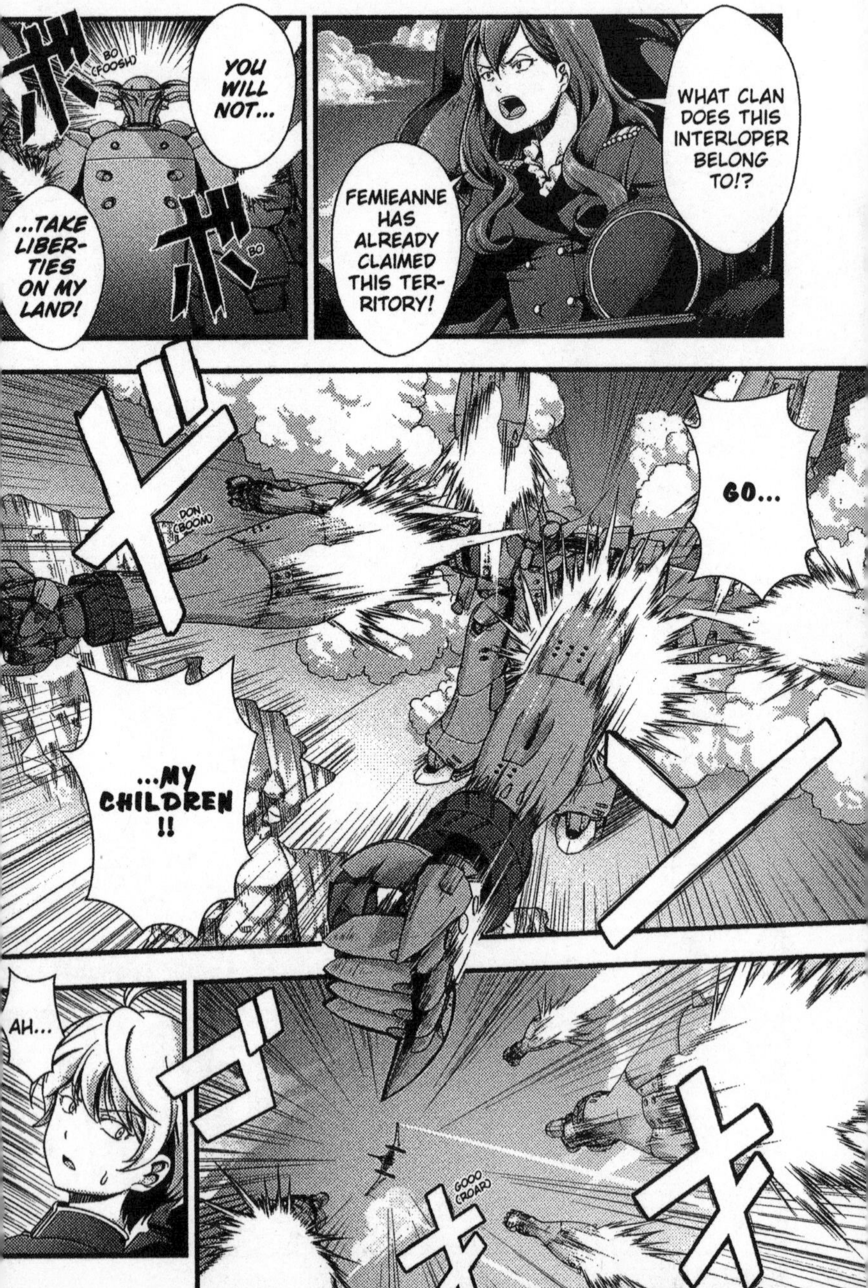
WHAT CLAN DOES THIS INTERLOPER BELONG TO!?
FEMIEANNE HAS ALREADY CLAIMED THIS TERRITORY!
BO (FOOSH)
YOU WILL NOT...
...TAKE LIBER-TIES ON MY LAND!
BO
GO...
DON (BOOM)
...MY CHILDREN !!
GOOO (ROAR)
AH...

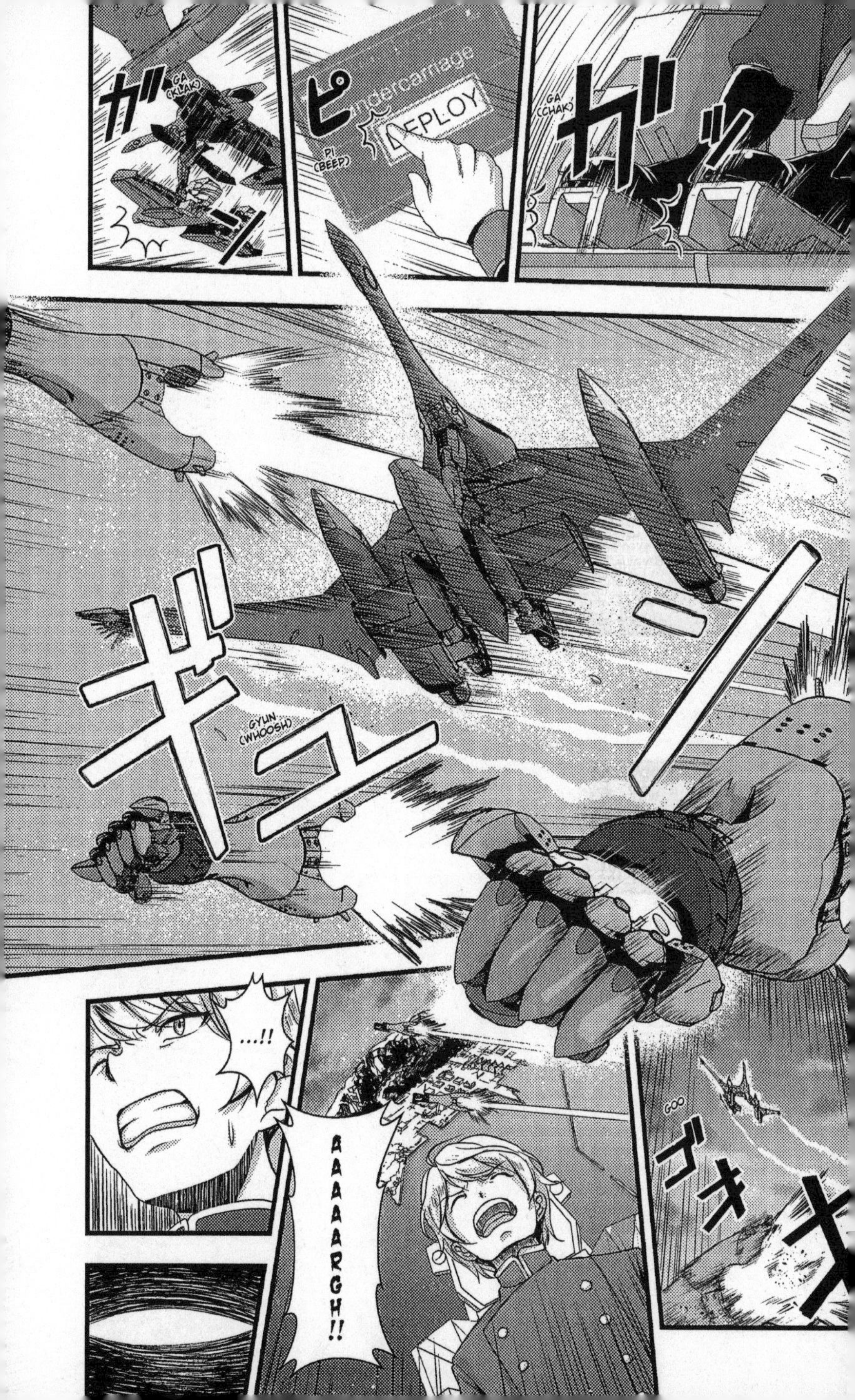
ガッ
GA (CHAK)
ピ
PI (BEEP)
ndercarriage
DEPLOY
ガ
GA (KLAK)
ギュ
GYUN (WHOOSH)
ゴキ
GOO
AAAAAARGH!!
...!!

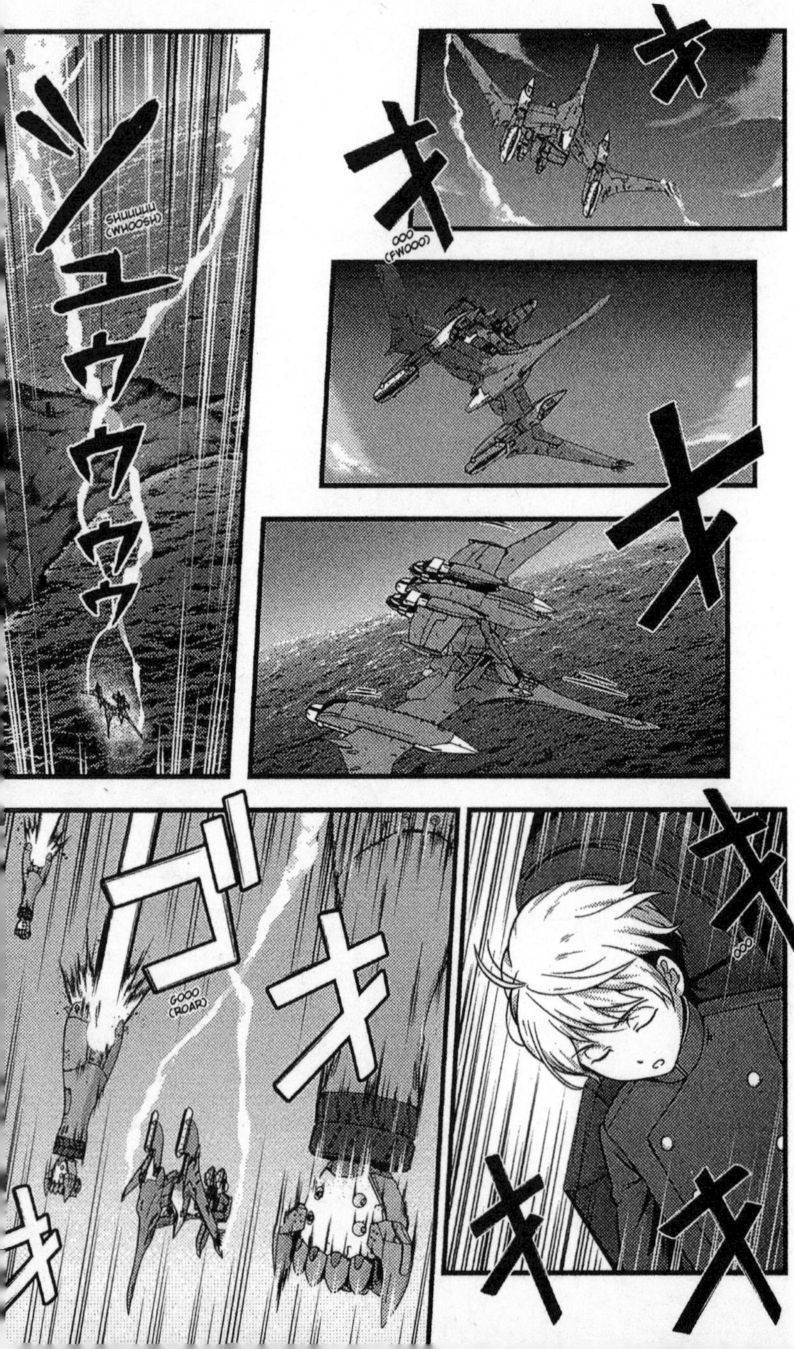
OOO
(FWOOO)
SHUUUUU
(WHOOSH)
OOO
GOOO
(ROAR)

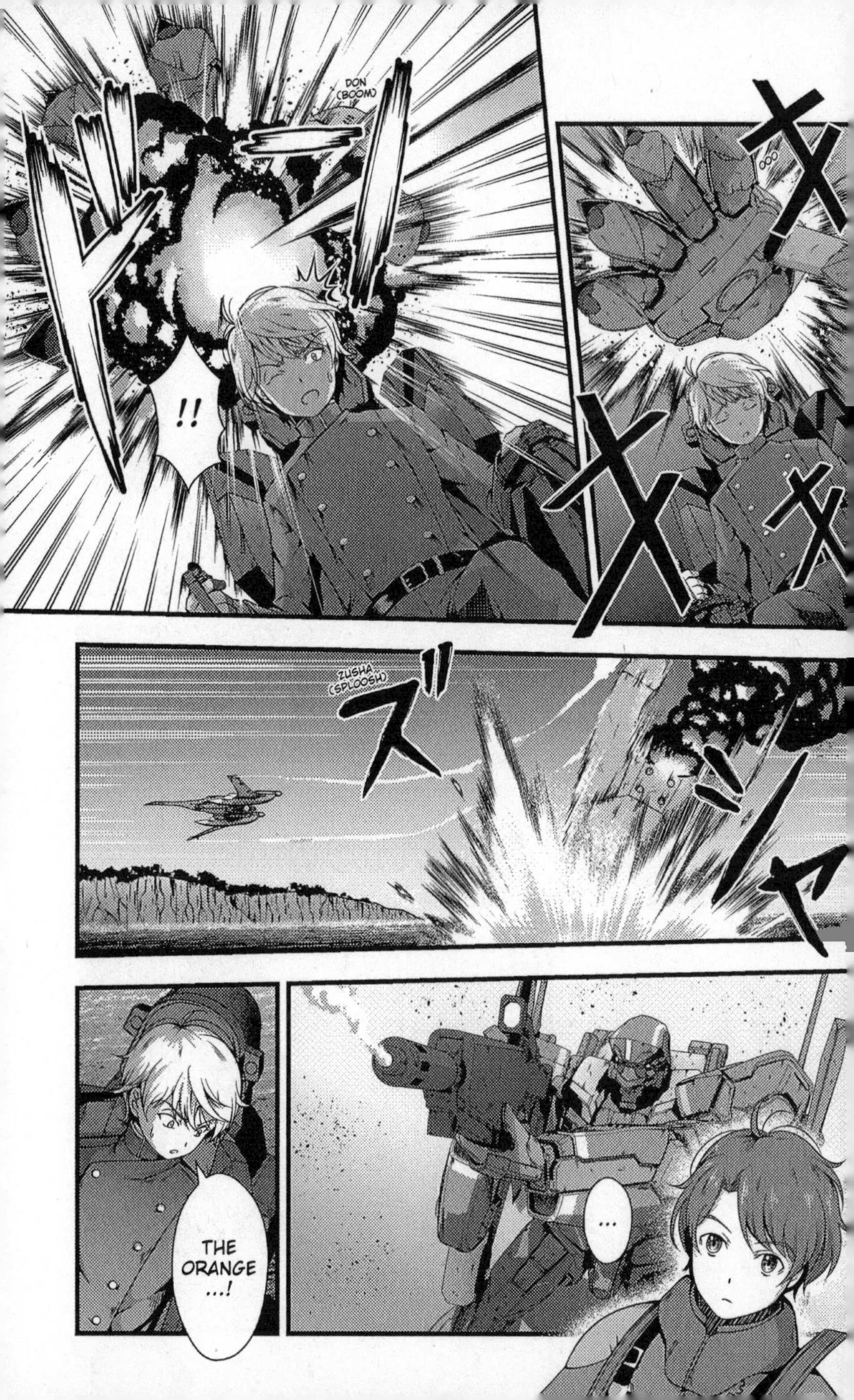
DON (BOOM)
!!
ZUSHA (SPLOOSH)
...
THE ORANGE ...!

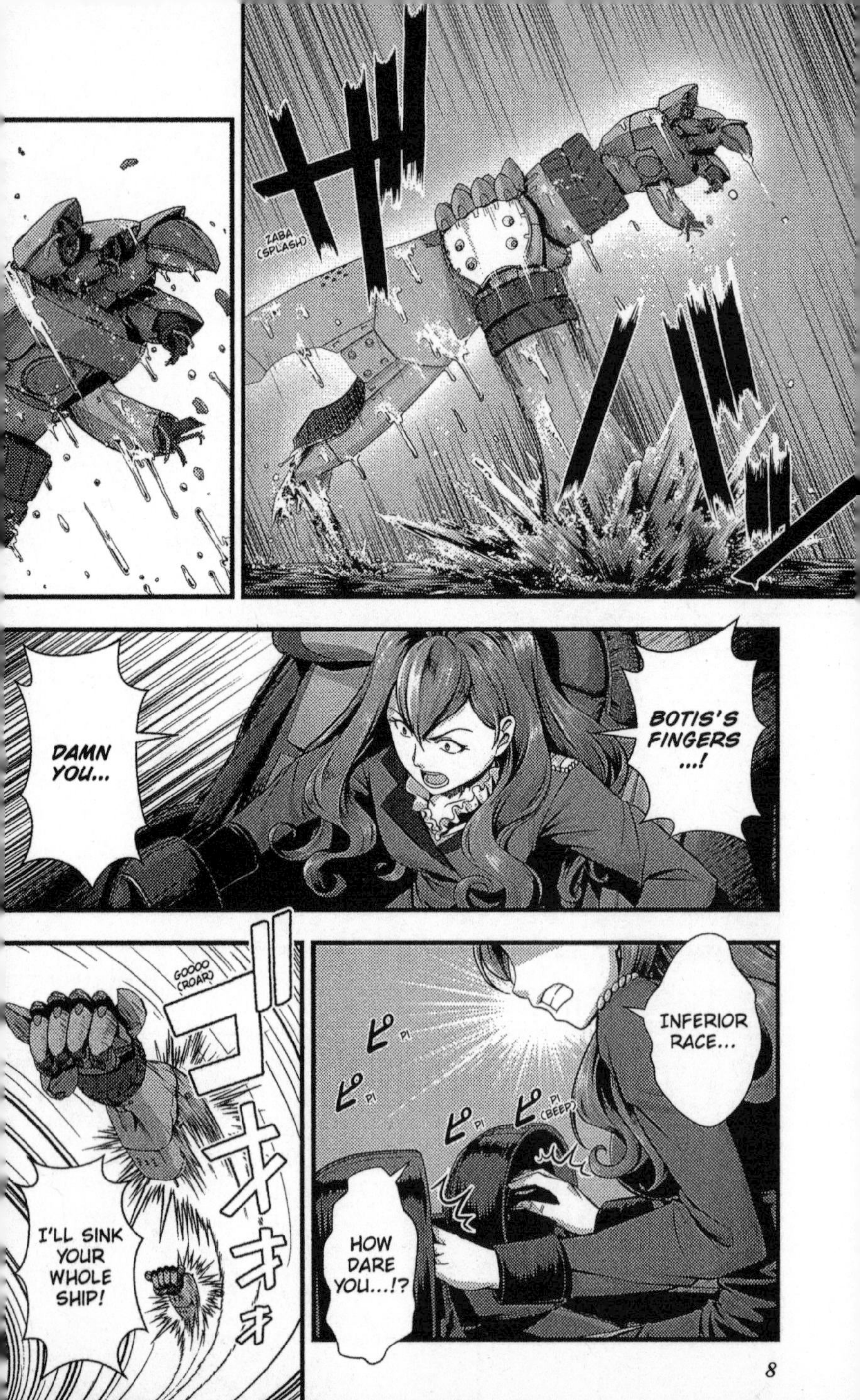
ZABA (SPLASH)
BOTIS'S FINGERS ...!
DAMN YOU...
INFERIOR RACE...
ピ PI
ピ PI
ピ PI
ピ PI (BEEP)
HOW DARE YOU...!?
GOOOO (ROAR)
ゴオオォ
I'LL SINK YOUR WHOLE SHIP!

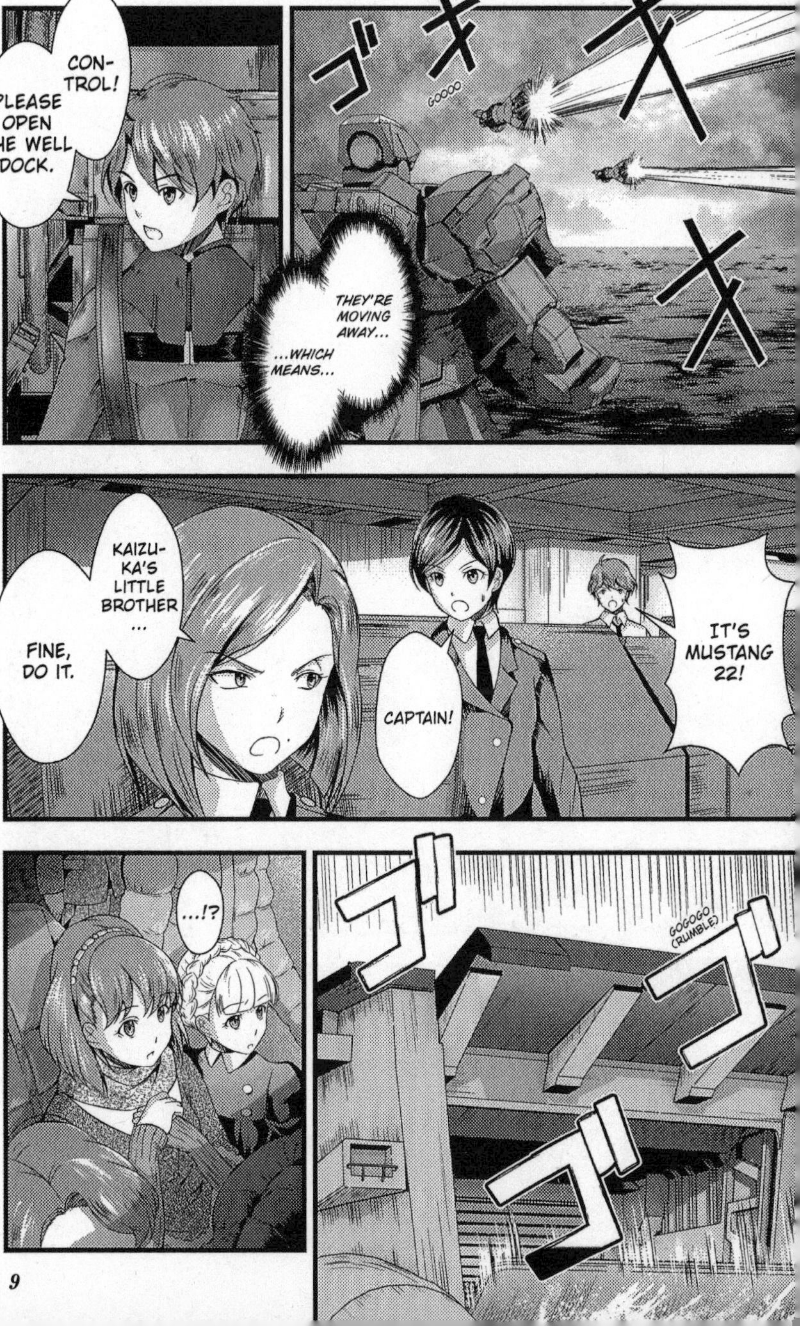
ゴオオオ
GOOOO
THEY'RE MOVING AWAY...
...WHICH MEANS...
CONTROL! PLEASE OPEN THE WELL DOCK.
IT'S MUSTANG 22!
CAPTAIN!
KAIZUKA'S LITTLE BROTHER...
FINE, DO IT.
ゴゴゴ
GOGOGO (RUMBLE)
...!?

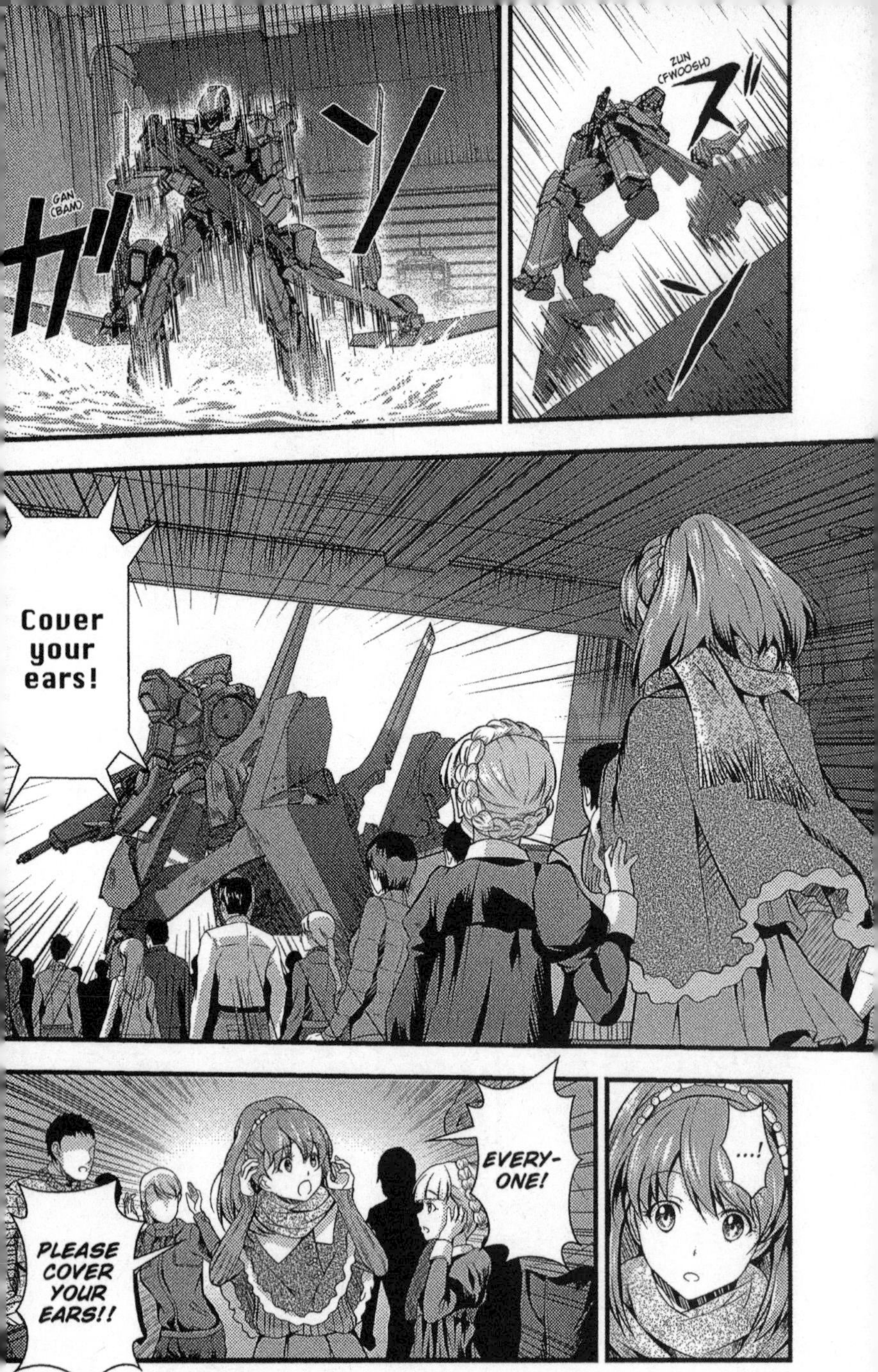

ZUN (FWOOSH)
ズ
GAN (BAM)
ガン
Cover your ears!
...!
EVERY-ONE!
PLEASE COVER YOUR EARS!!

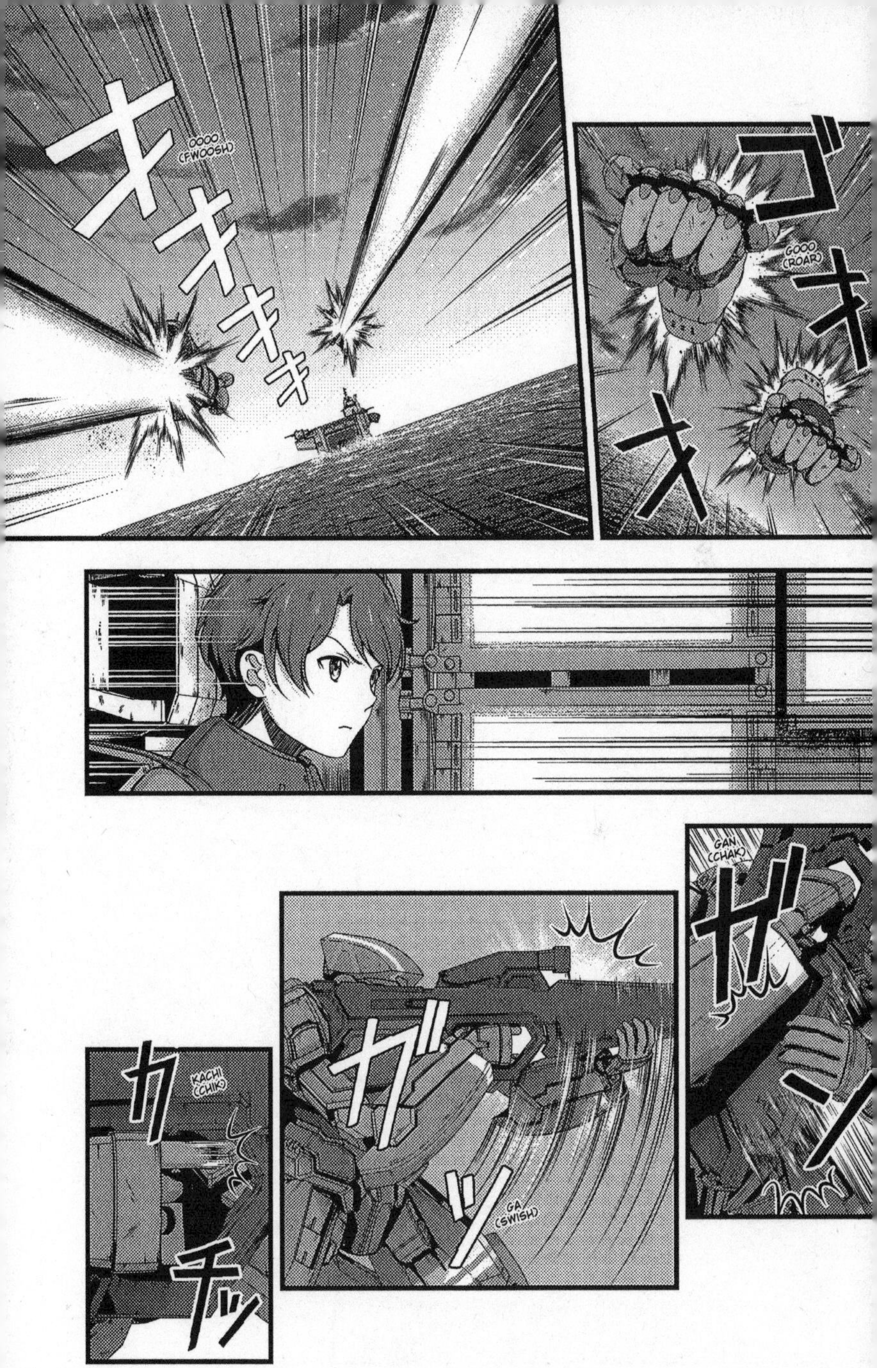
GOOO (ROAR)
OOOO (F.WOOSH)
GAN (CHAK)
GA (SWISH)
KACHI (CHIK)

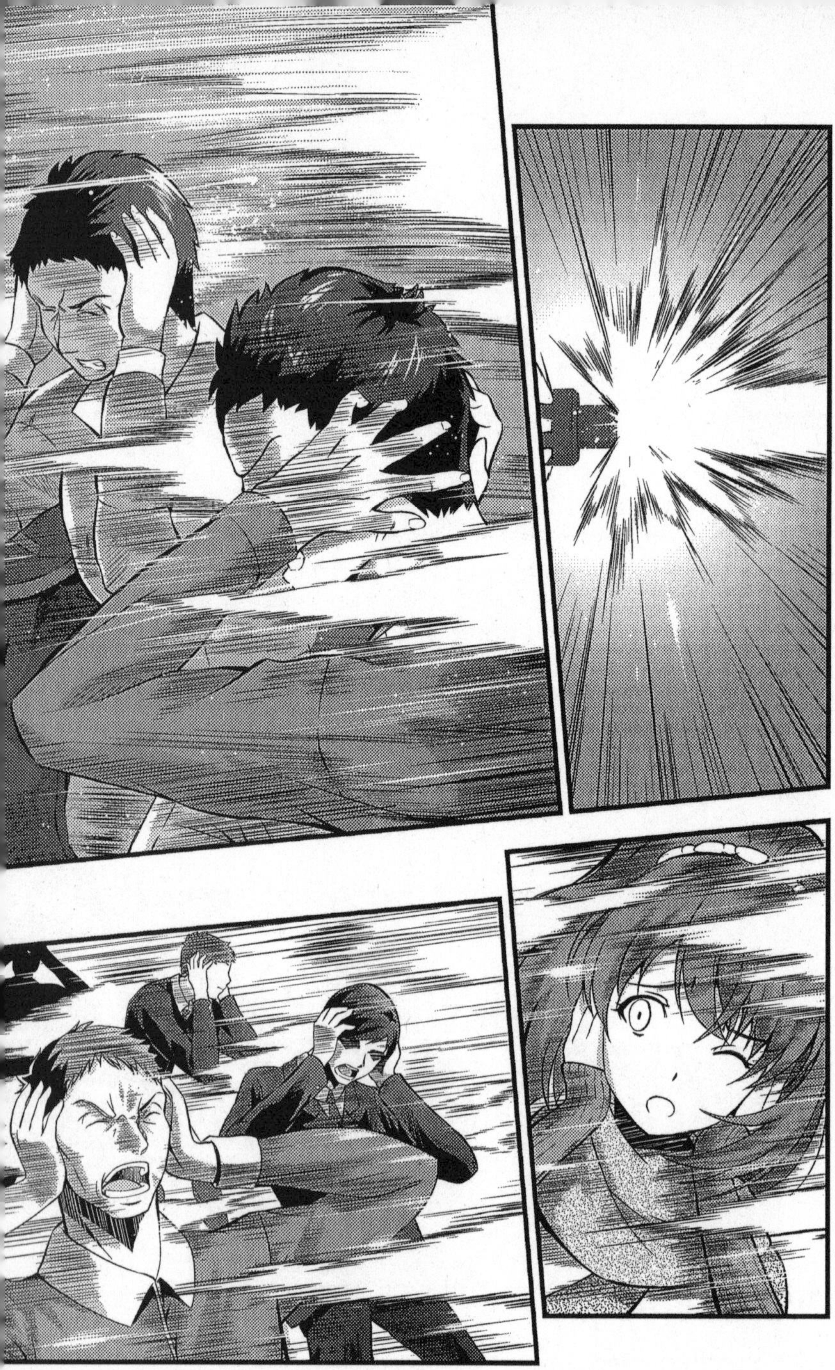

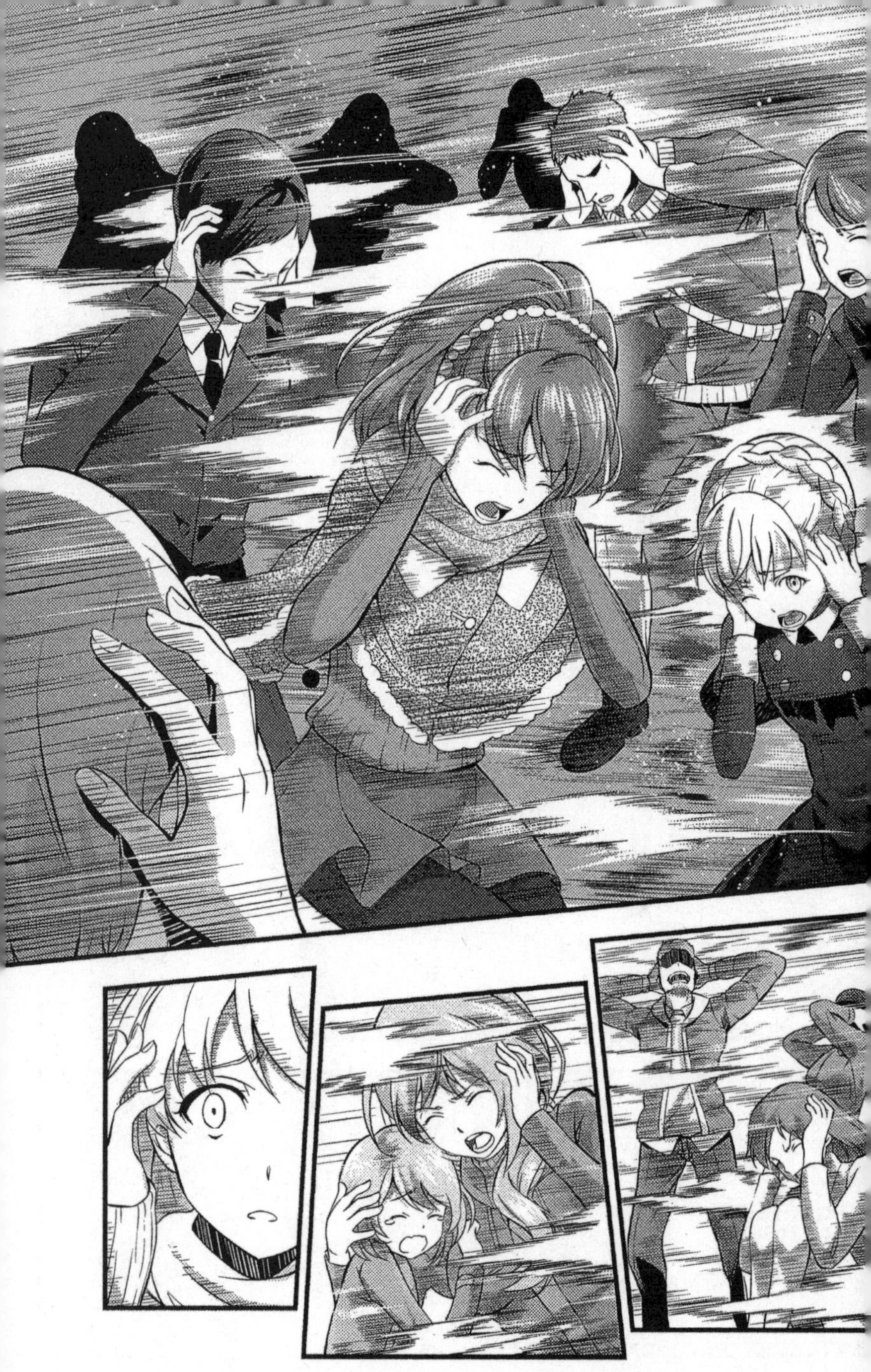

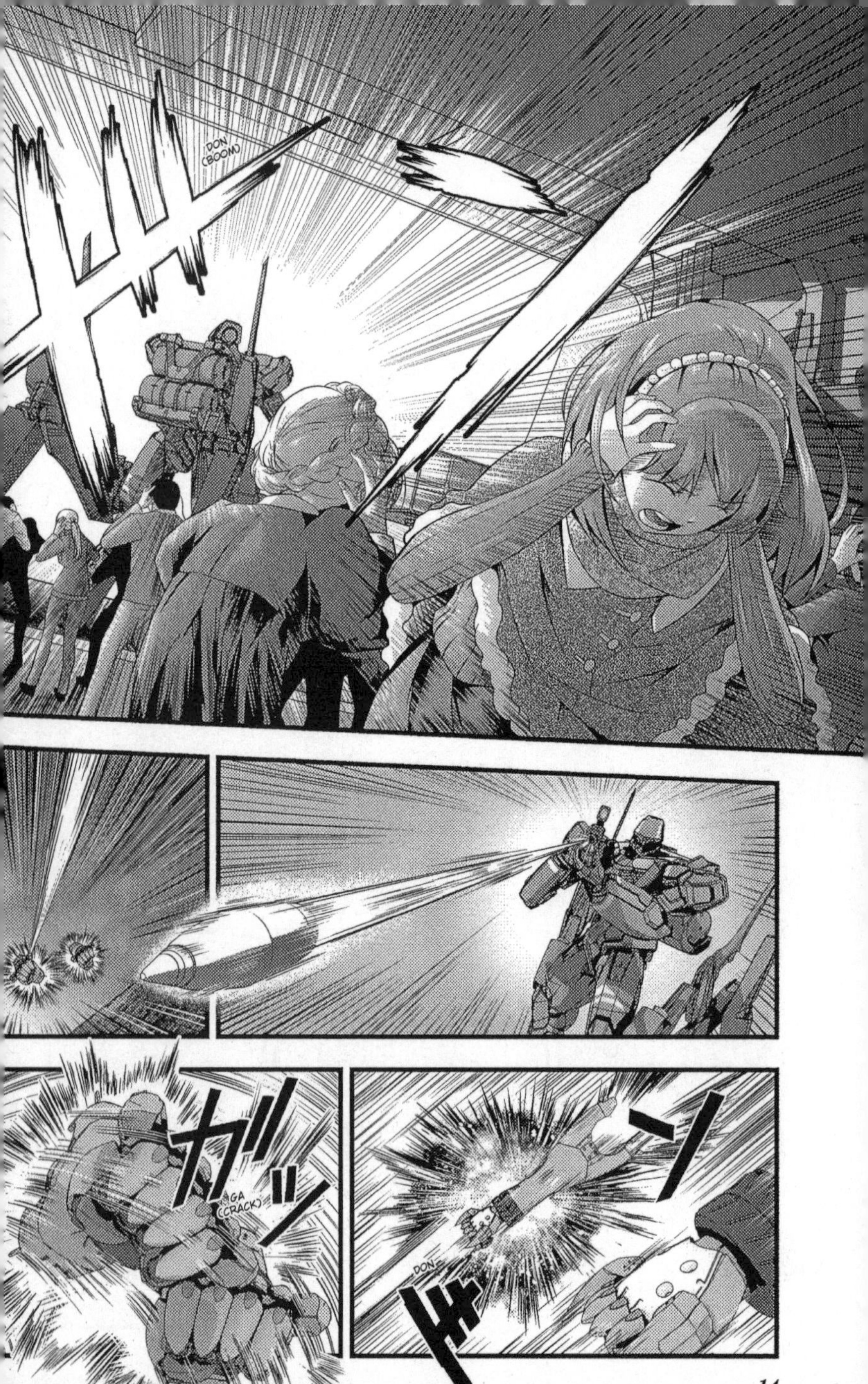
DON (BOOM)
DON
GA (CRACK)

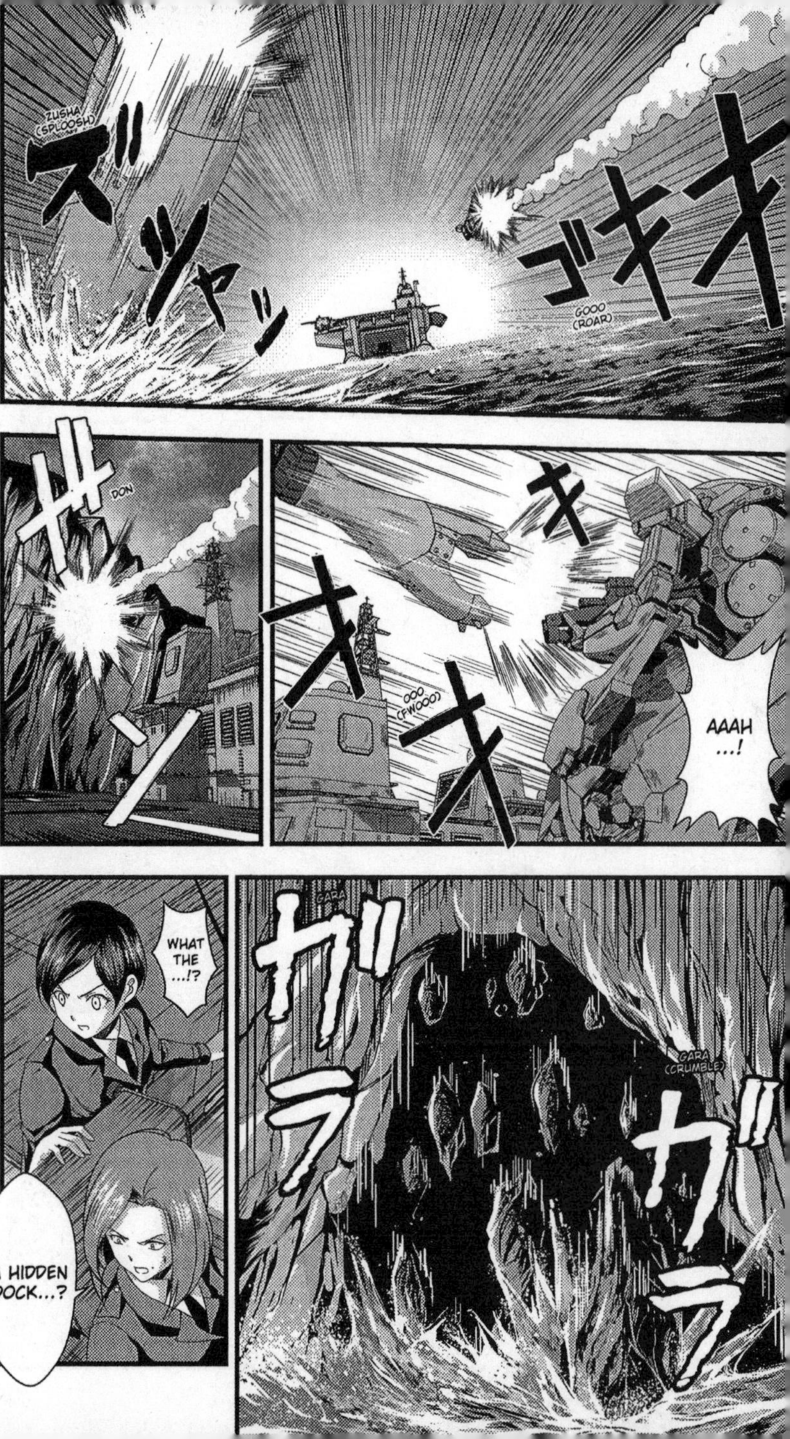
GOOO (ROAR)
ZUSHA (SPLOOSH)
AAAH ...!
OOO (FWOOO)
DON
GARA (CRUMBLE)
GARA
WHAT THE ...!?
A HIDDEN DOCK...?

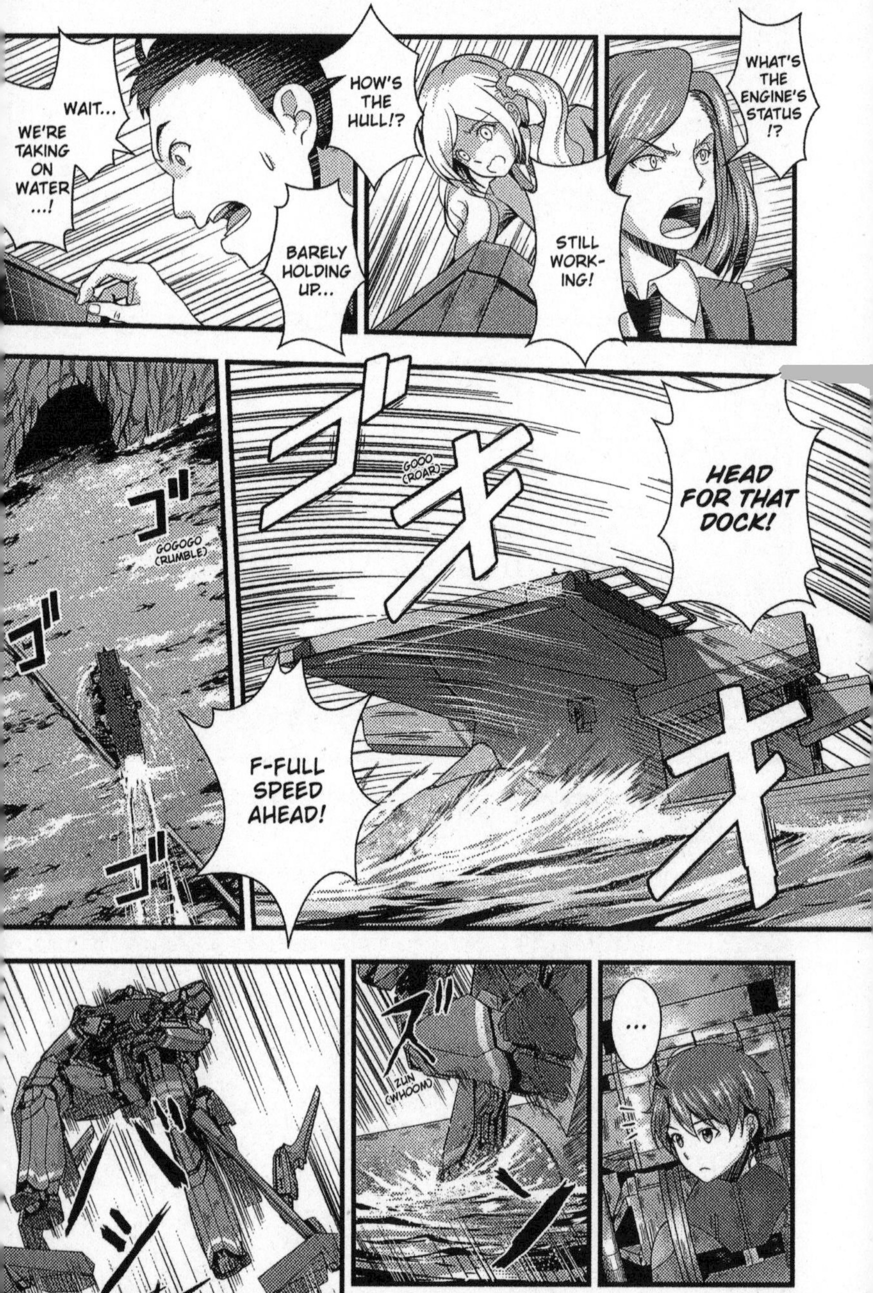
WHAT'S THE ENGINE'S STATUS !?
STILL WORKING!
HOW'S THE HULL!?
BARELY HOLDING UP...
WAIT... WE'RE TAKING ON WATER ...!
HEAD FOR THAT DOCK!
GOOO (ROAR)
F-FULL SPEED AHEAD!
GOGOGO (RUMBLE)
...
ZUN (WHOOM)
BASHU (SPLASH)

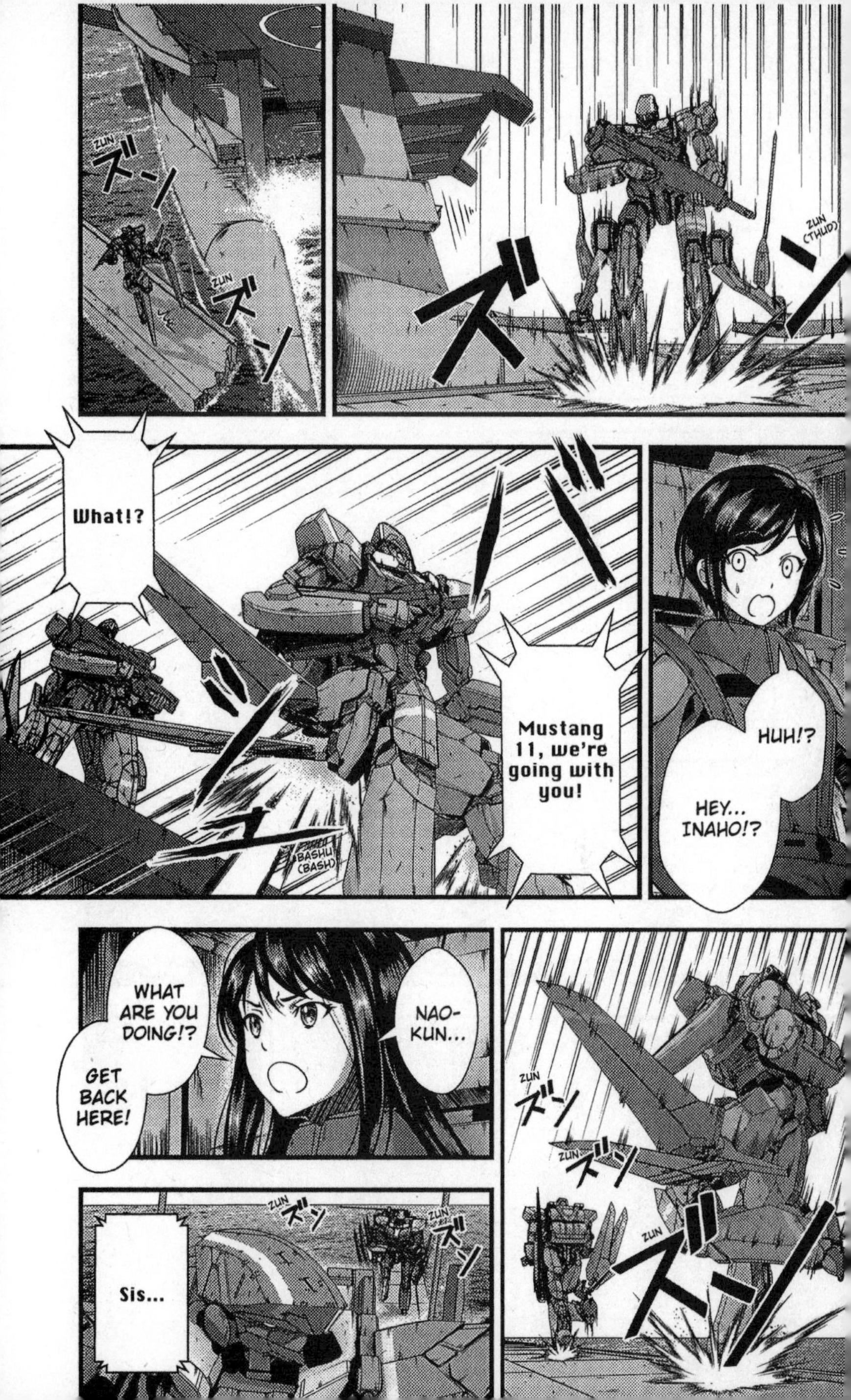
ZUN (THUD)
ZUN
ZUN
HUH!?
HEY... INAHO!?
What!?
Mustang 11, we're going with you!
BASHU (BASH)
ZUN
ZUN
ZUN
NAO-KUN...
WHAT ARE YOU DOING!?
GET BACK HERE!
ZUN
ZUN
Sis...

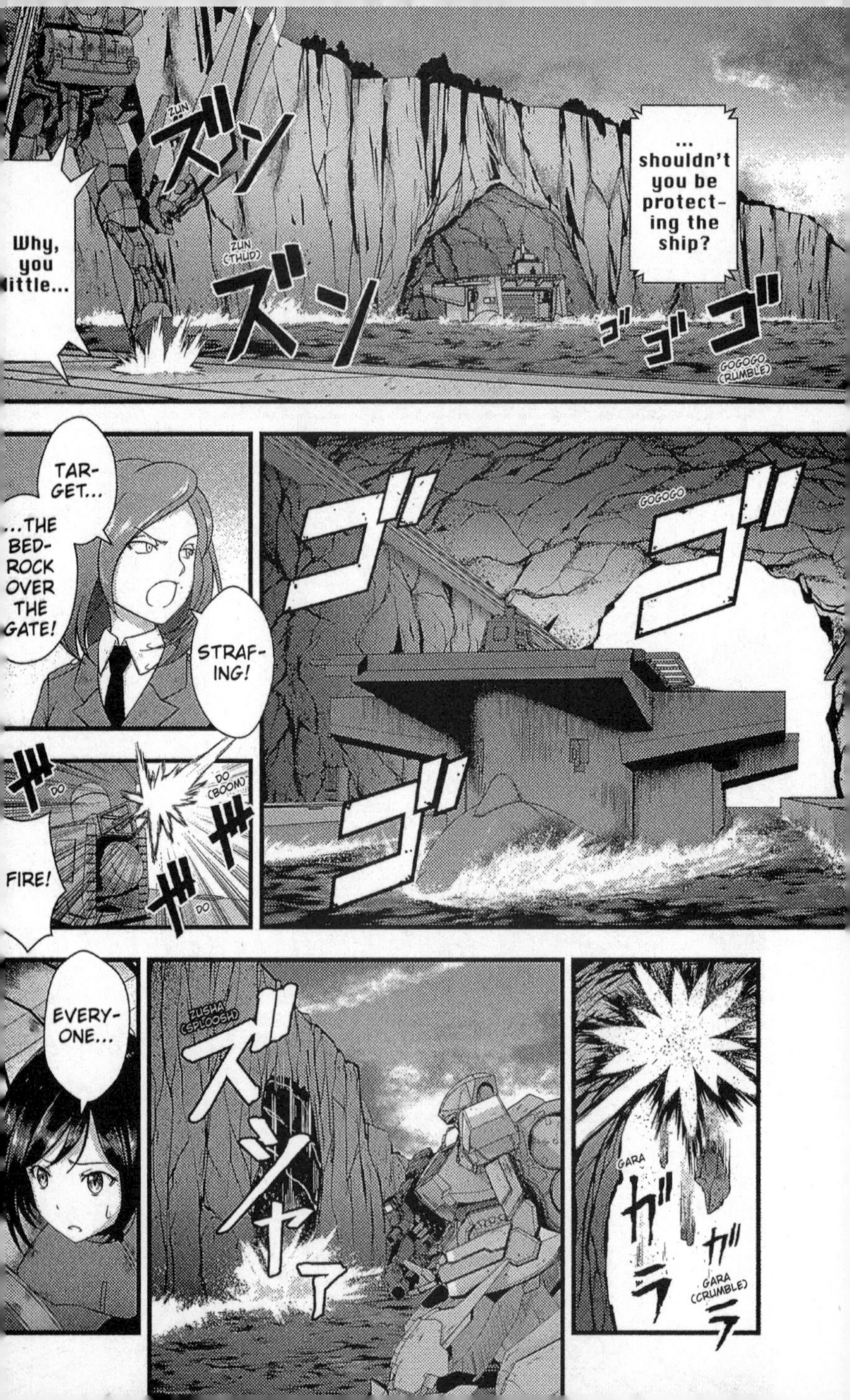

...shouldn't you be protecting the ship?
ZUN
ZUN (THUD)
GOGOGO (RUMBLE)
Why, you little...
GOGOGO
TARGET...
...THE BEDROCK OVER THE GATE!
STRAFING!
DO (BOOM)
DO
DO
FIRE!
GARA
GARA (CRUMBLE)
ZUSHA (SPLOOSH)
EVERYONE...

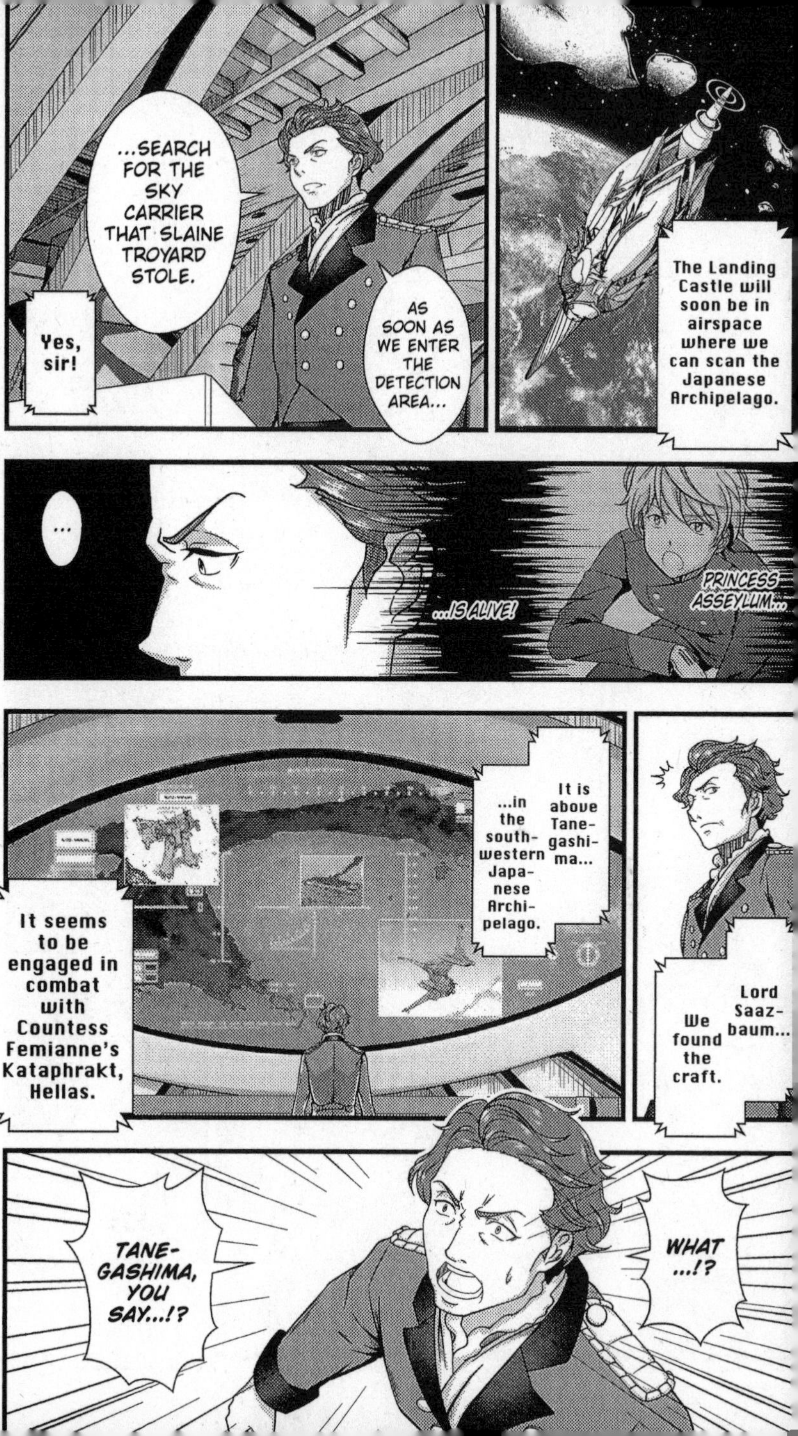
The Landing Castle will soon be in airspace where we can scan the Japanese Archipelago.
AS SOON AS WE ENTER THE DETECTION AREA...
...SEARCH FOR THE SKY CARRIER THAT SLAINE TROYARD STOLE.
Yes, sir!
PRINCESS ASSEYLUM...
...IS ALIVE!
...
Lord Saazbaum...
We found the craft.
It is above Tane-gashima...
...in the south-western Japa-nese Archi-pelago.
It seems to be engaged in combat with Countess Femianne's Kataphrakt, Hellas.
WHAT ...!?
TANE-GASHIMA, YOU SAY...!?

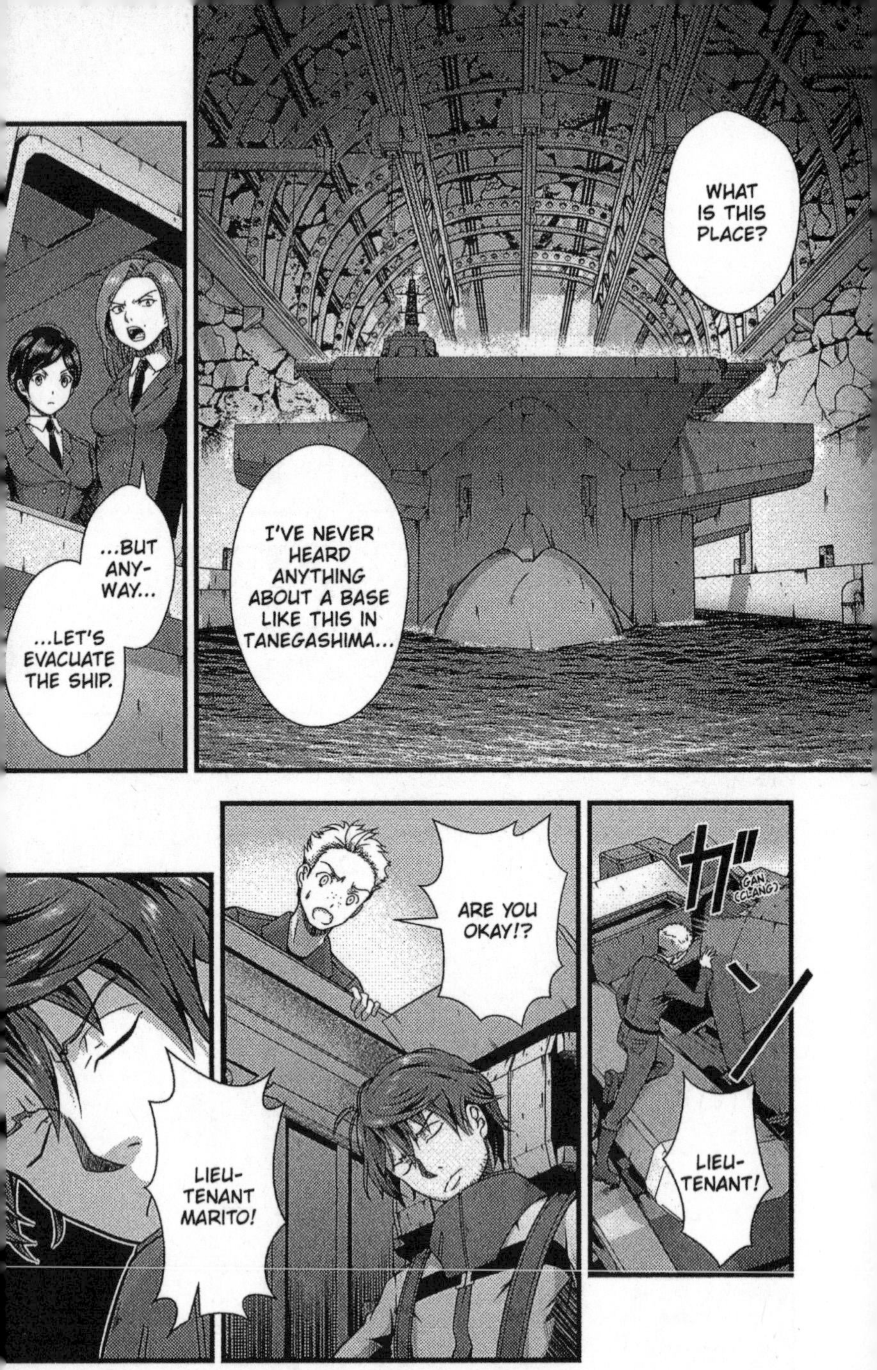
WHAT IS THIS PLACE?
I'VE NEVER HEARD ANYTHING ABOUT A BASE LIKE THIS IN TANEGASHIMA...
...BUT ANY-WAY...
...LET'S EVACUATE THE SHIP.
GAN (CLANG)
LIEU-TENANT!
ARE YOU OKAY!?
LIEU-TENANT MARITO!

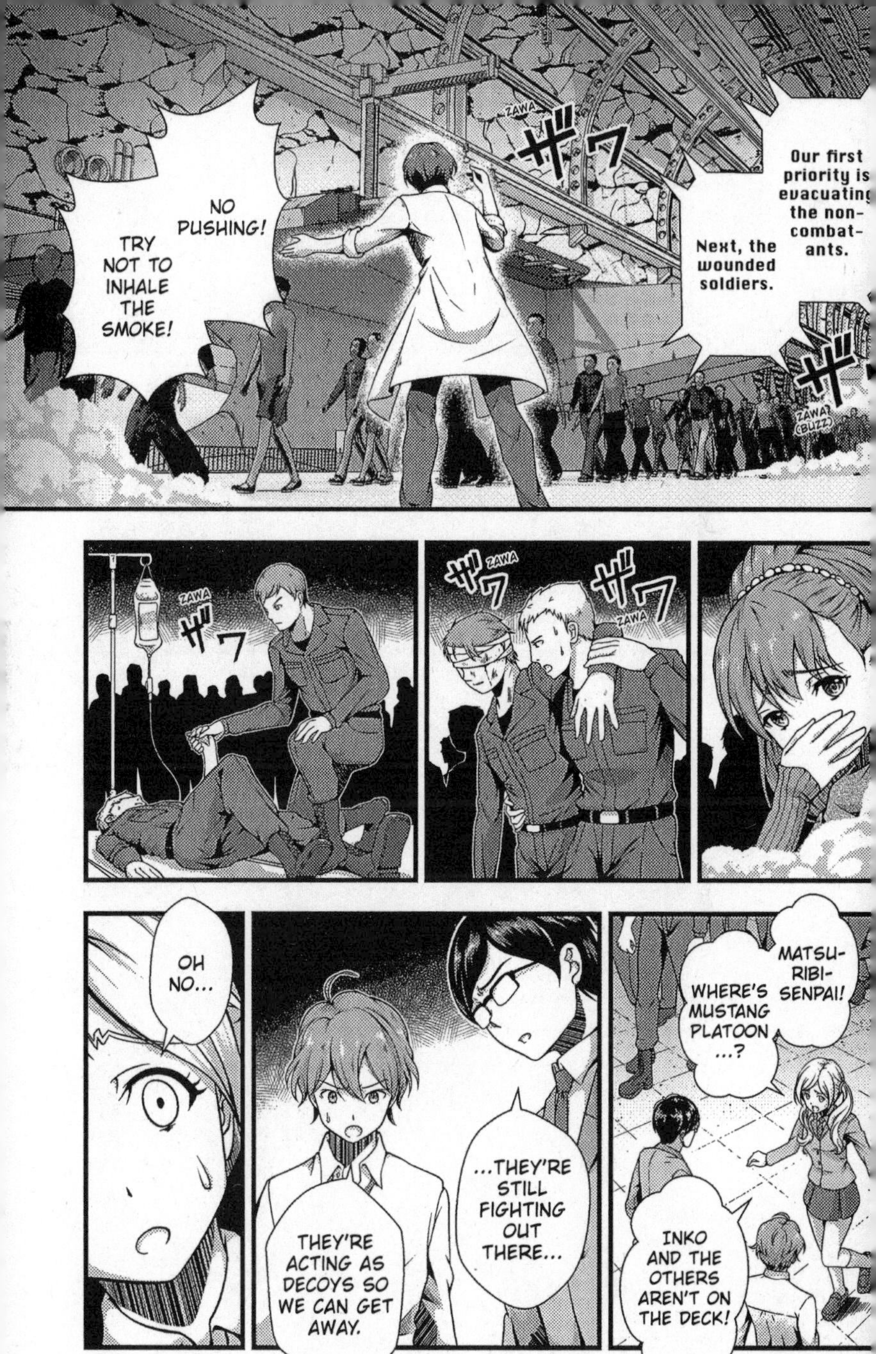
Our first priority is evacuating the non-combatants.
Next, the wounded soldiers.
ZAWA
ZAWA (BUZZ)
ZAWA
NO PUSHING!
TRY NOT TO INHALE THE SMOKE!
ZAWA
ZAWA
ZAWA
MATSURIBI-SENPAI!
WHERE'S MUSTANG PLATOON...?
INKO AND THE OTHERS AREN'T ON THE DECK!
...THEY'RE STILL FIGHTING OUT THERE...
THEY'RE ACTING AS DECOYS SO WE CAN GET AWAY.
OH NO...

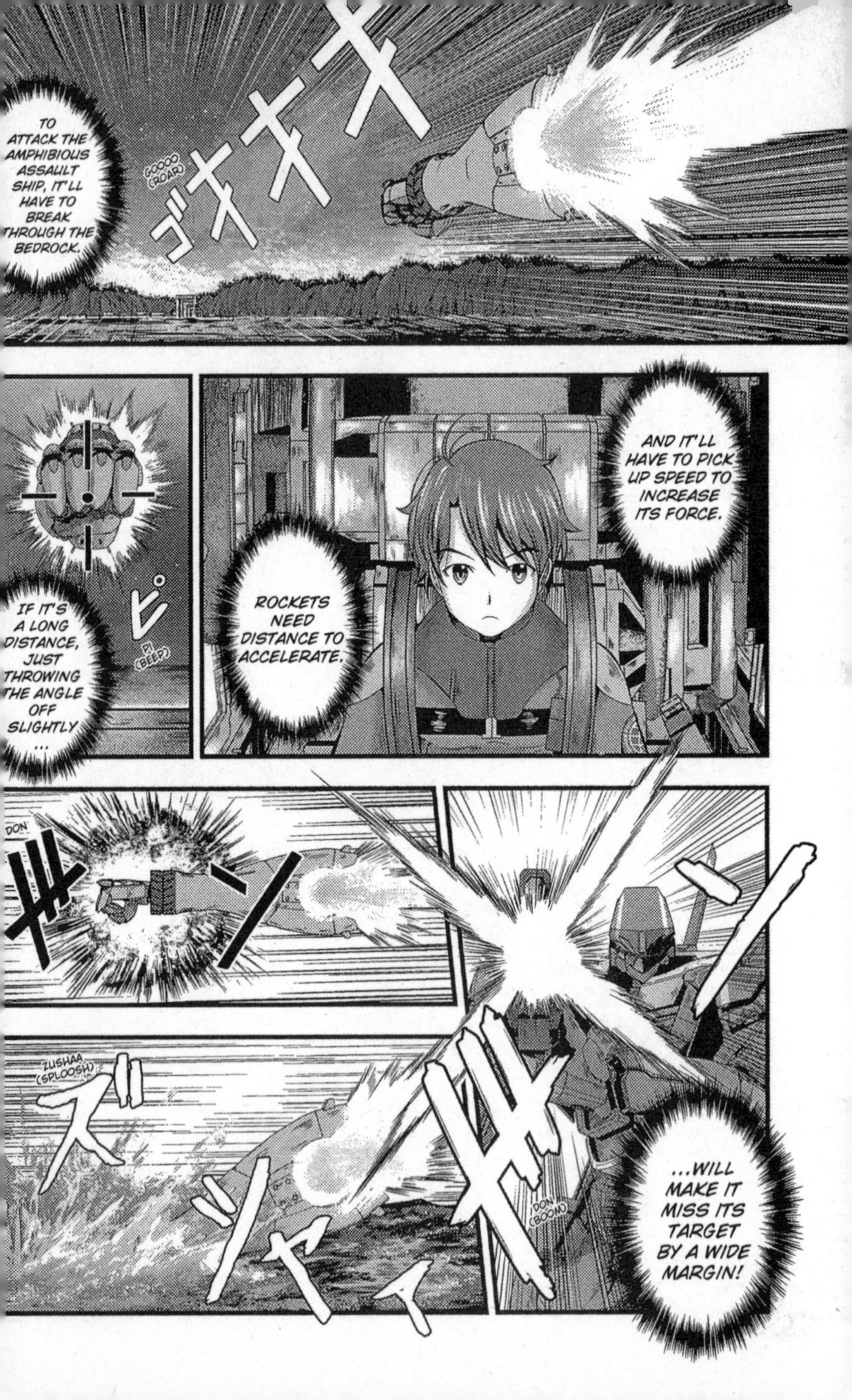
GOOOO (ROAR)
TO ATTACK THE AMPHIBIOUS ASSAULT SHIP, IT'LL HAVE TO BREAK THROUGH THE BEDROCK.
AND IT'LL HAVE TO PICK UP SPEED TO INCREASE ITS FORCE.
ROCKETS NEED DISTANCE TO ACCELERATE.
PI (BEEP)
IF IT'S A LONG DISTANCE, JUST THROWING THE ANGLE OFF SLIGHTLY ...
DON (BOOM)
...WILL MAKE IT MISS ITS TARGET BY A WIDE MARGIN!
DON
ZUSHAA (SPLOOSH)

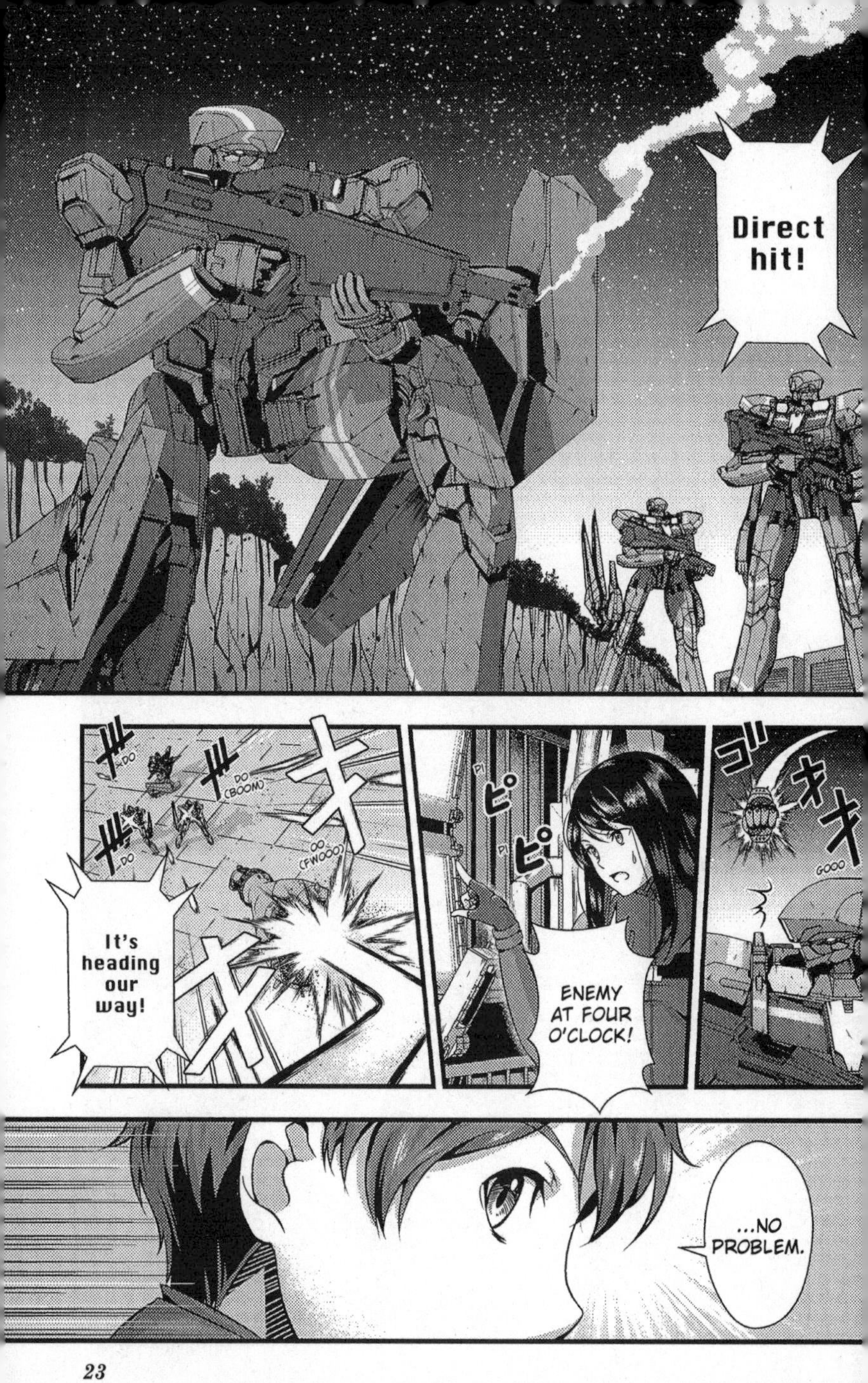
Direct hit!
GOOO
PI
PI
ENEMY AT FOUR O'CLOCK!
DO
DO (BOOM)
DO
OO (FWOOO)
It's heading our way!
...NO PROBLEM.

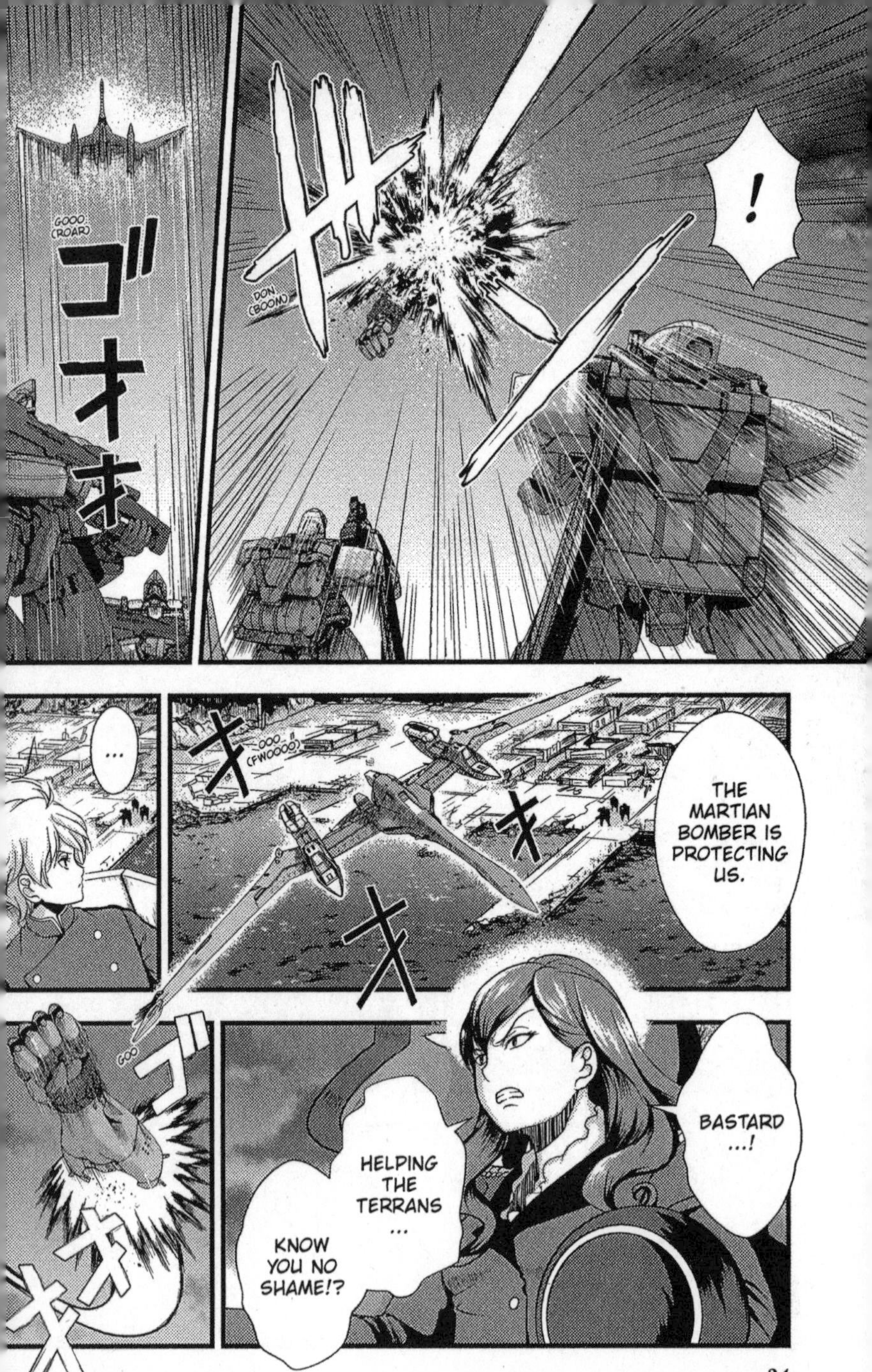
!
DON (BOOM)
GOOO (ROAR)
ゴオォ
THE MARTIAN BOMBER IS PROTECTING US.
OOO (FWOOOO)
...
BASTARD ...!
HELPING THE TERRANS ...
KNOW YOU NO SHAME!?
GOO
ゴオォ

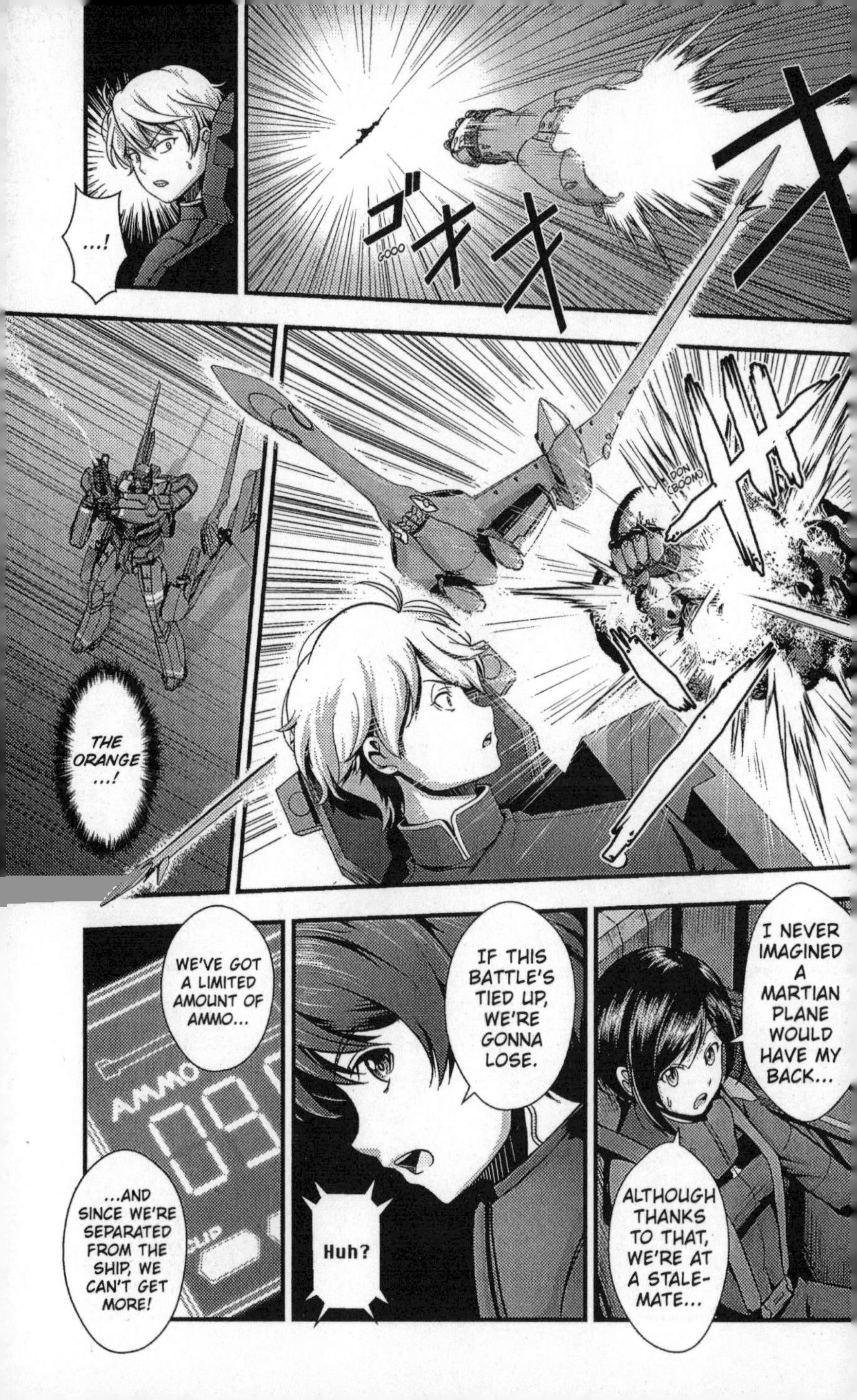

ゴォォ
GOOO
...!
DON (BOOM)
THE ORANGE...!
I NEVER IMAGINED A MARTIAN PLANE WOULD HAVE MY BACK...
ALTHOUGH THANKS TO THAT, WE'RE AT A STALEMATE...
IF THIS BATTLE'S TIED UP, WE'RE GONNA LOSE.
Huh?
WE'VE GOT A LIMITED AMOUNT OF AMMO...
AMMO
09
...AND SINCE WE'RE SEPARATED FROM THE SHIP, WE CAN'T GET MORE!

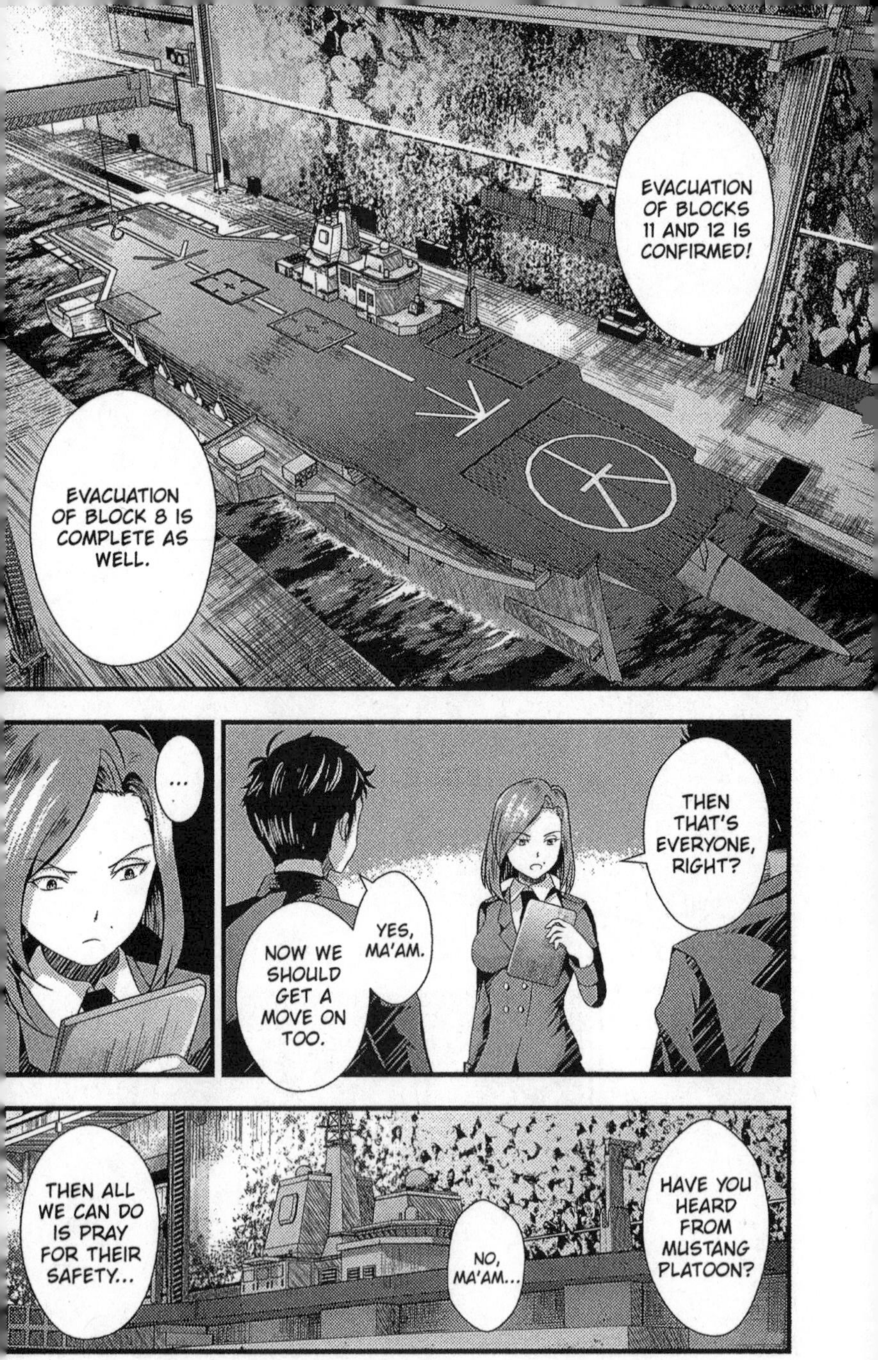
EVACUATION OF BLOCKS 11 AND 12 IS CONFIRMED!
EVACUATION OF BLOCK 8 IS COMPLETE AS WELL.
THEN THAT'S EVERYONE, RIGHT?
YES, MA'AM.
NOW WE SHOULD GET A MOVE ON TOO.
...
HAVE YOU HEARD FROM MUSTANG PLATOON?
NO, MA'AM...
THEN ALL WE CAN DO IS PRAY FOR THEIR SAFETY...

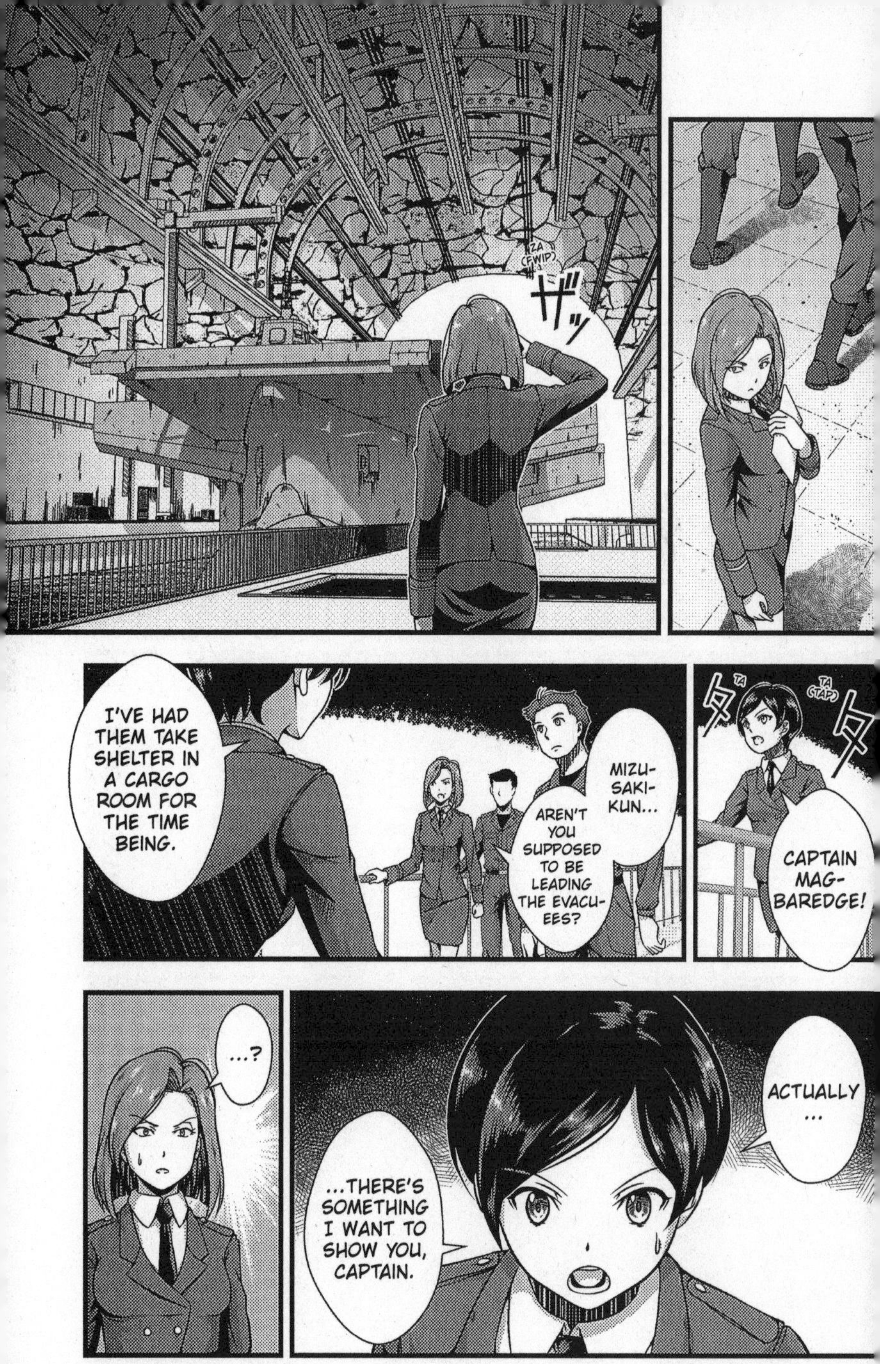
ZA (FWIP)
ザッ
TA (TAP)
タ
TA
タ
CAPTAIN MAG-BAREDGE!
MIZUSAKI-KUN...
AREN'T YOU SUPPOSED TO BE LEADING THE EVACUEES?
I'VE HAD THEM TAKE SHELTER IN A CARGO ROOM FOR THE TIME BEING.
ACTUALLY...
...THERE'S SOMETHING I WANT TO SHOW YOU, CAPTAIN.
...?

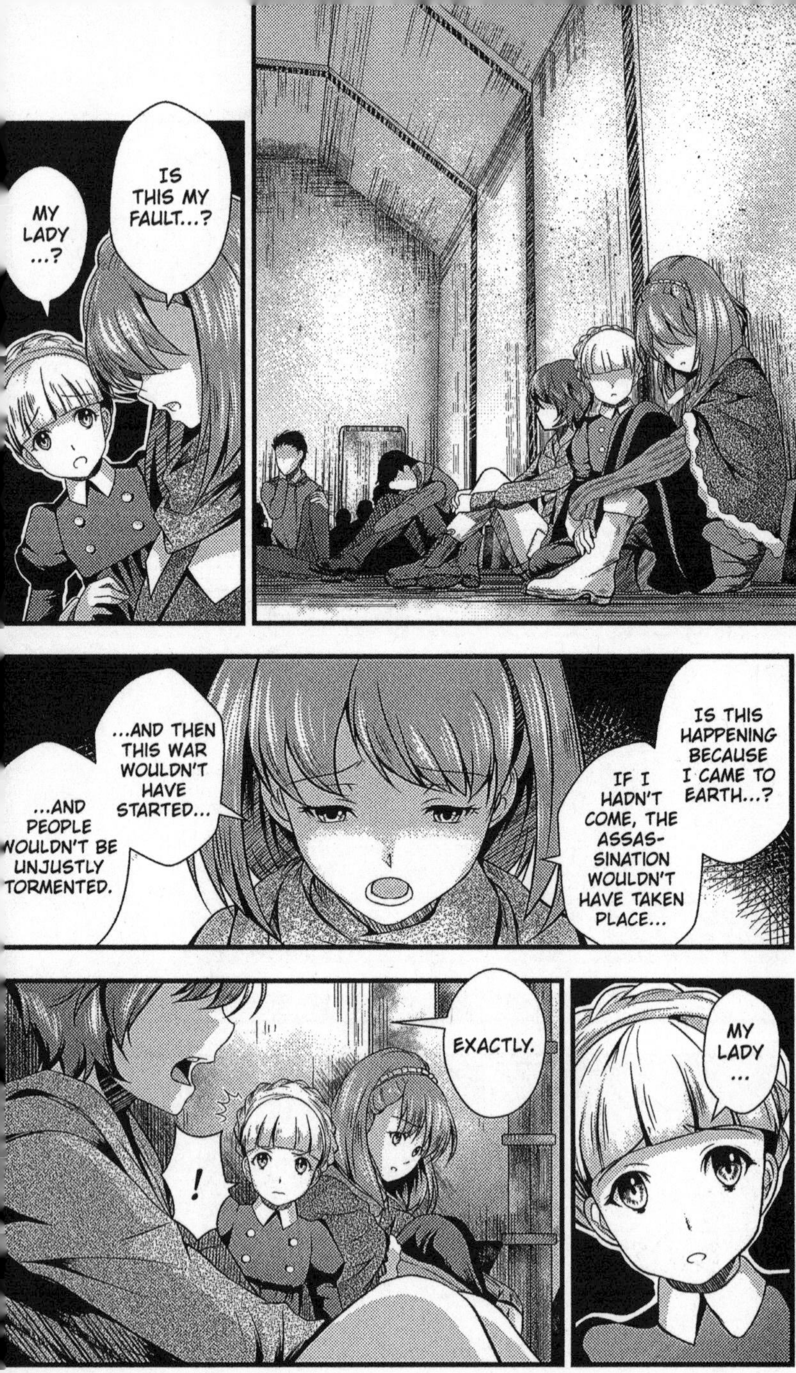
IS THIS MY FAULT...?
MY LADY ...?
IS THIS HAPPENING BECAUSE I CAME TO EARTH...?
IF I HADN'T COME, THE ASSAS-SINATION WOULDN'T HAVE TAKEN PLACE...
...AND THEN THIS WAR WOULDN'T HAVE STARTED...
...AND PEOPLE WOULDN'T BE UNJUSTLY TORMENTED.
MY LADY ...
EXACTLY.
!

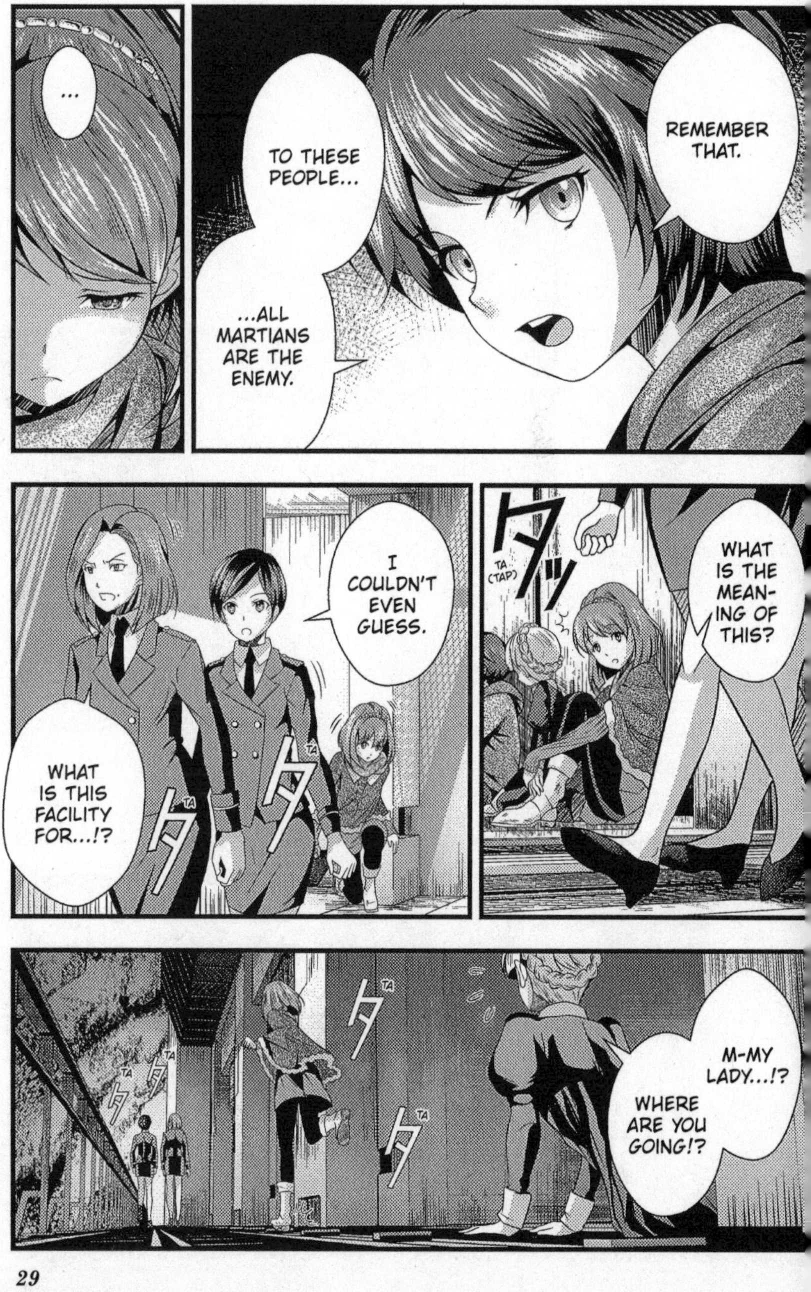
REMEMBER THAT.
TO THESE PEOPLE...
...ALL MARTIANS ARE THE ENEMY.
...
TA (TAP)
WHAT IS THE MEANING OF THIS?
I COULDN'T EVEN GUESS.
TA
TA
WHAT IS THIS FACILITY FOR...!?
M-MY LADY...!?
WHERE ARE YOU GOING!?
TA
TA
TA
TA

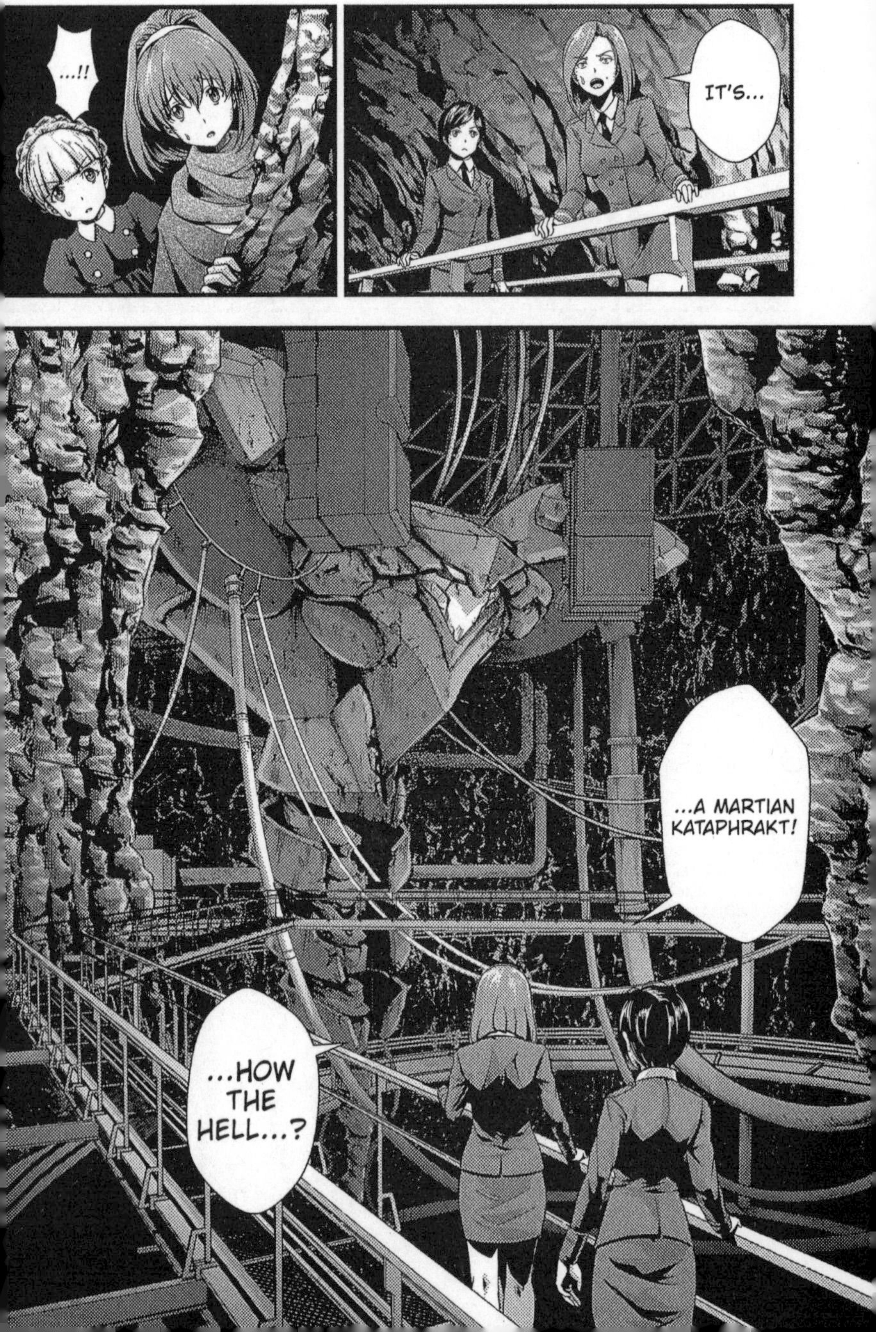
IT'S...
...!!
...A MARTIAN KATAPHRAKT!
...HOW THE HELL...?

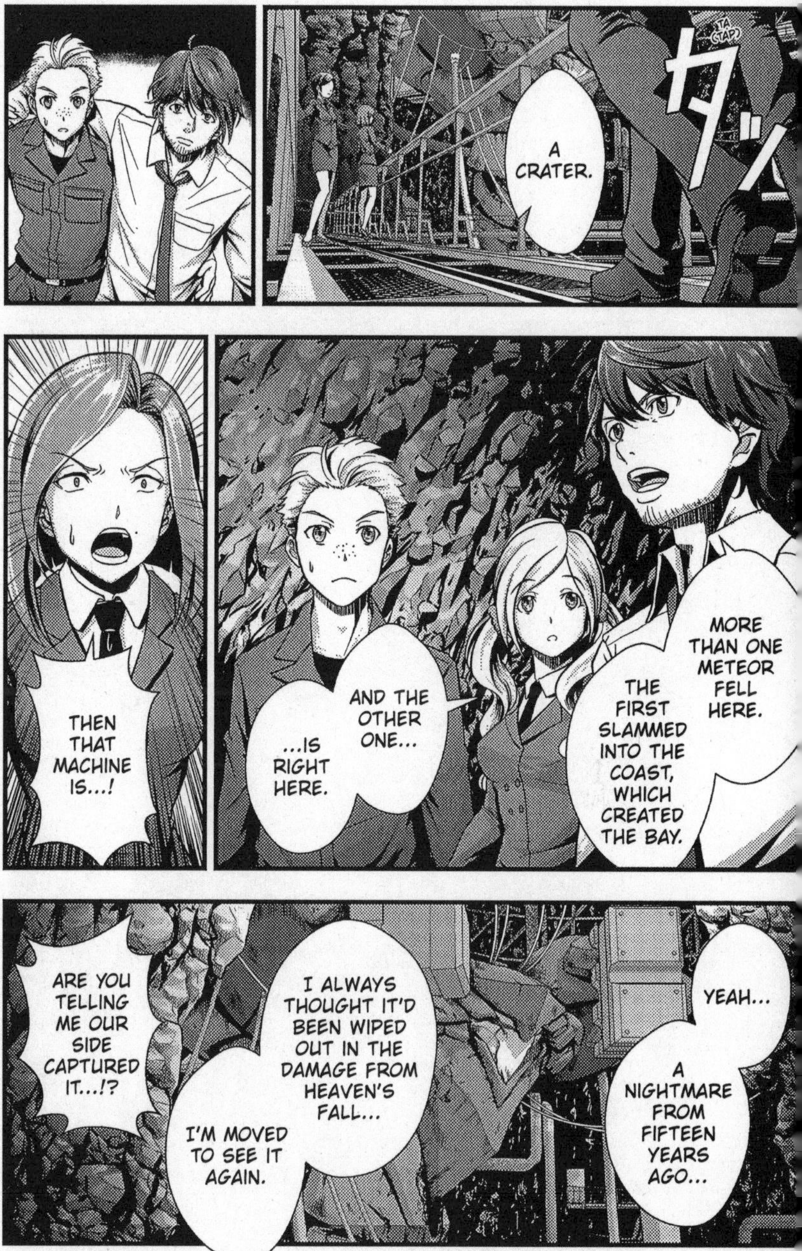
TA (TAP)
A CRATER.
MORE THAN ONE METEOR FELL HERE.
THE FIRST SLAMMED INTO THE COAST, WHICH CREATED THE BAY.
AND THE OTHER ONE...
...IS RIGHT HERE.
THEN THAT MACHINE IS...!
YEAH...
A NIGHTMARE FROM FIFTEEN YEARS AGO...
I ALWAYS THOUGHT IT'D BEEN WIPED OUT IN THE DAMAGE FROM HEAVEN'S FALL...
I'M MOVED TO SEE IT AGAIN.
ARE YOU TELLING ME OUR SIDE CAPTURED IT...!?

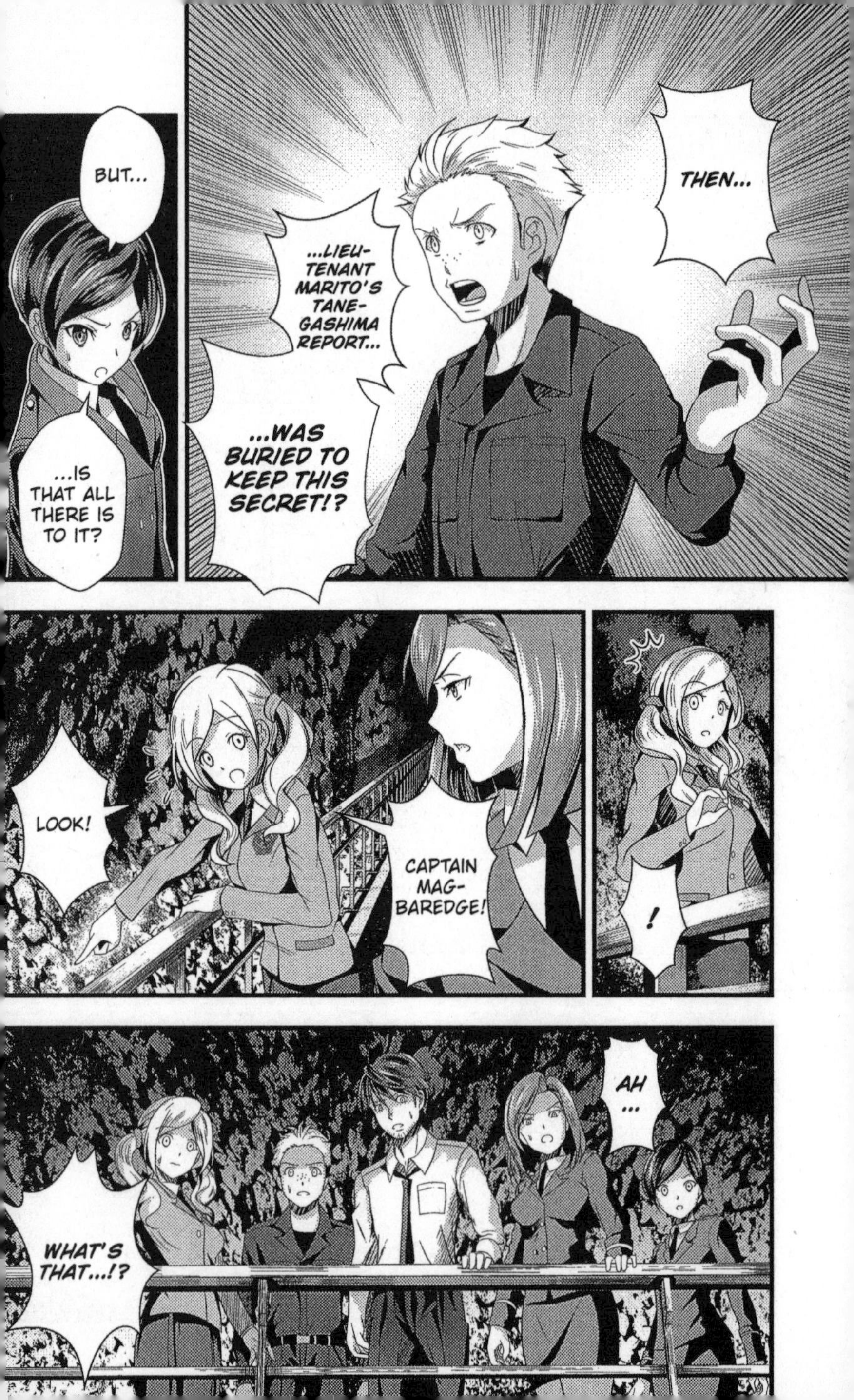
THEN...
...LIEU-TENANT MARITO'S TANE-GASHIMA REPORT...
...WAS BURIED TO KEEP THIS SECRET!?
BUT...
...IS THAT ALL THERE IS TO IT?
!
CAPTAIN MAG-BAREDGE!
LOOK!
AH ...
WHAT'S THAT...!?

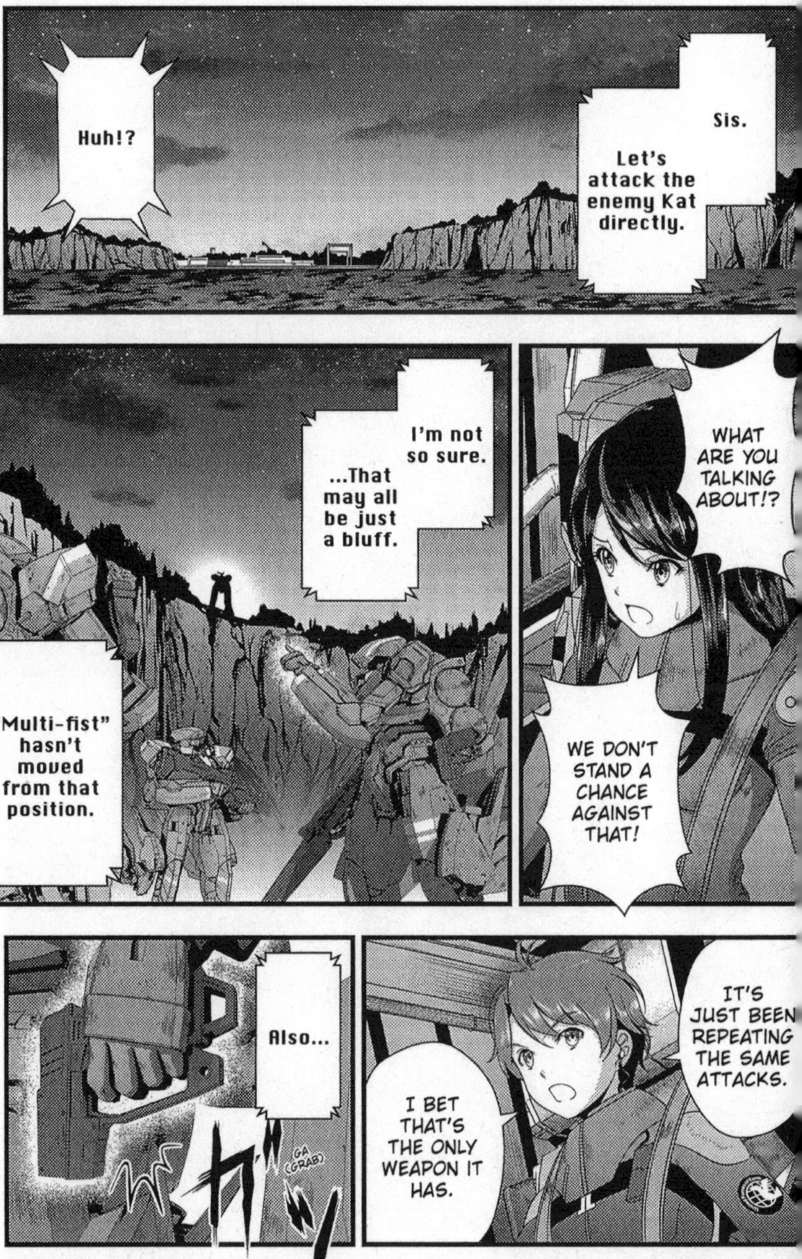
Sis.
Let's attack the enemy Kat directly.
Huh!?
WHAT ARE YOU TALKING ABOUT!?
WE DON'T STAND A CHANCE AGAINST THAT!
I'm not so sure.
...That may all be just a bluff.
“Multi-fist” hasn't moved from that position.
IT'S JUST BEEN REPEATING THE SAME ATTACKS.
I BET THAT'S THE ONLY WEAPON IT HAS.
Also...
GA (GRAB)

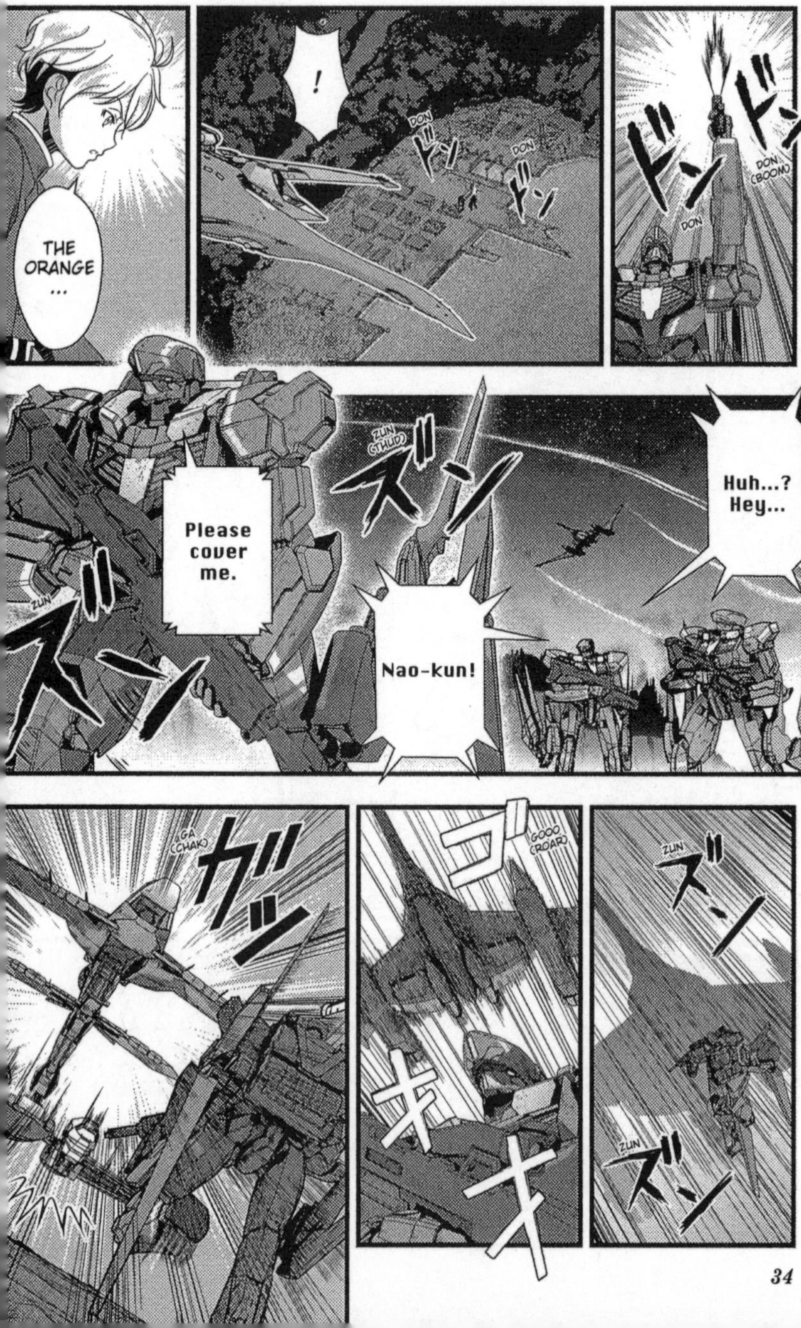
DON (BOOM)
DON
DON
!
DON
THE ORANGE ...
Huh...? Hey...
ZUN (THUD)
Please cover me.
Nao-kun!
ZUN
ZUN
ZUN
GOOO (ROAR)
GA (CHAK)

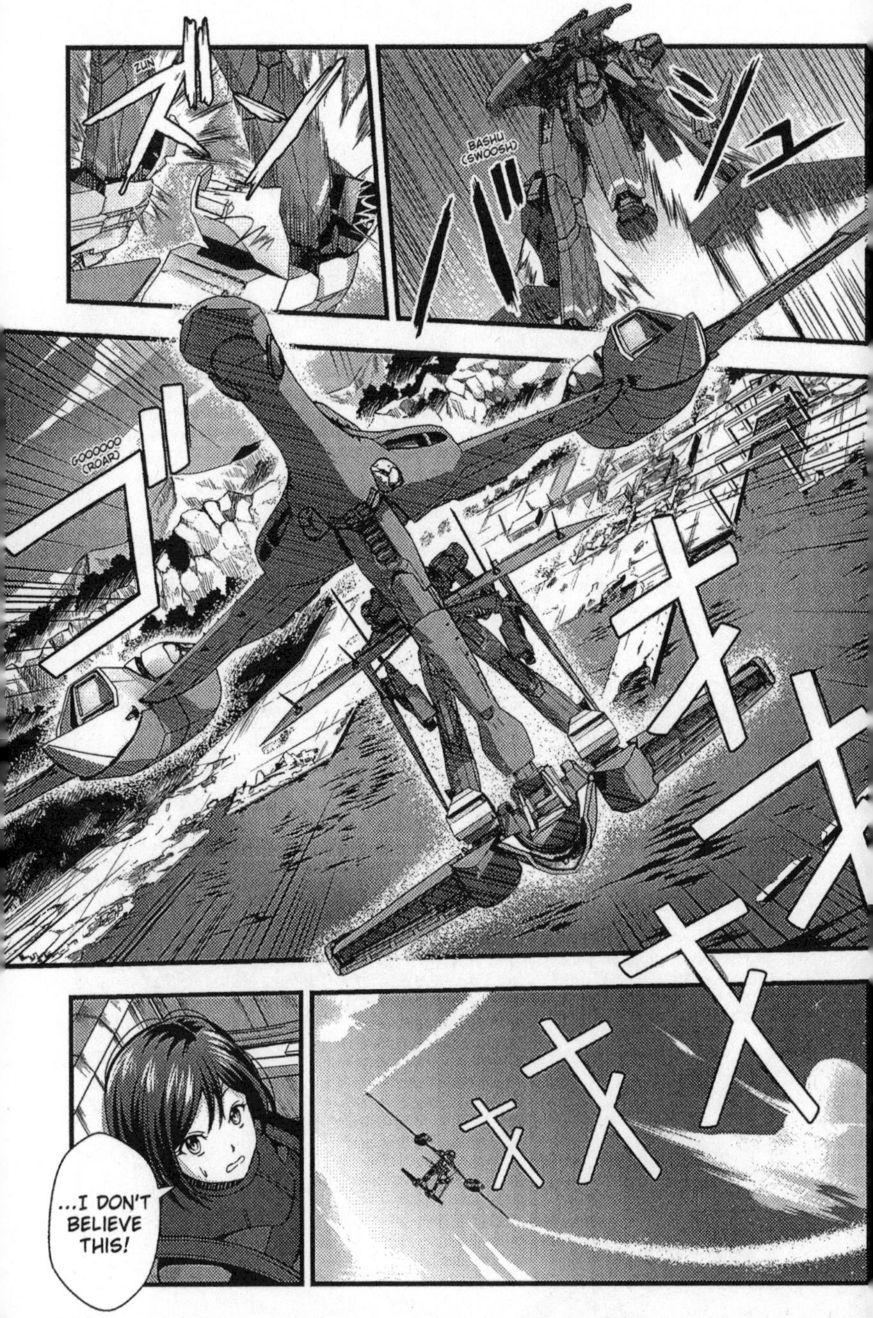
BASHU (SWOOSH)
ZUN
GOOOOOO (ROAR)
...I DON'T BELIEVE THIS!

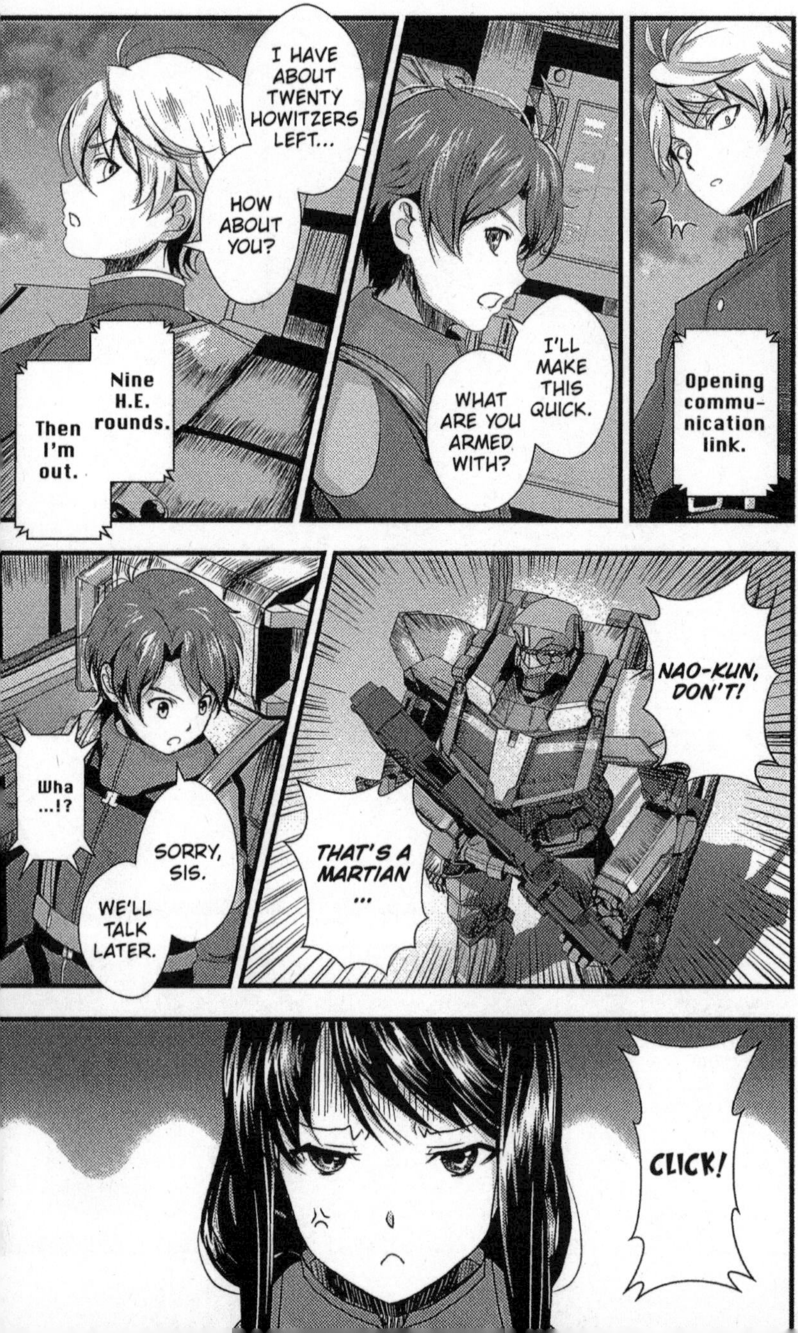
Opening communication link.
I'LL MAKE THIS QUICK.
WHAT ARE YOU ARMED WITH?
I HAVE ABOUT TWENTY HOWITZERS LEFT...
HOW ABOUT YOU?
Nine H.E. rounds.
Then I'm out.
NAO-KUN, DON'T!
THAT'S A MARTIAN ...
Wha ...!?
SORRY, SIS.
WE'LL TALK LATER.
CLICK!

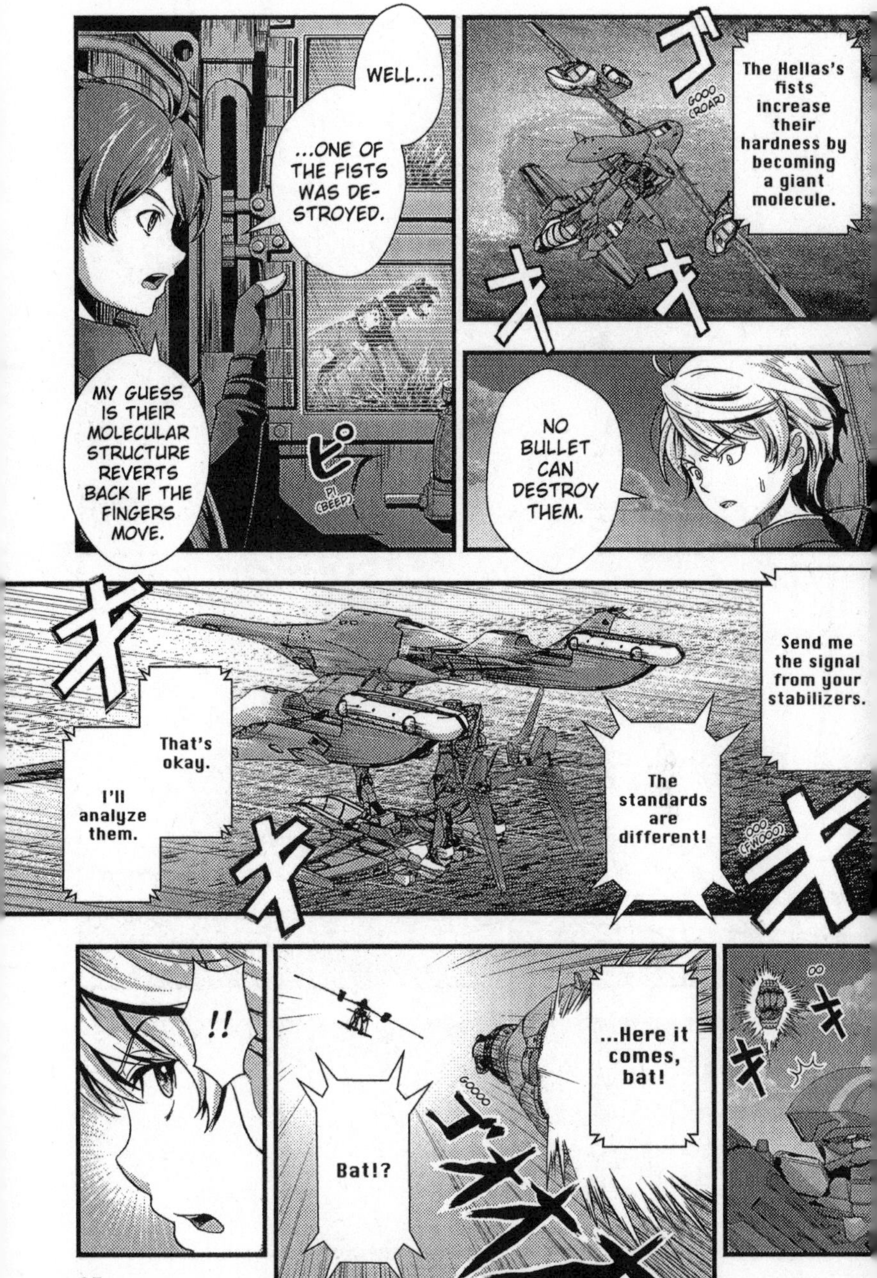
GOOO (ROAR)
The Hellas's fists increase their hardness by becoming a giant molecule.
NO BULLET CAN DESTROY THEM.
WELL...
...ONE OF THE FISTS WAS DE-STROYED.
PI (BEEP)
MY GUESS IS THEIR MOLECULAR STRUCTURE REVERTS BACK IF THE FINGERS MOVE.
Send me the signal from your stabilizers.
OOO (FWOOO)
The standards are different!
That's okay.
I'll analyze them.
...Here it comes, bat!
GOOOO
Bat!?
!!

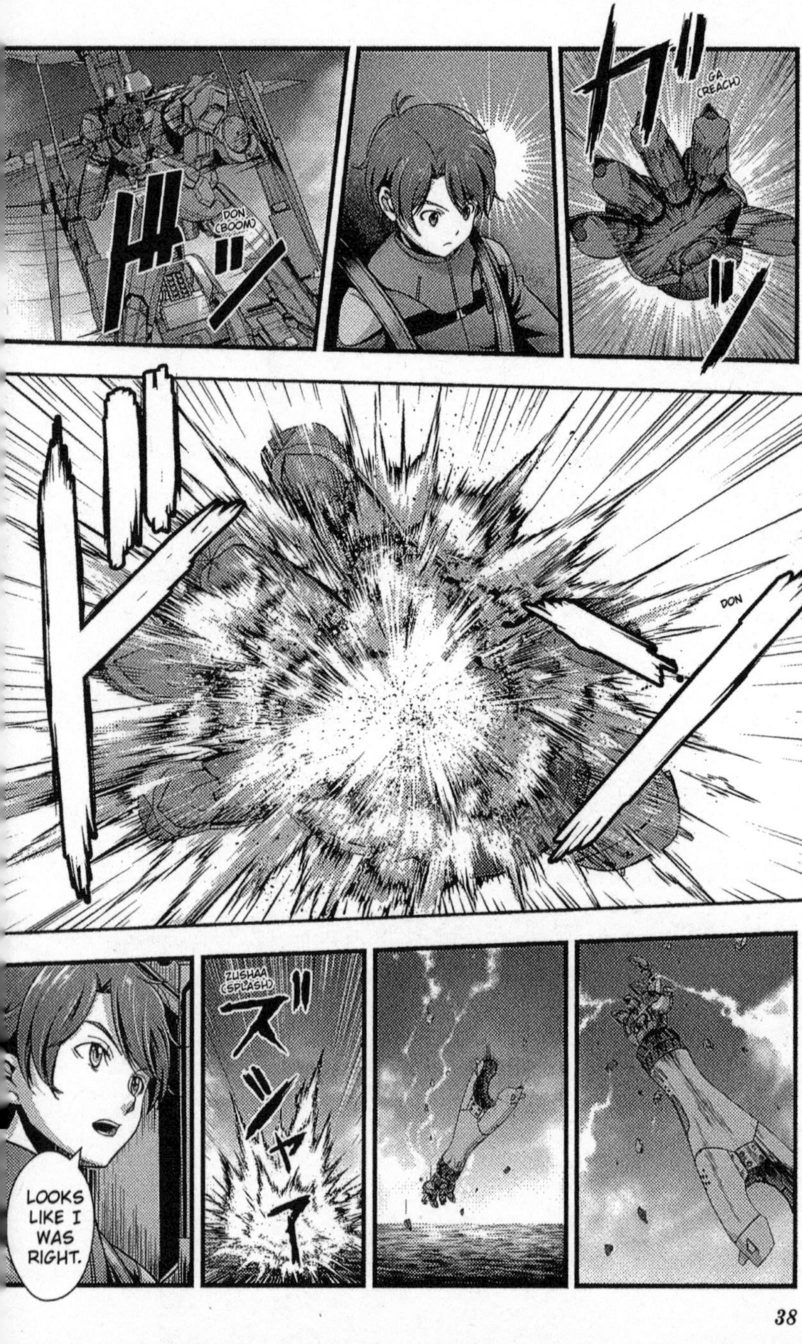
GA (REACH)
DON (BOOM)
DON
ZUSHAA (SPLASH)
LOOKS LIKE I WAS RIGHT.

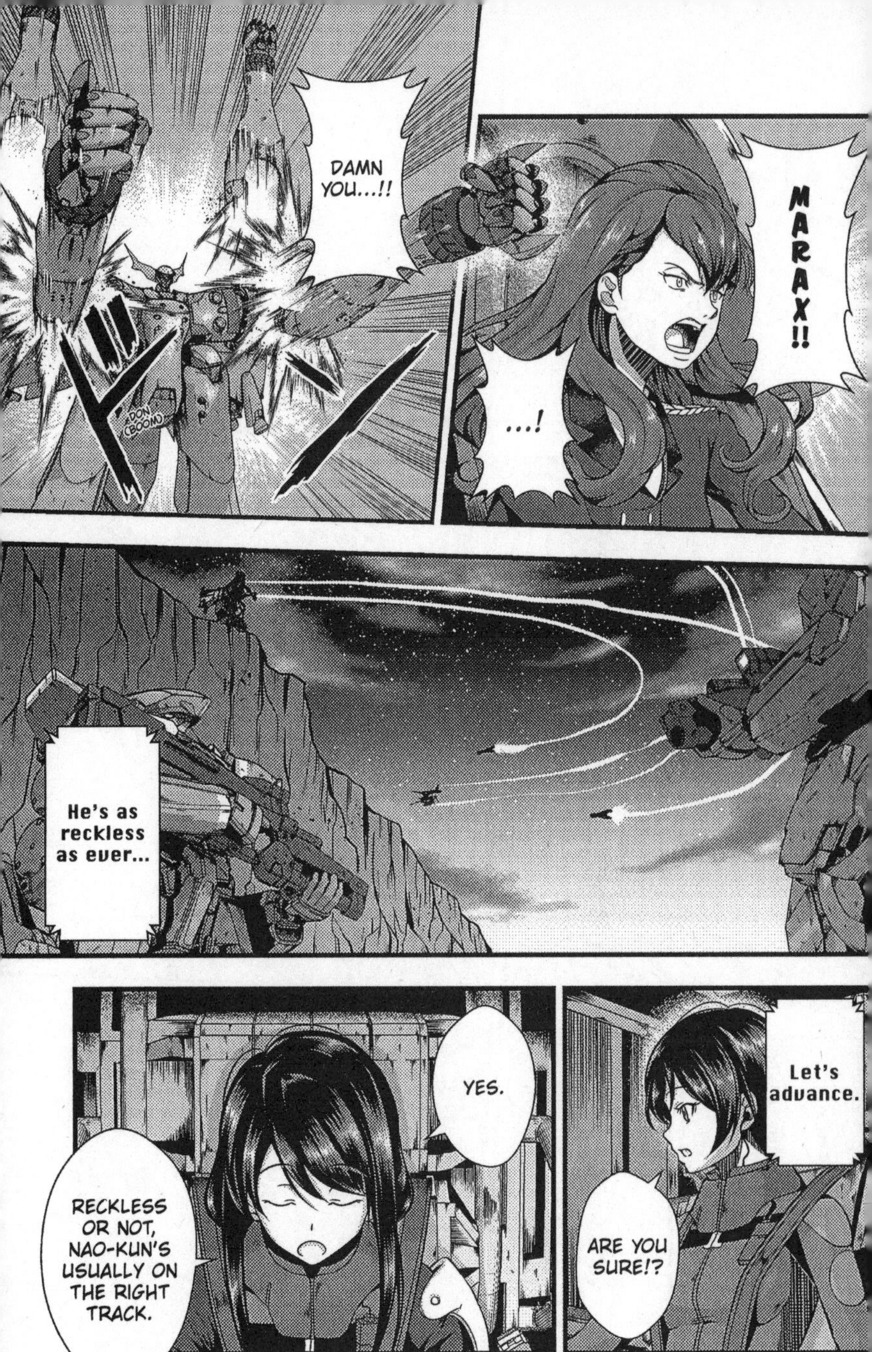
MARAX!!
...!
DAMN YOU...!!
DON (BOOM)
He's as reckless as ever...
Let's advance.
ARE YOU SURE!?
YES.
RECKLESS OR NOT, NAO-KUN'S USUALLY ON THE RIGHT TRACK.

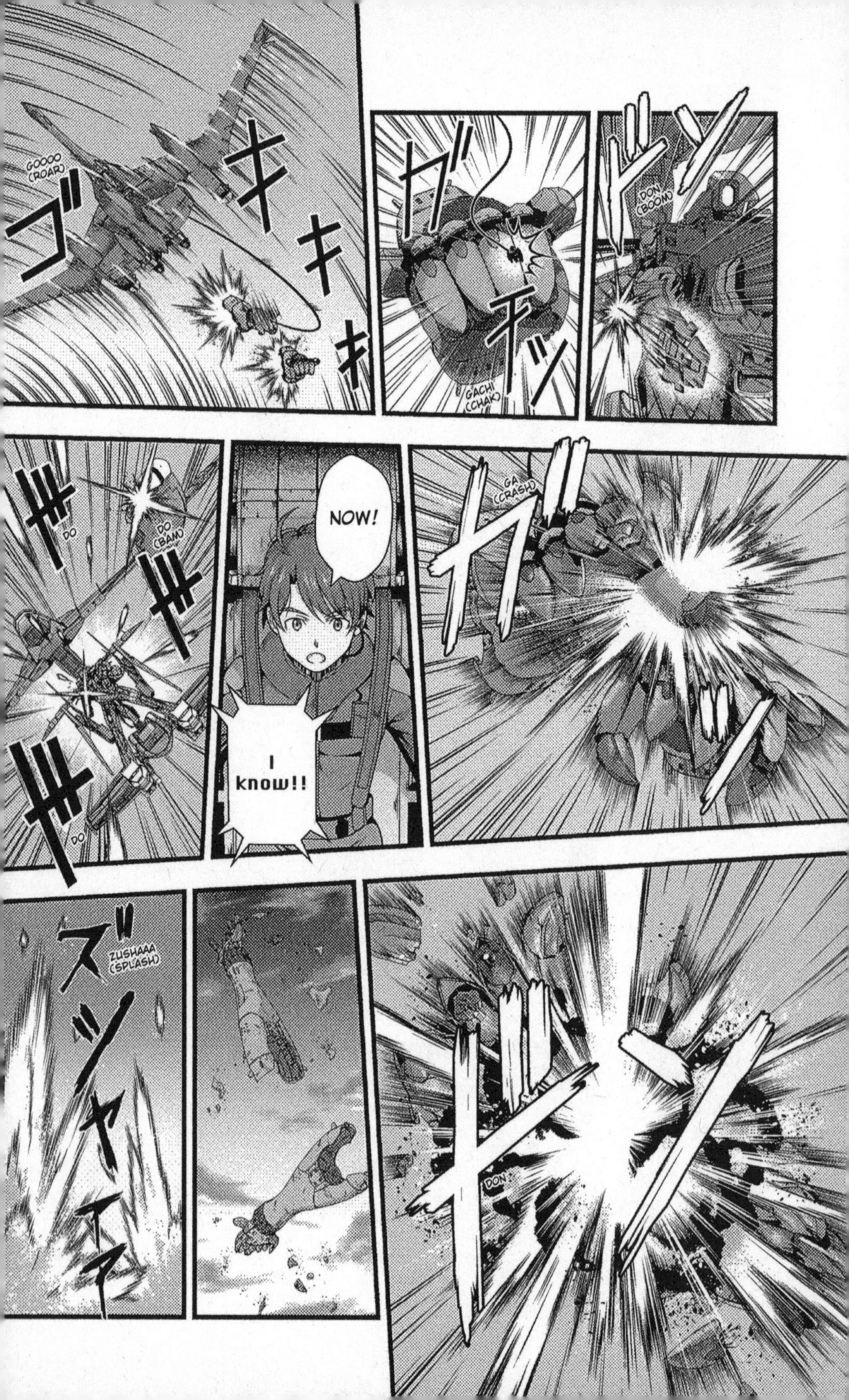

DON (BOOM)
GACHI (CHAK)
GOOOO (ROAR)
GA (CRASH)
NOW!
I know!!
DO
DO (BAM)
DO
DON
ZUSHAAA (SPLASH)

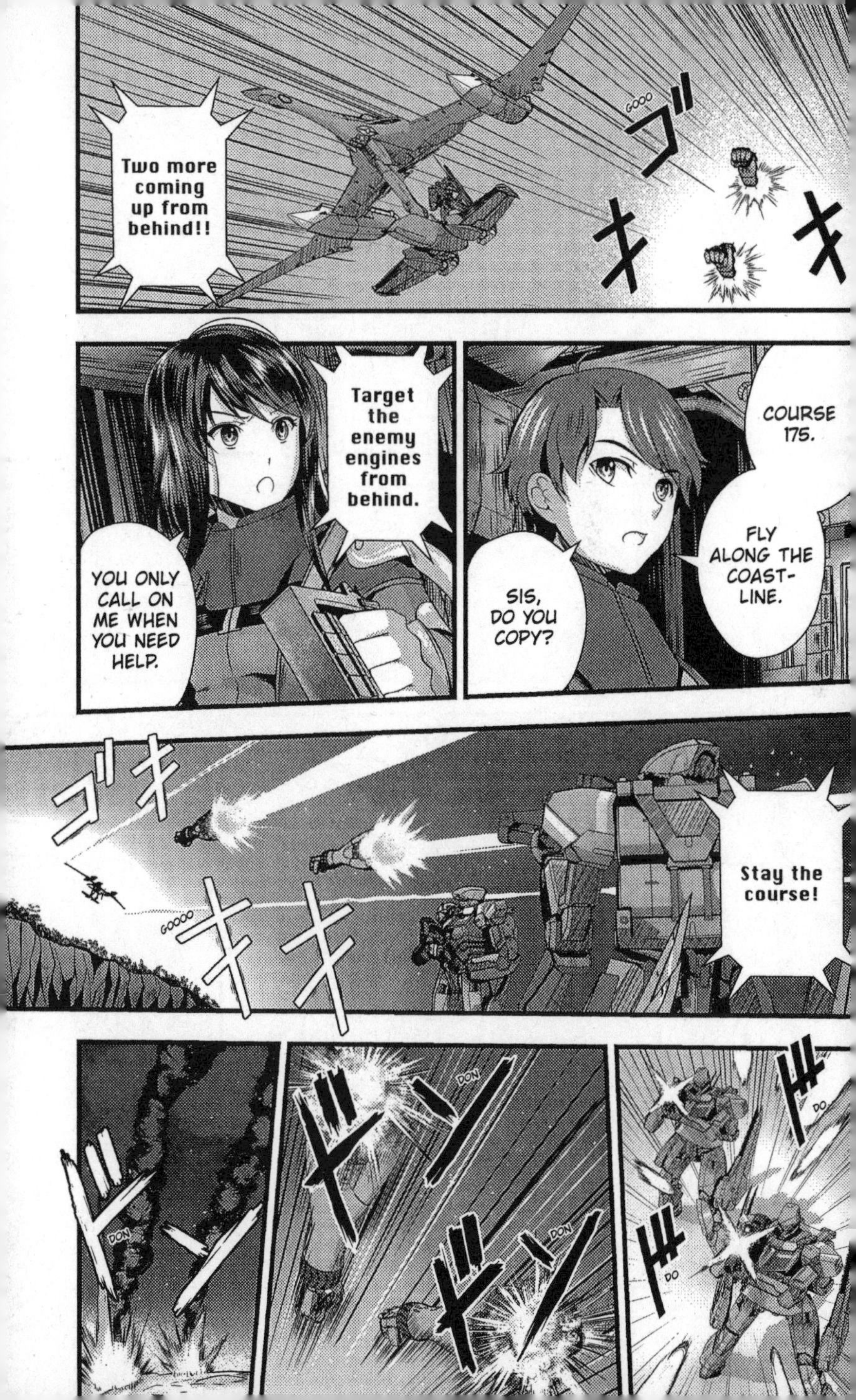
GOOO
Two more coming up from behind!!
COURSE 175.
FLY ALONG THE COAST-LINE.
SIS, DO YOU COPY?
Target the enemy engines from behind.
YOU ONLY CALL ON ME WHEN YOU NEED HELP.
Stay the course!
GOOOO
DO
DO
DON
DON
DON

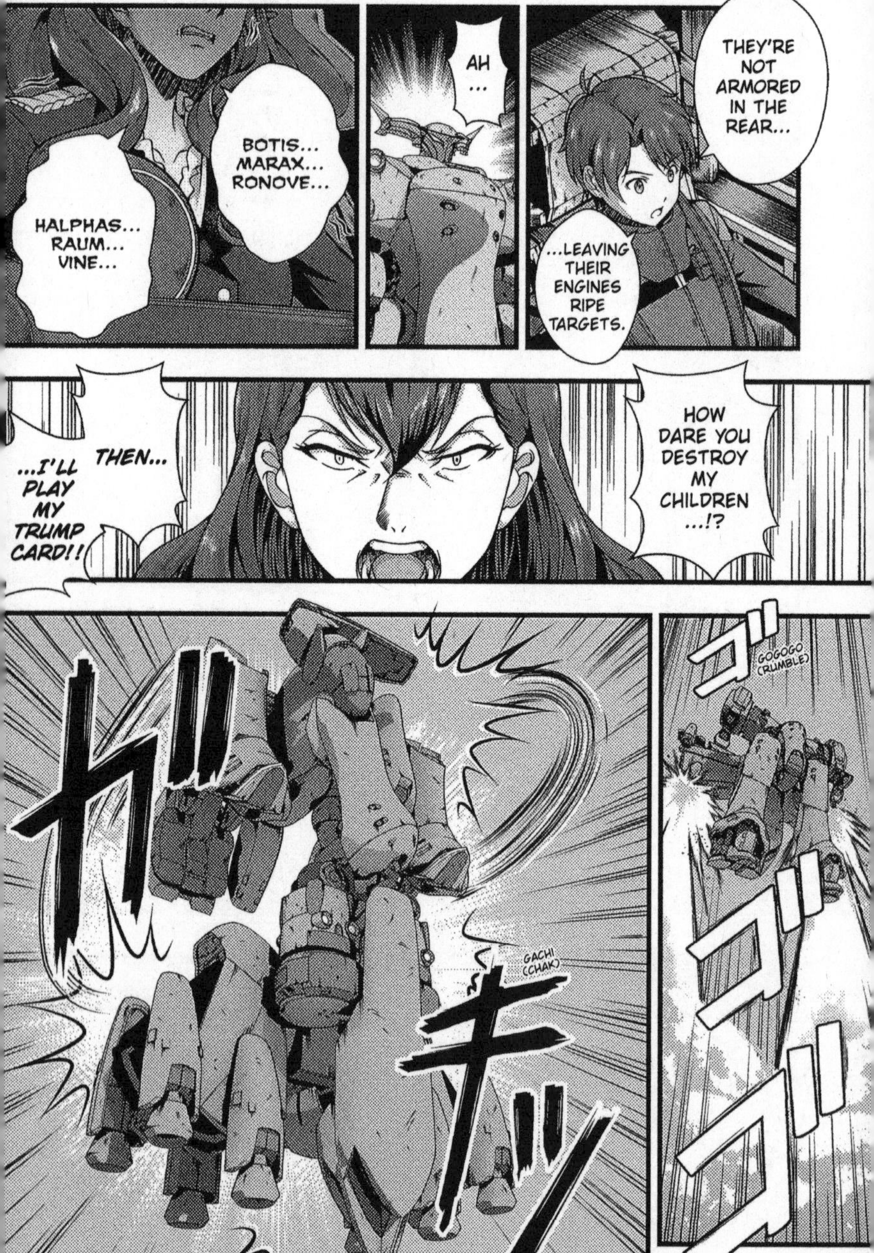
THEY'RE NOT ARMORED IN THE REAR...
...LEAVING THEIR ENGINES RIPE TARGETS.
AH ...
BOTIS... MARAX... RONOVE...
HALPHAS... RAUM... VINE...
HOW DARE YOU DESTROY MY CHILDREN ...!?
THEN...
...I'LL PLAY MY TRUMP CARD!!
GOGOGO (RUMBLE)
GACHI (CHAK)

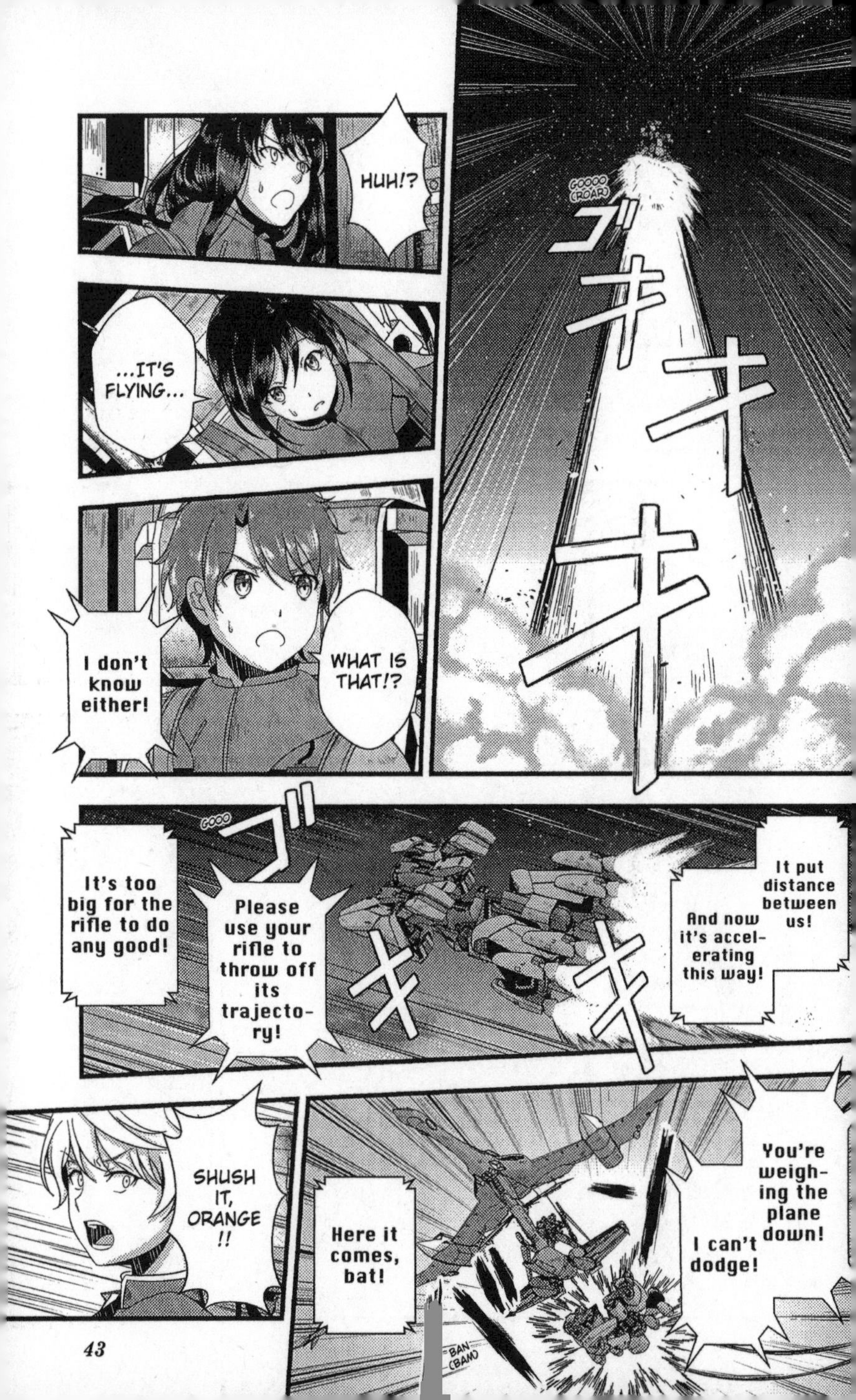
GOOOO (ROAR)
HUH!?
...IT'S FLYING...
WHAT IS THAT!?
I don't know either!
It put distance between us!
And now it's accel-erating this way!
GOOO
Please use your rifle to throw off its trajecto-ry!
It's too big for the rifle to do any good!
You're weigh-ing the plane down!
I can't dodge!
Here it comes, bat!
BAN (BAM)
SHUSH IT, ORANGE !!

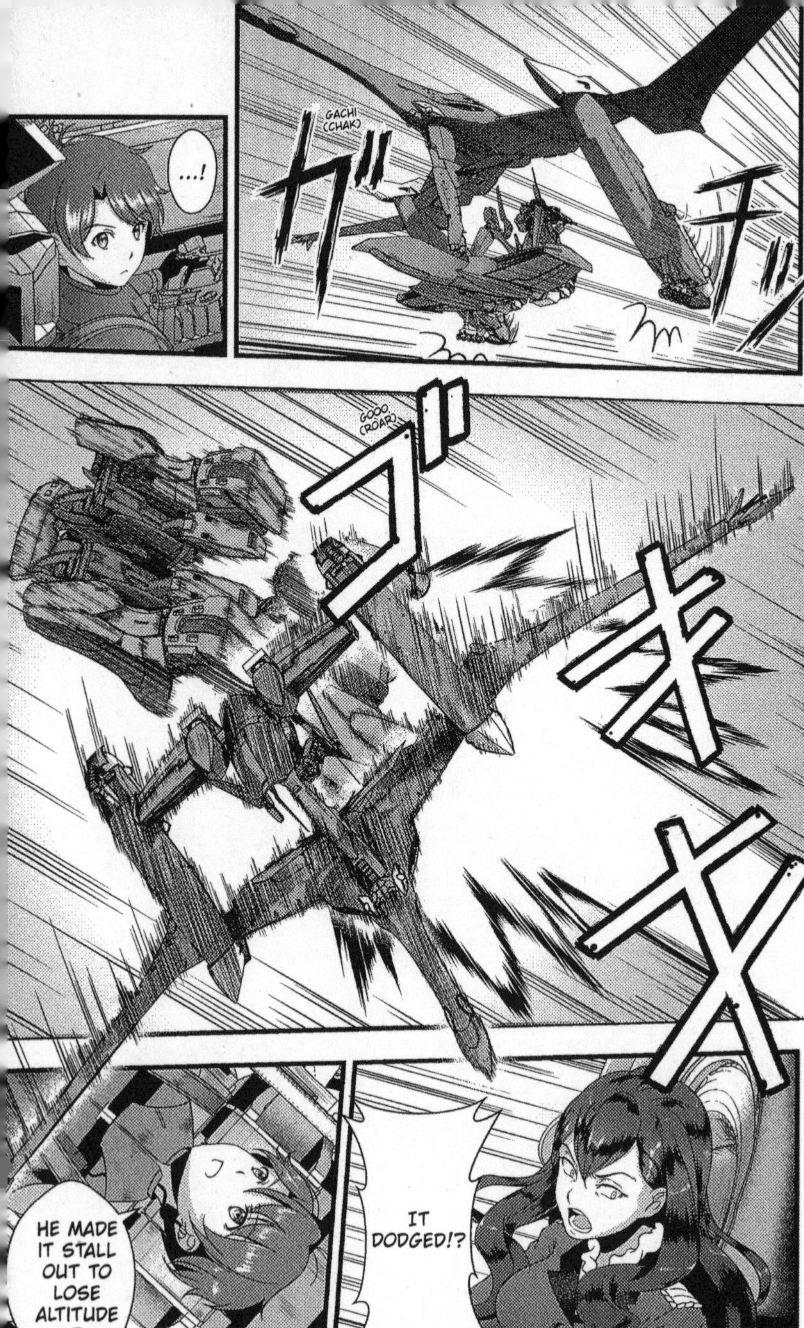
GACHI (CHAK)
ガチッ
...!
GOOO (ROAR)
IT DODGED!?
HE MADE IT STALL OUT TO LOSE ALTITUDE?

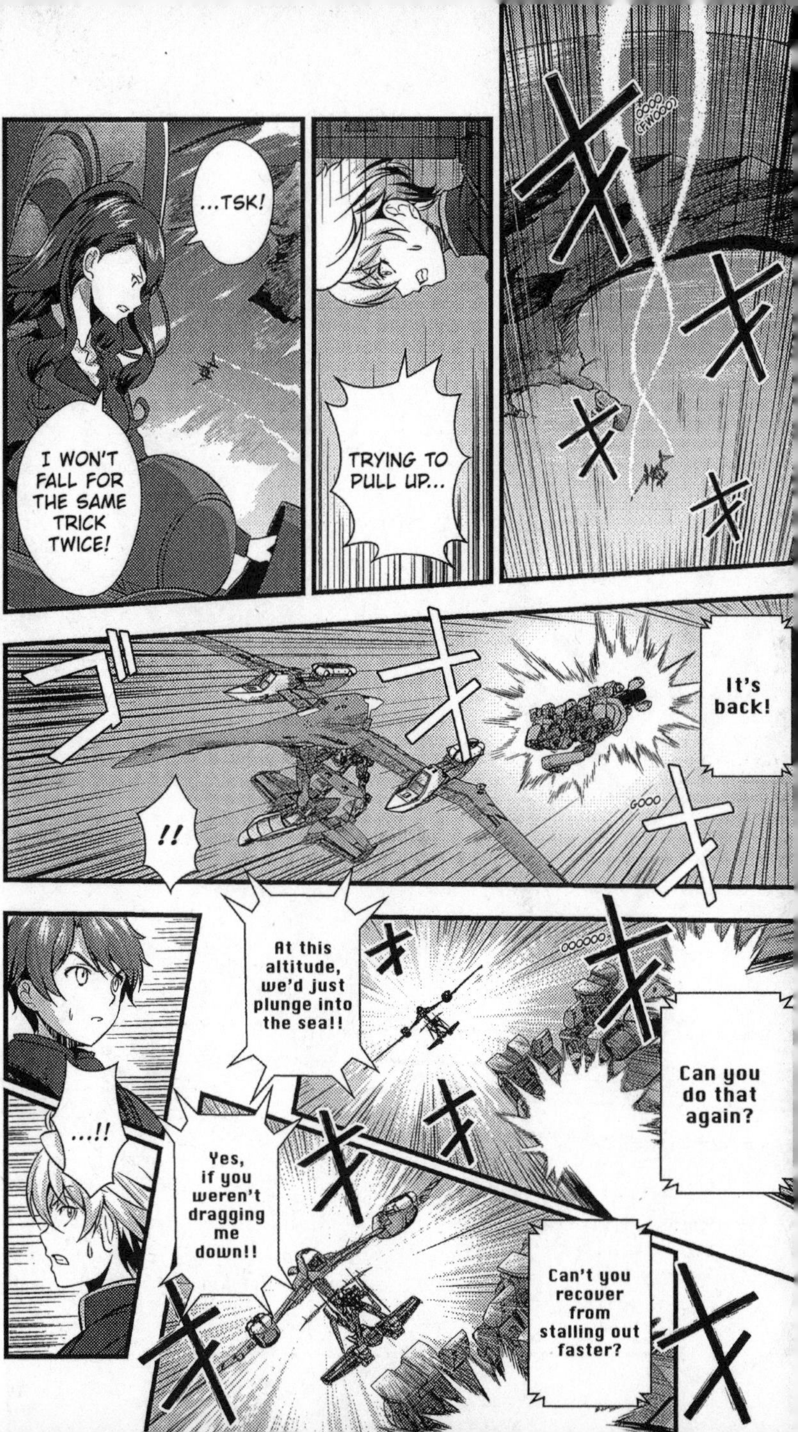
OOOO (FWOOO)
TRYING TO PULL UP...
...TSK!
I WON'T FALL FOR THE SAME TRICK TWICE!
It's back!
GOOO
!!
OOOOOO
Can you do that again?
At this altitude, we'd just plunge into the sea!!
Can't you recover from stalling out faster?
Yes, if you weren't dragging me down!!
...!!

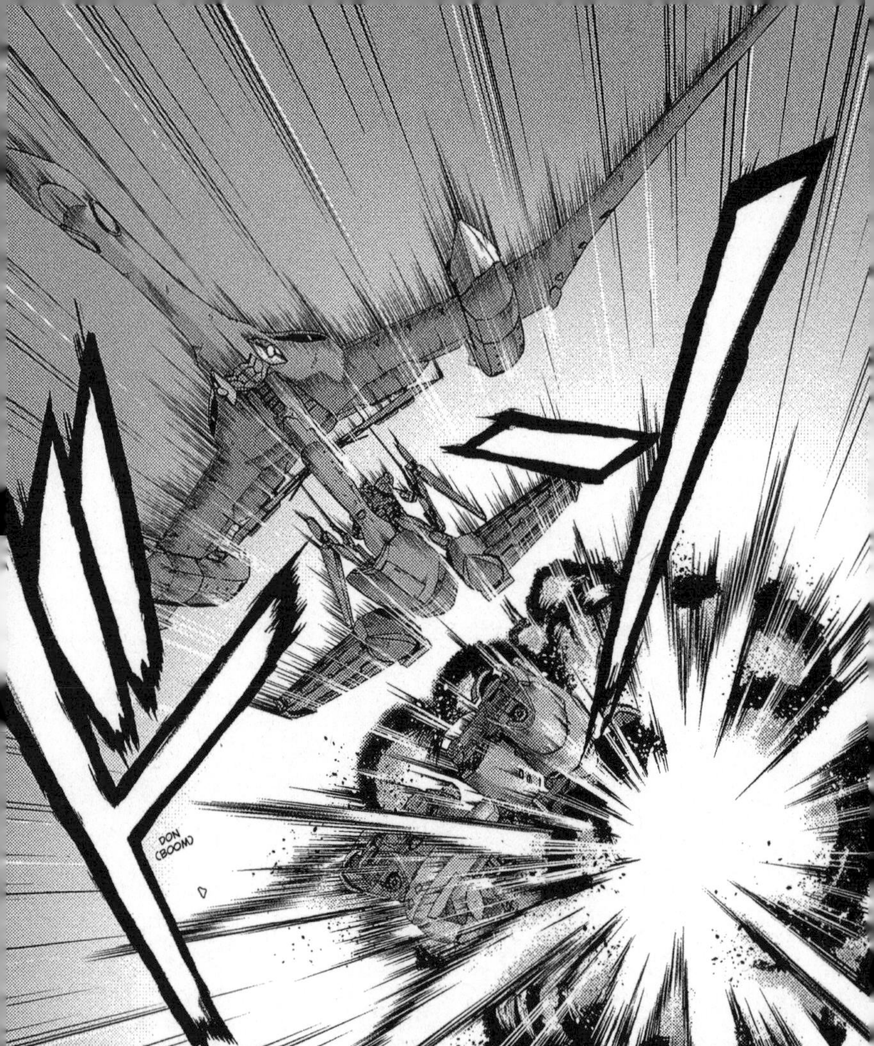
DON
(BOOM)
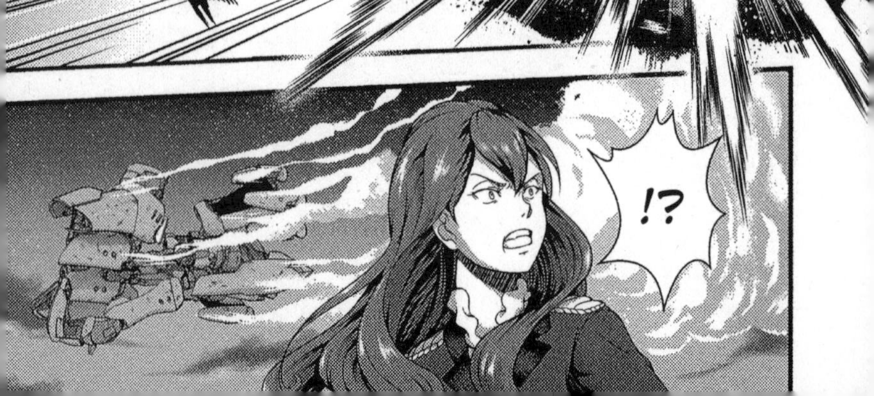
!?

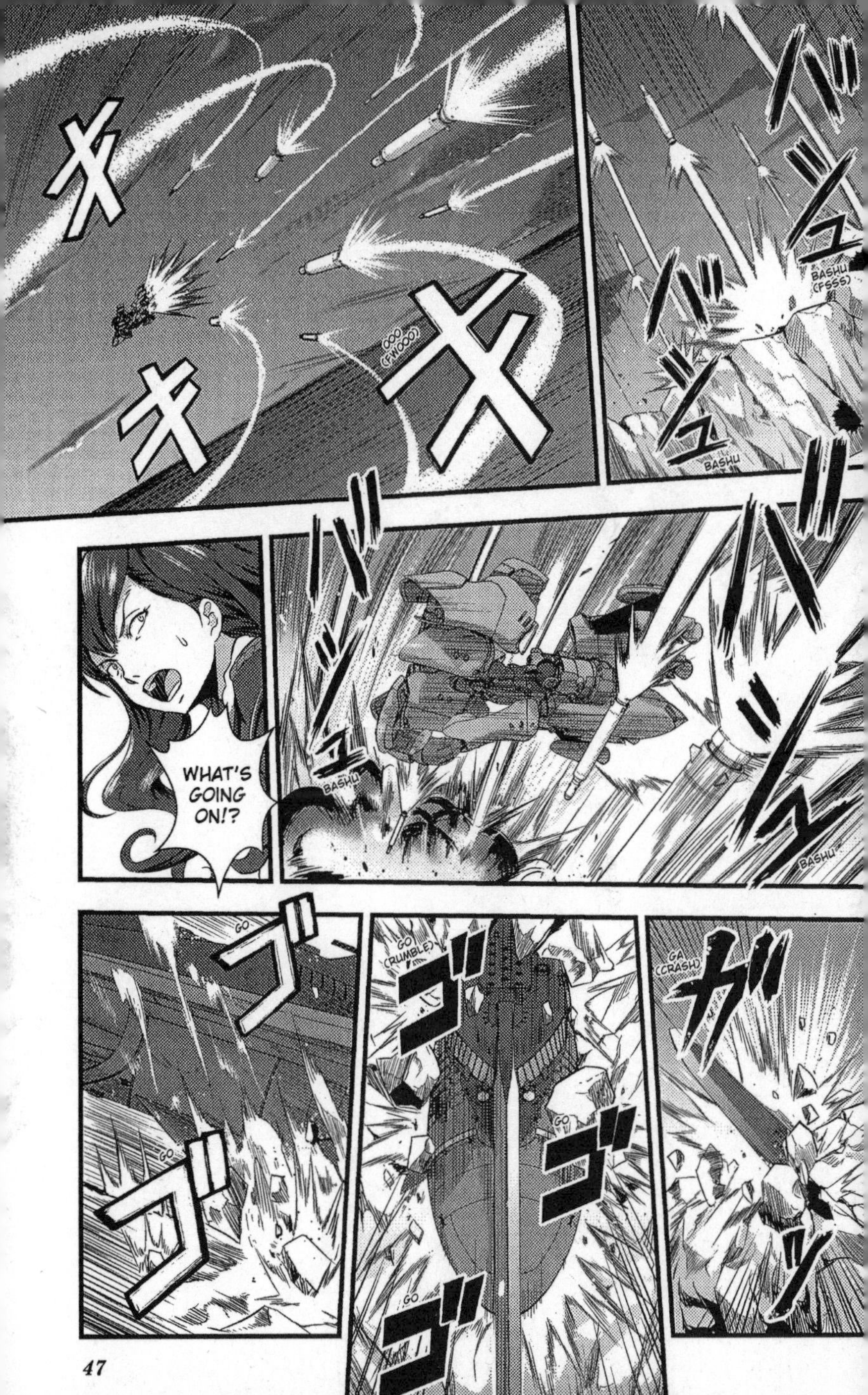
BASHU (FSSS)
BASHU
OOO (FWOOO)
BASHU
BASHU
WHAT'S GOING ON!?
GA (CRASH)
GO (RUMBLE)
GO
GO
GO
GO

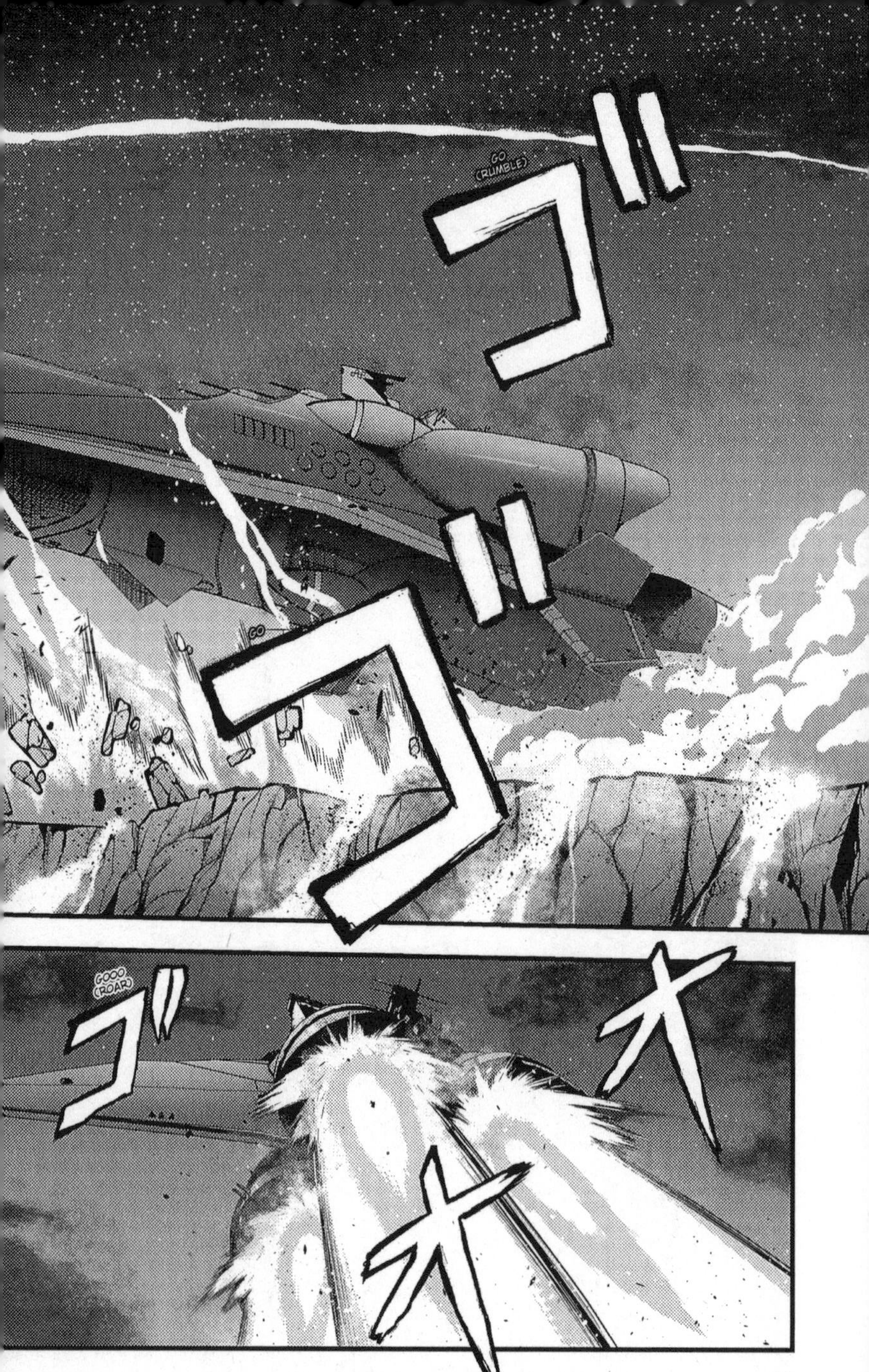

GO (RUMBLE)
ゴ
GO
ゴ
GOOO (ROAR)
ゴオオ

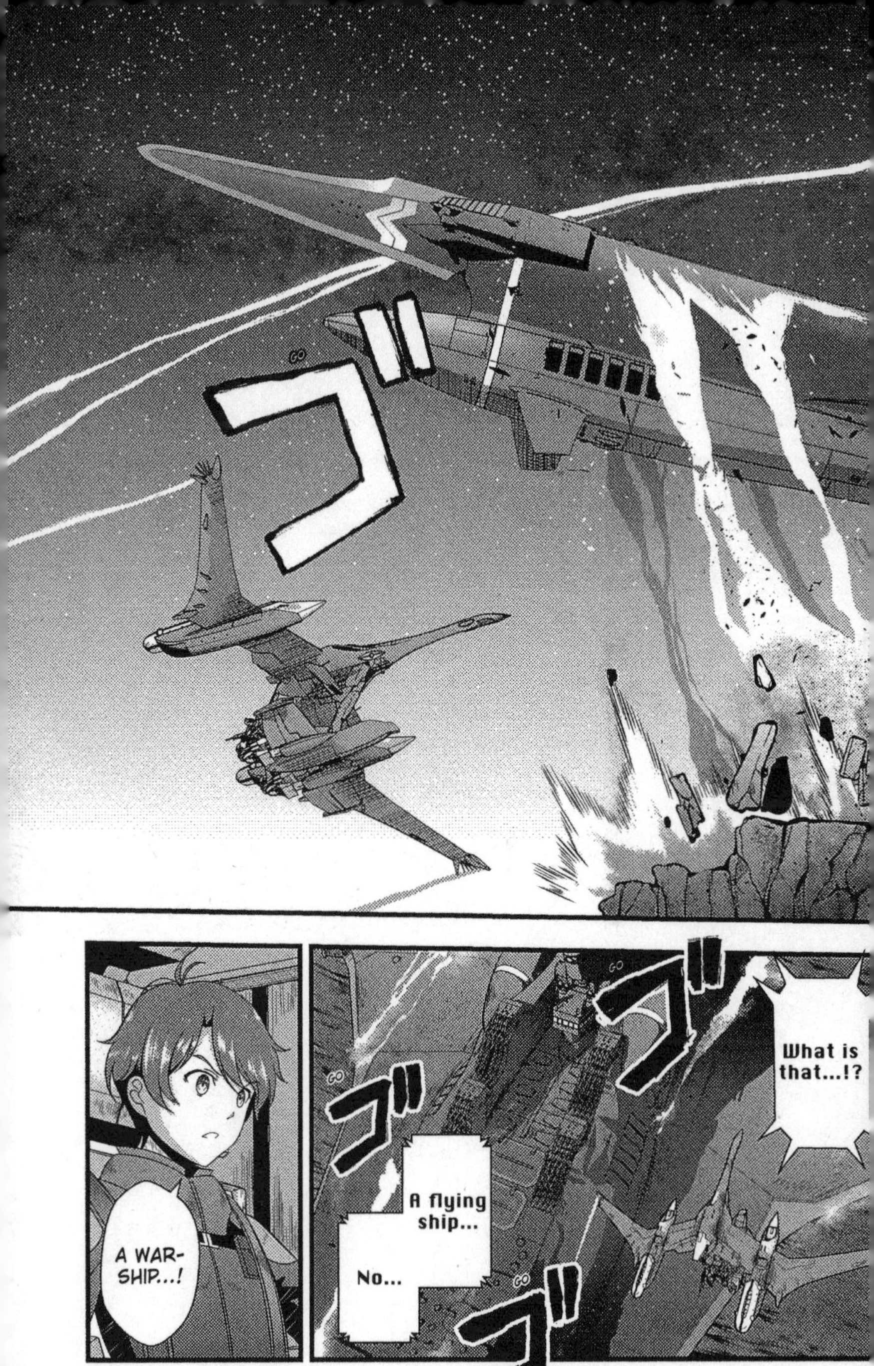
GO
GO
What is that...!?
GO
A flying ship...
No...
GO
A WAR-SHIP...!

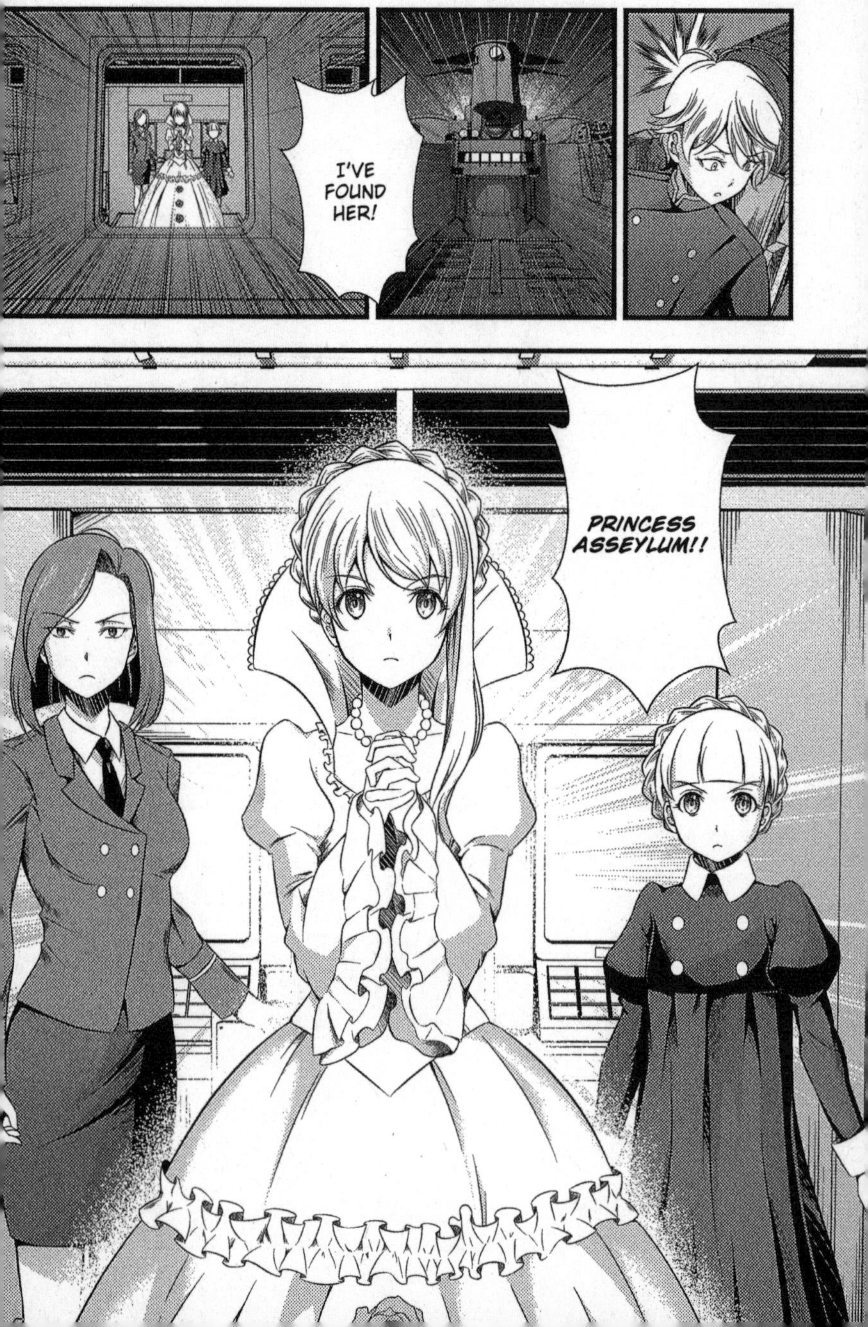
I'VE FOUND HER!
PRINCESS ASSEYLUM!!

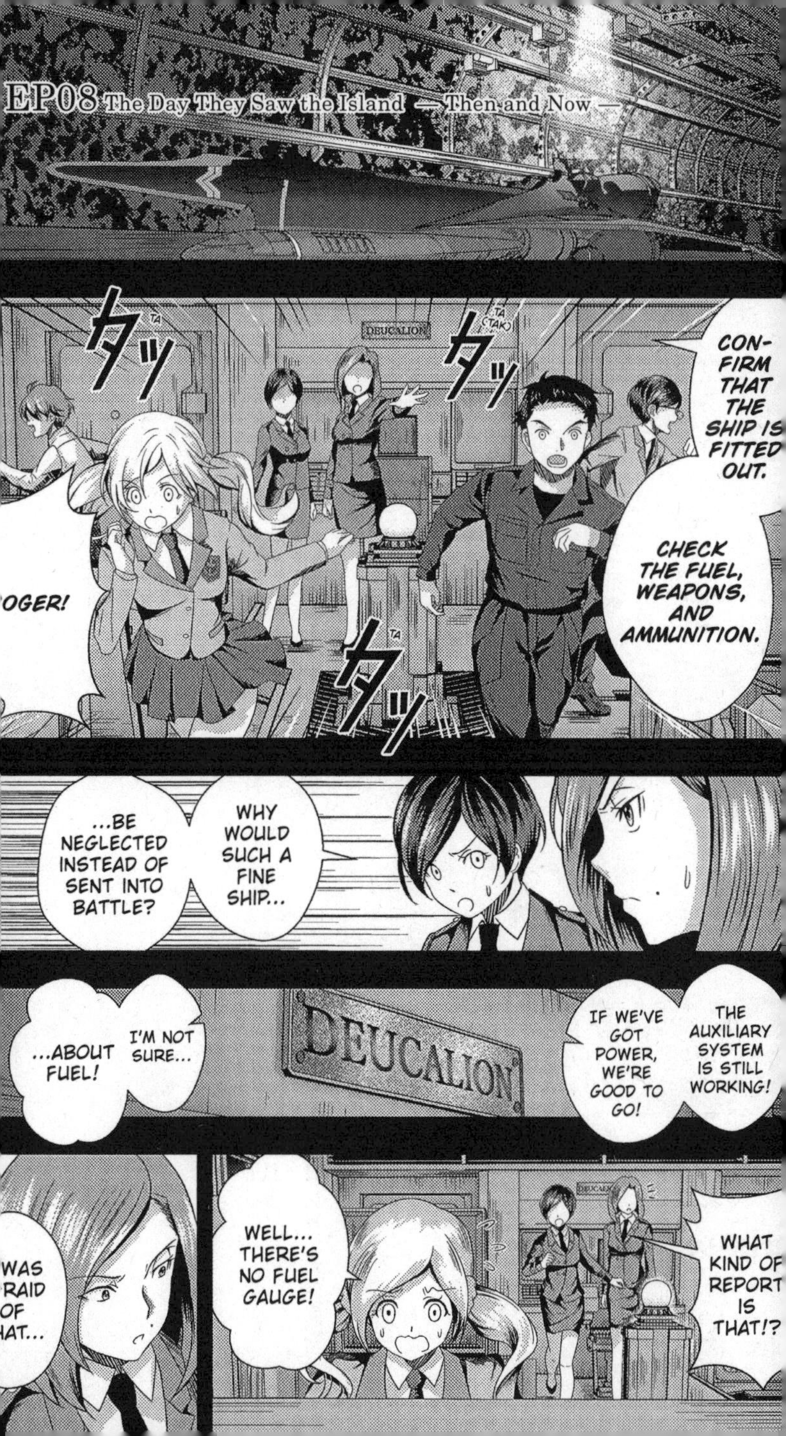
EP08 The Day They Saw the Island —Then and Now—
CON-FIRM THAT THE SHIP IS FITTED OUT.
CHECK THE FUEL, WEAPONS, AND AMMUNITION.
TA (TAK)
DEUCALION
TA
TA
OGER!
WHY WOULD SUCH A FINE SHIP...
...BE NEGLECTED INSTEAD OF SENT INTO BATTLE?
THE AUXILIARY SYSTEM IS STILL WORKING!
IF WE'VE GOT POWER, WE'RE GOOD TO GO!
DEUCALION
I'M NOT SURE...
...ABOUT FUEL!
WHAT KIND OF REPORT IS THAT!?
WELL... THERE'S NO FUEL GAUGE!
WAS RAID OF HAT...

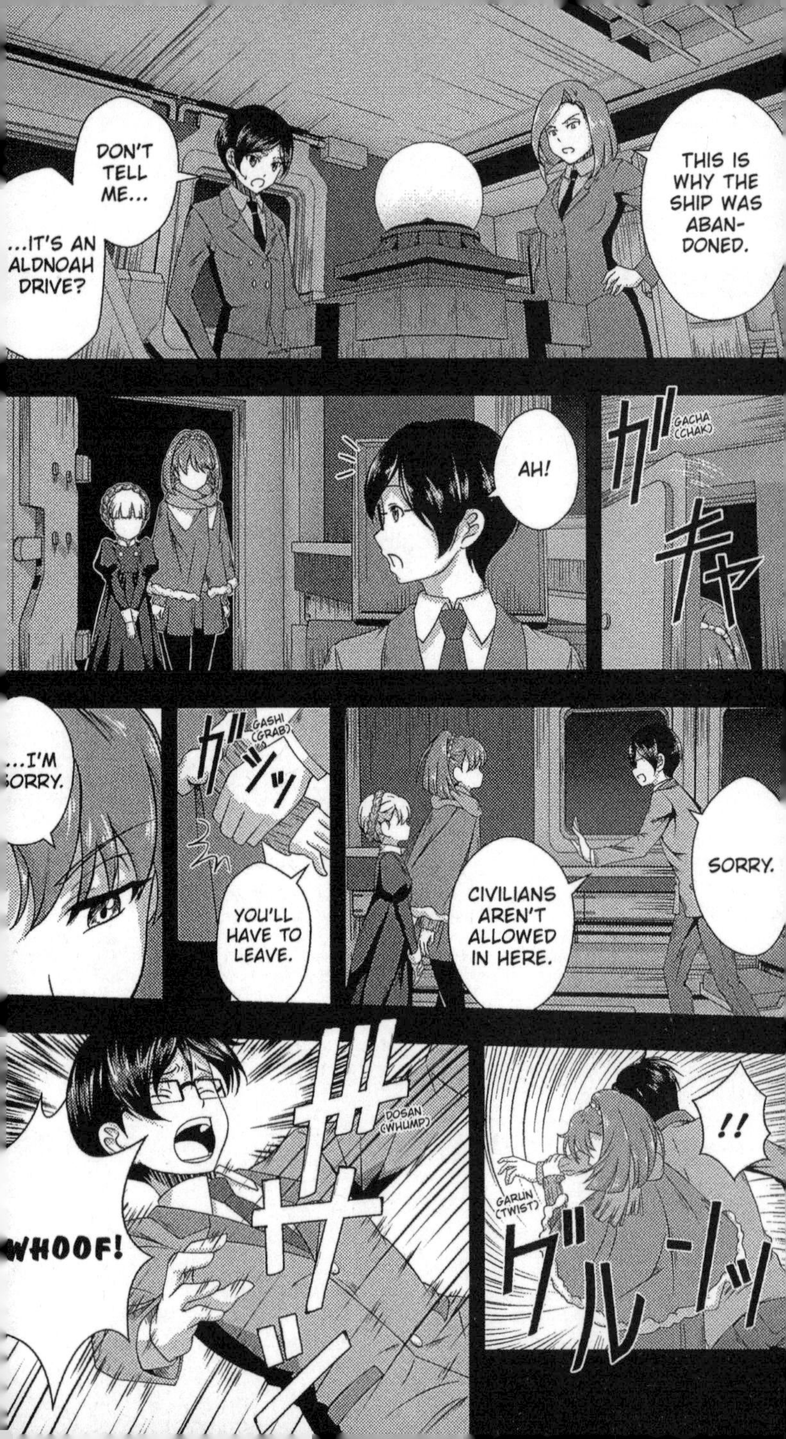
THIS IS WHY THE SHIP WAS ABAN-DONED.
DON'T TELL ME...
...IT'S AN ALDNOAH DRIVE?
ガチャ
GACHA (CHAK)
AH!
SORRY.
CIVILIANS AREN'T ALLOWED IN HERE.
ガシッ
GASHI (GRAB)
YOU'LL HAVE TO LEAVE.
...I'M SORRY.
!!
ヴルーッ
GARUN (TWIST)
ドサッ
DOSAN (WHUMP)
WHOOF!

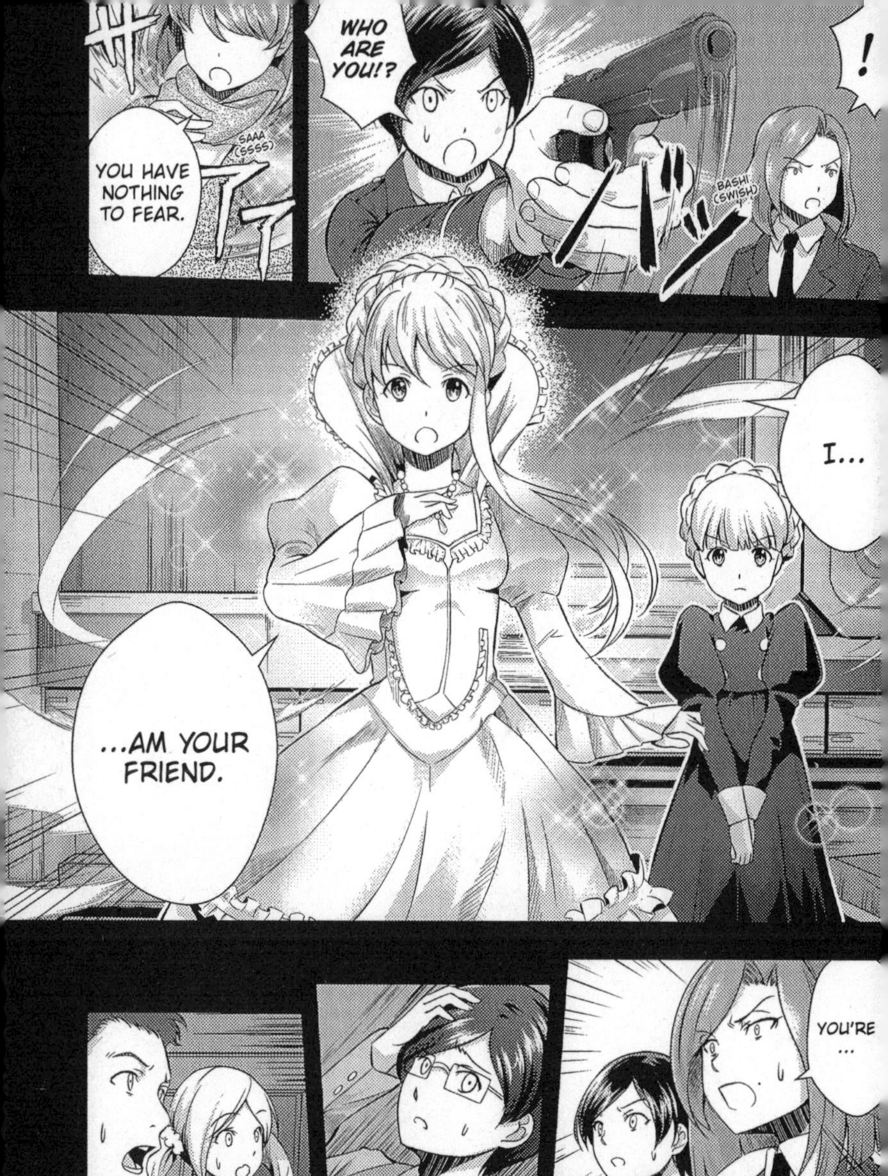
!
BASHI (SWISH)
WHO ARE YOU!?
SAAA (SSSS)
YOU HAVE NOTHING TO FEAR.
I...
...AM YOUR FRIEND.
YOU'RE ...

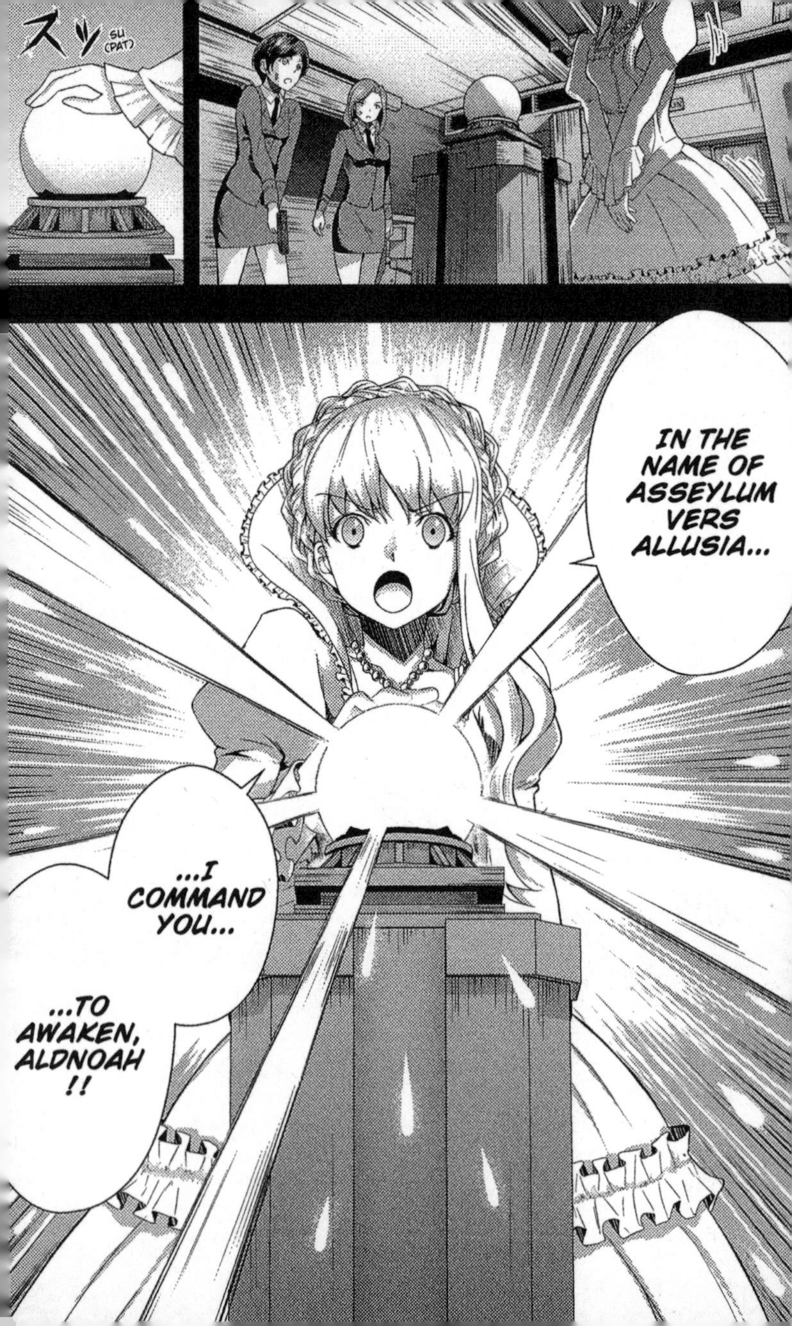
スッ
SU (PAT)
IN THE NAME OF ASSEYLUM VERS ALLUSIA...
...I COMMAND YOU...
...TO AWAKEN, ALDNOAH !!

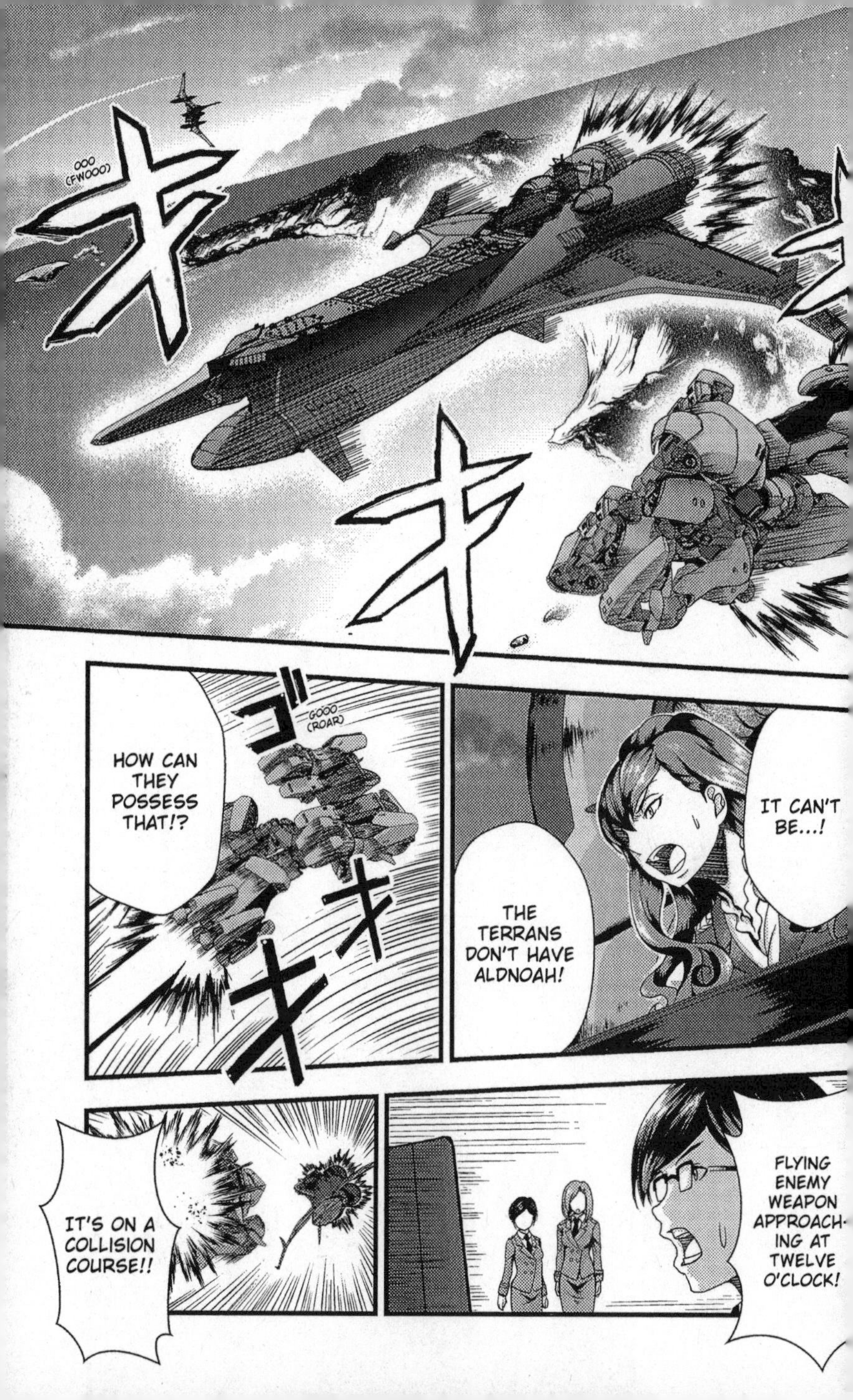
OOO (FWOOO)
GOOO (ROAR)
IT CAN'T BE...!
THE TERRANS DON'T HAVE ALDNOAH!
HOW CAN THEY POSSESS THAT!?
FLYING ENEMY WEAPON APPROACHING AT TWELVE O'CLOCK!
IT'S ON A COLLISION COURSE!!

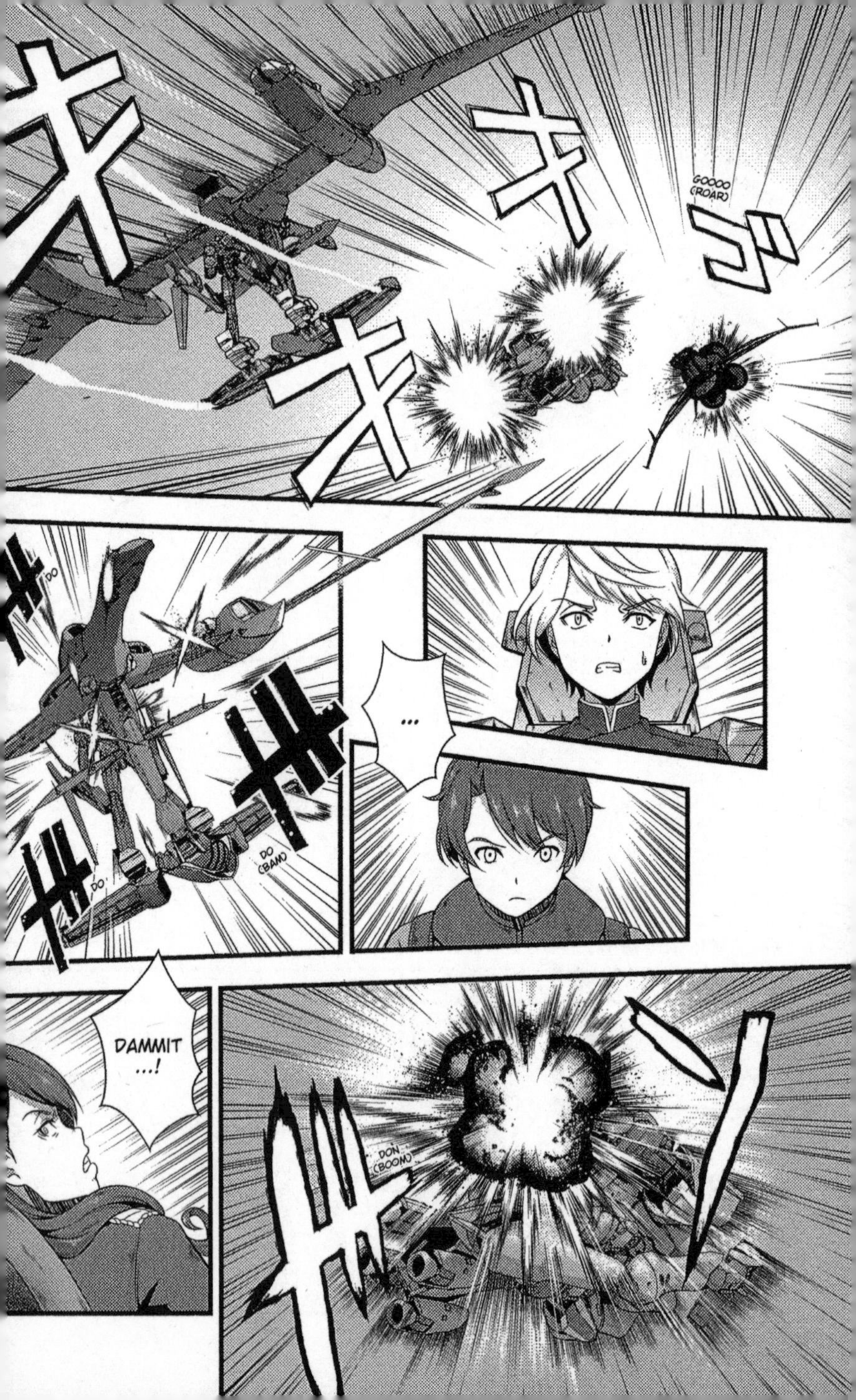
GOOOO (ROAR)
DO
DO (BAM)
DO
...
DAMMIT ...!
DON (BOOM)

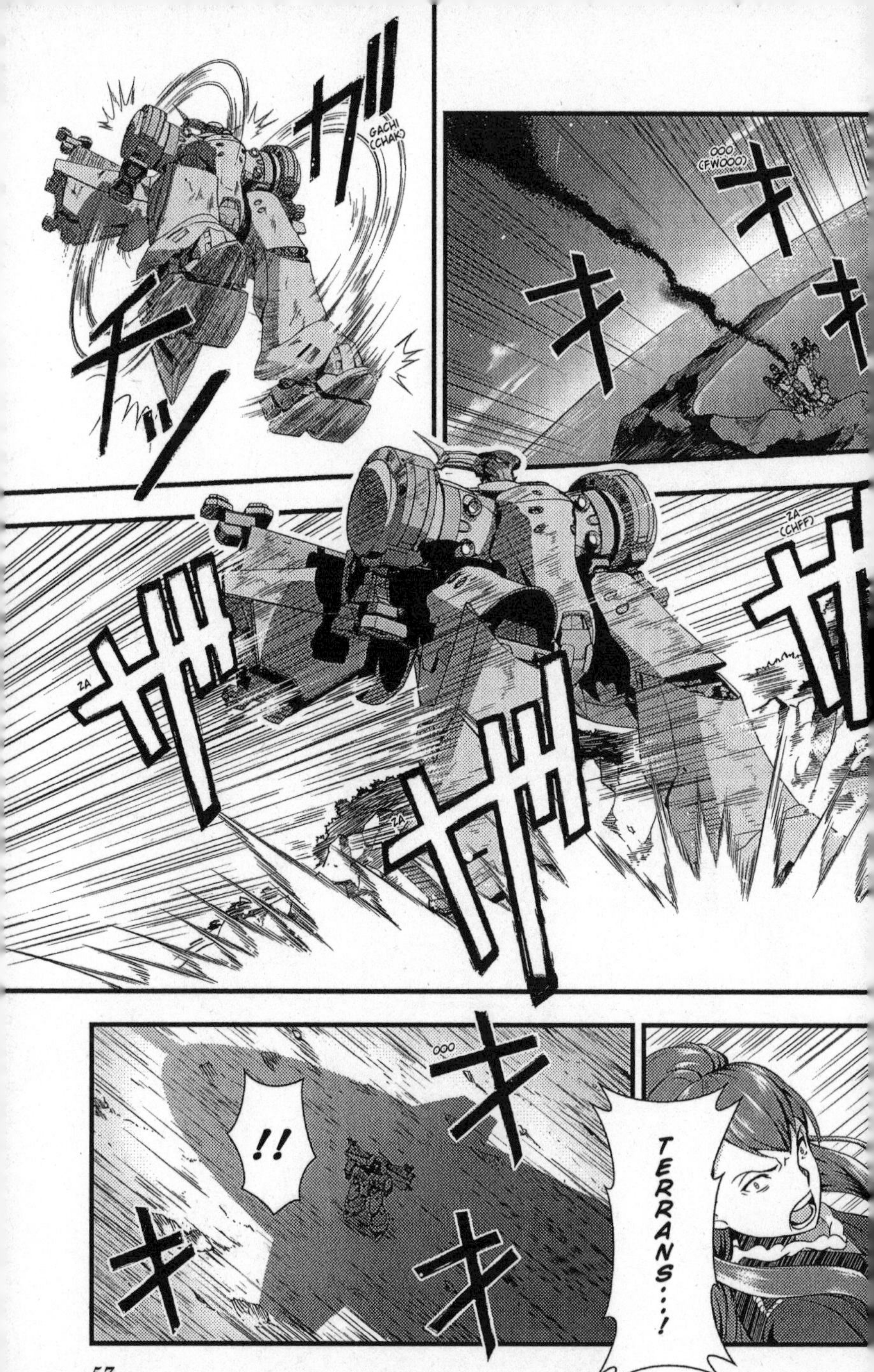
OOO (FWOOO)
GACHI (CHAK)
ZA (CHFF)
ZA
ZA
TERRANS...!
OOO
!!

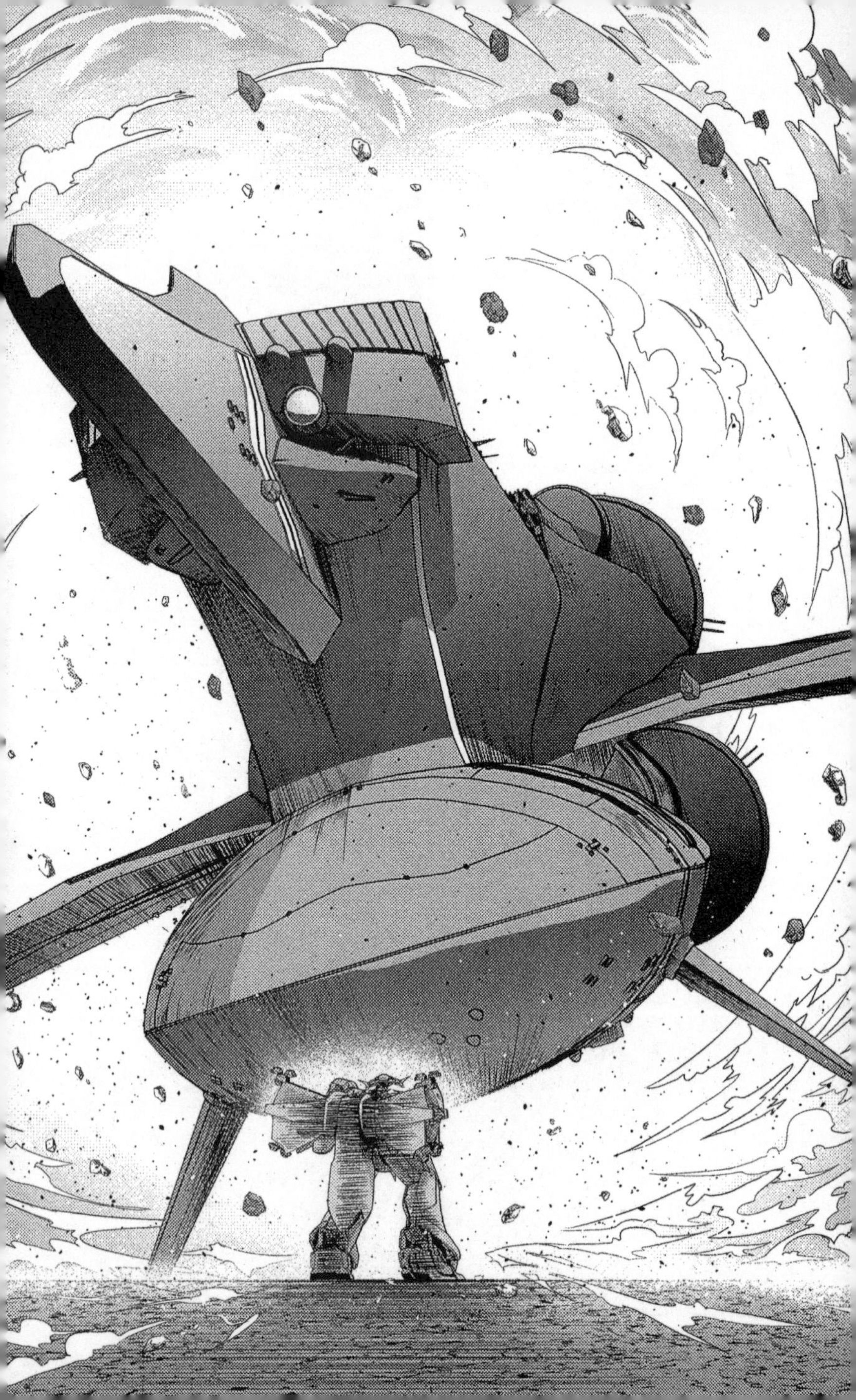

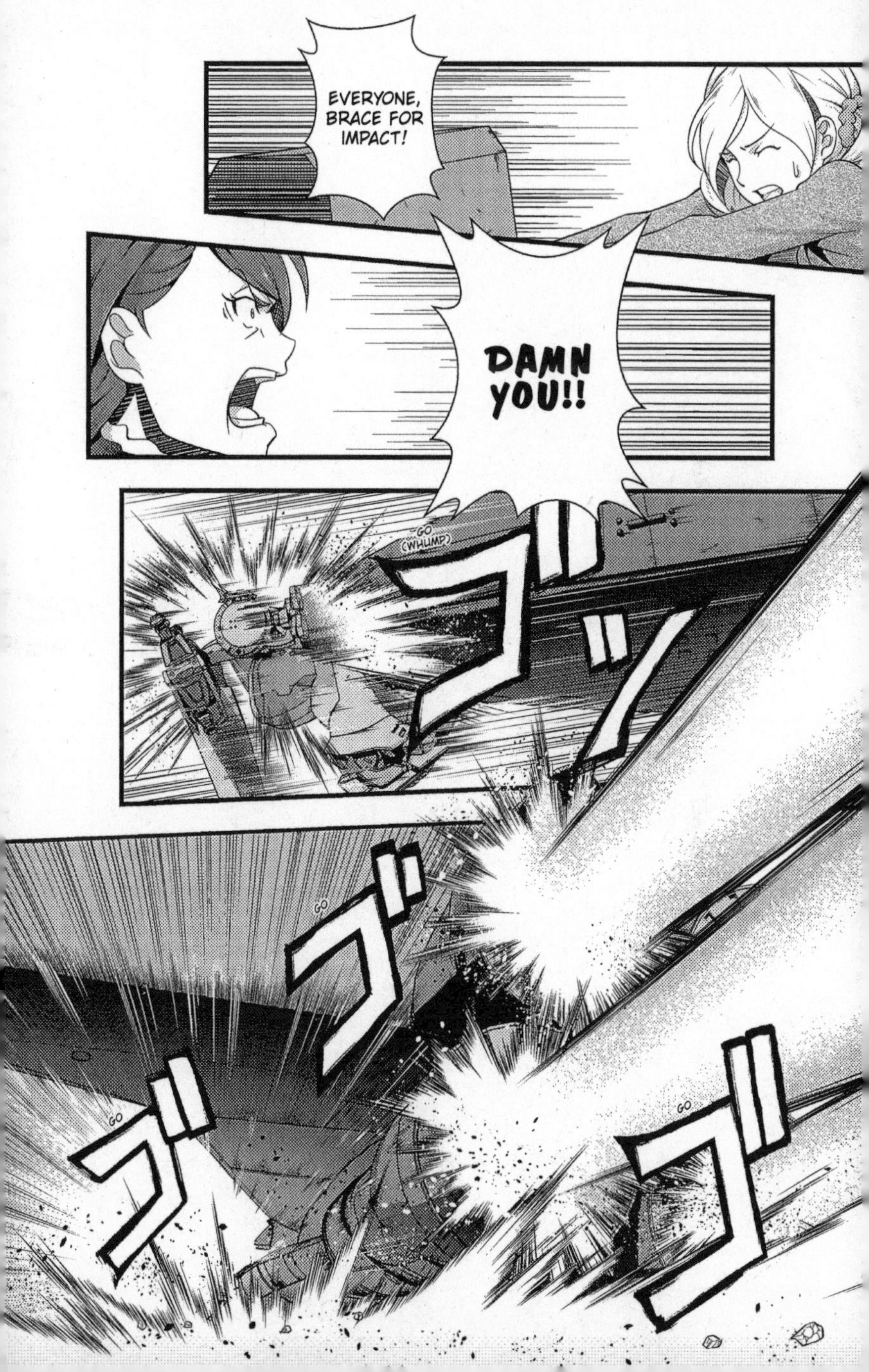
EVERYONE, BRACE FOR IMPACT!
DAMN YOU!!
GO (WHUMP)
GO
GO
GO

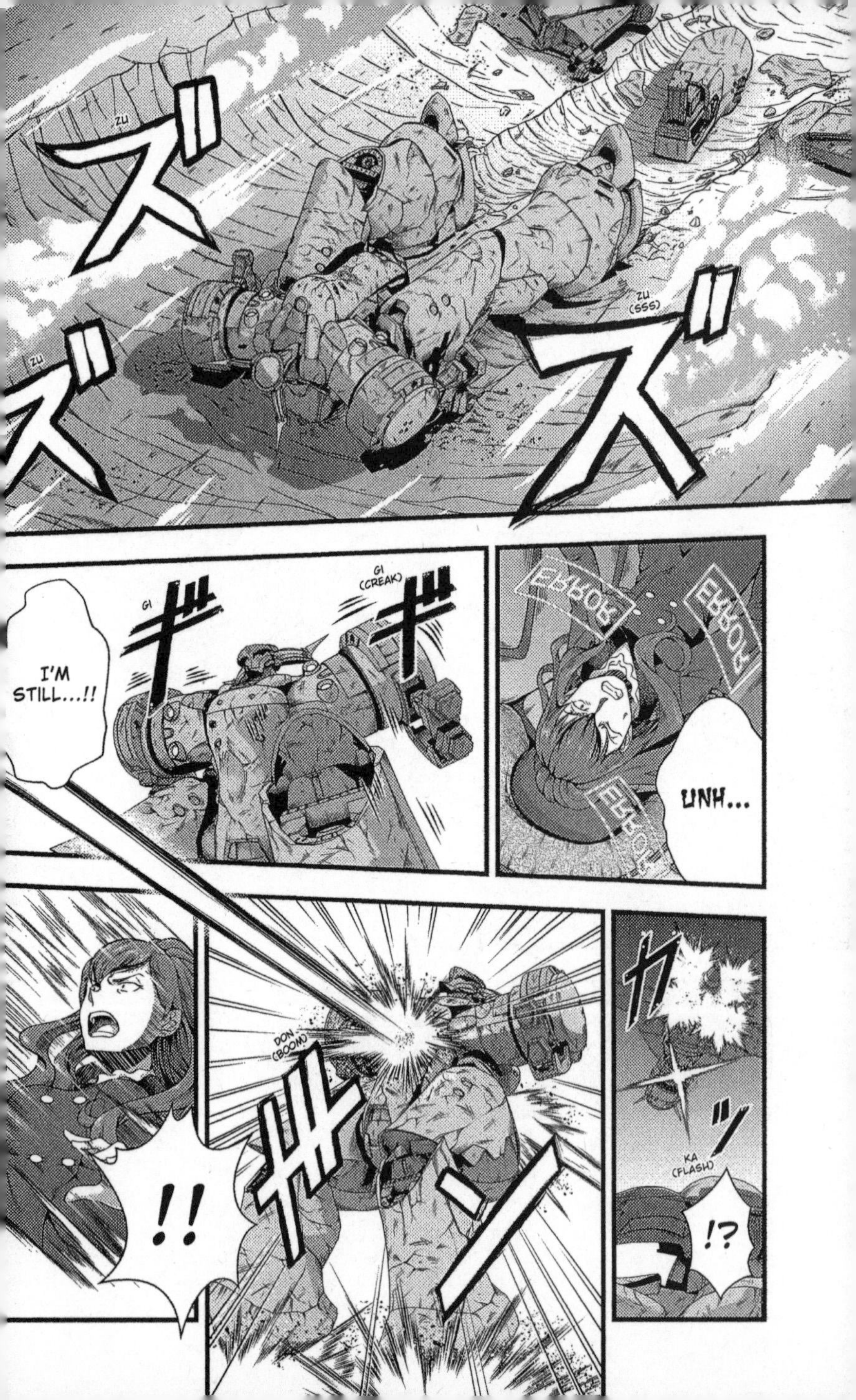
ZU
ZU (SSS)
ZU
ERROR
ERROR
ERROR
UNH...
GI (CREAK)
GI
I'M STILL...!!
KA (FLASH)
!?
DON (BOOM)
!!

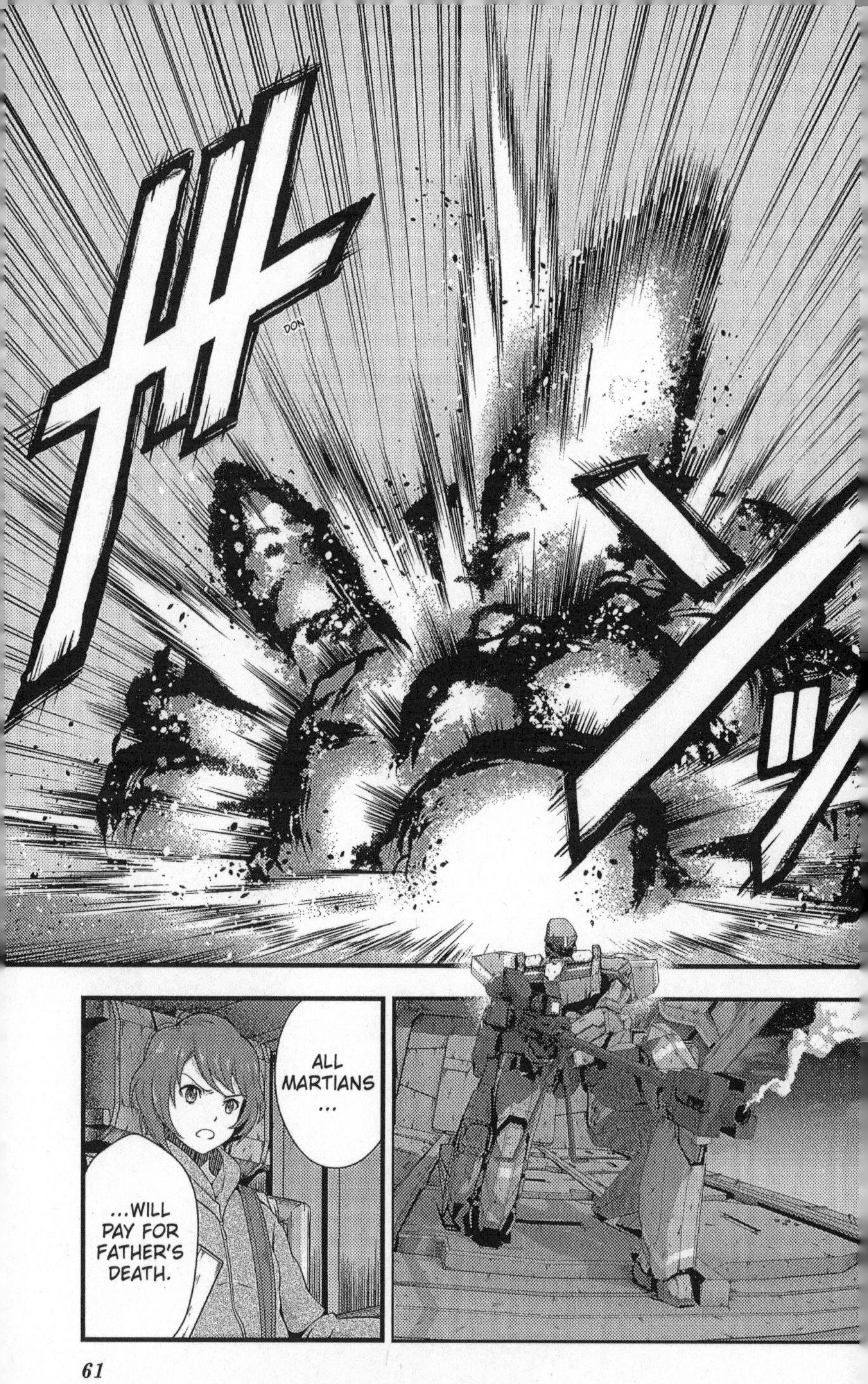
DON
ALL MARTIANS ...
...WILL PAY FOR FATHER'S DEATH.

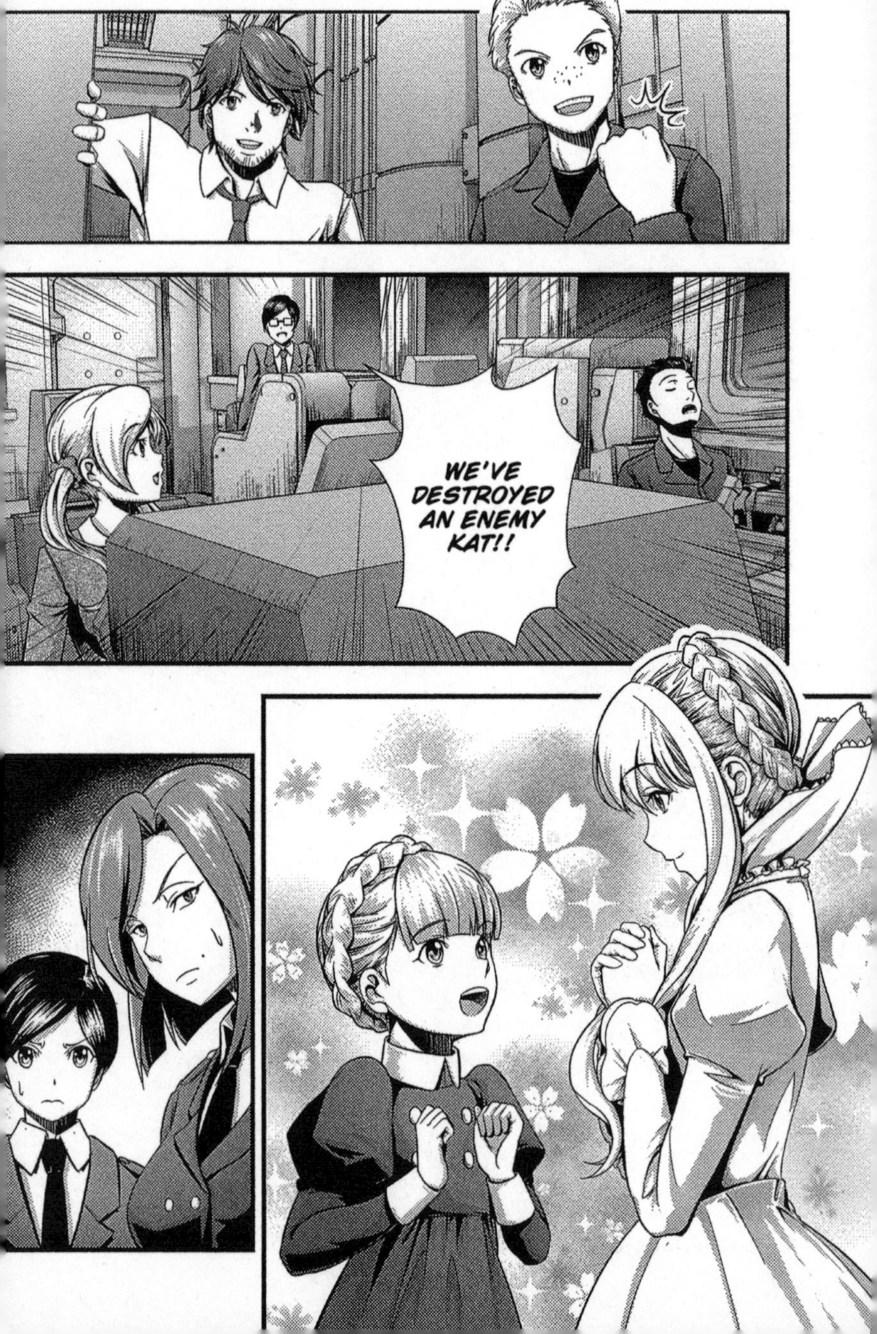
WE'VE DESTROYED AN ENEMY KAT!!

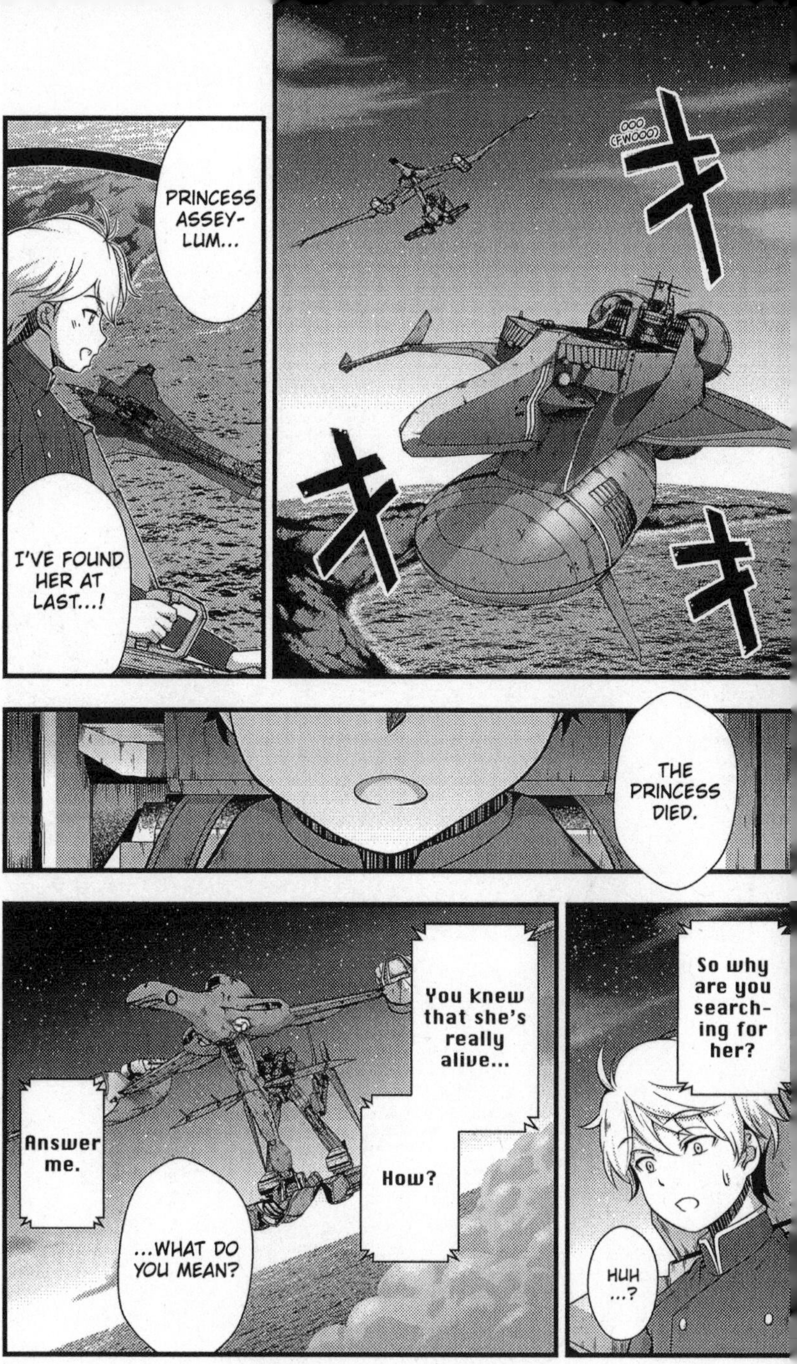
OOO (FWOOO)
PRINCESS ASSEY-LUM...
I'VE FOUND HER AT LAST...!
THE PRINCESS DIED.
So why are you search-ing for her?
HUH ...?
You knew that she's really alive...
How?
Answer me.
...WHAT DO YOU MEAN?

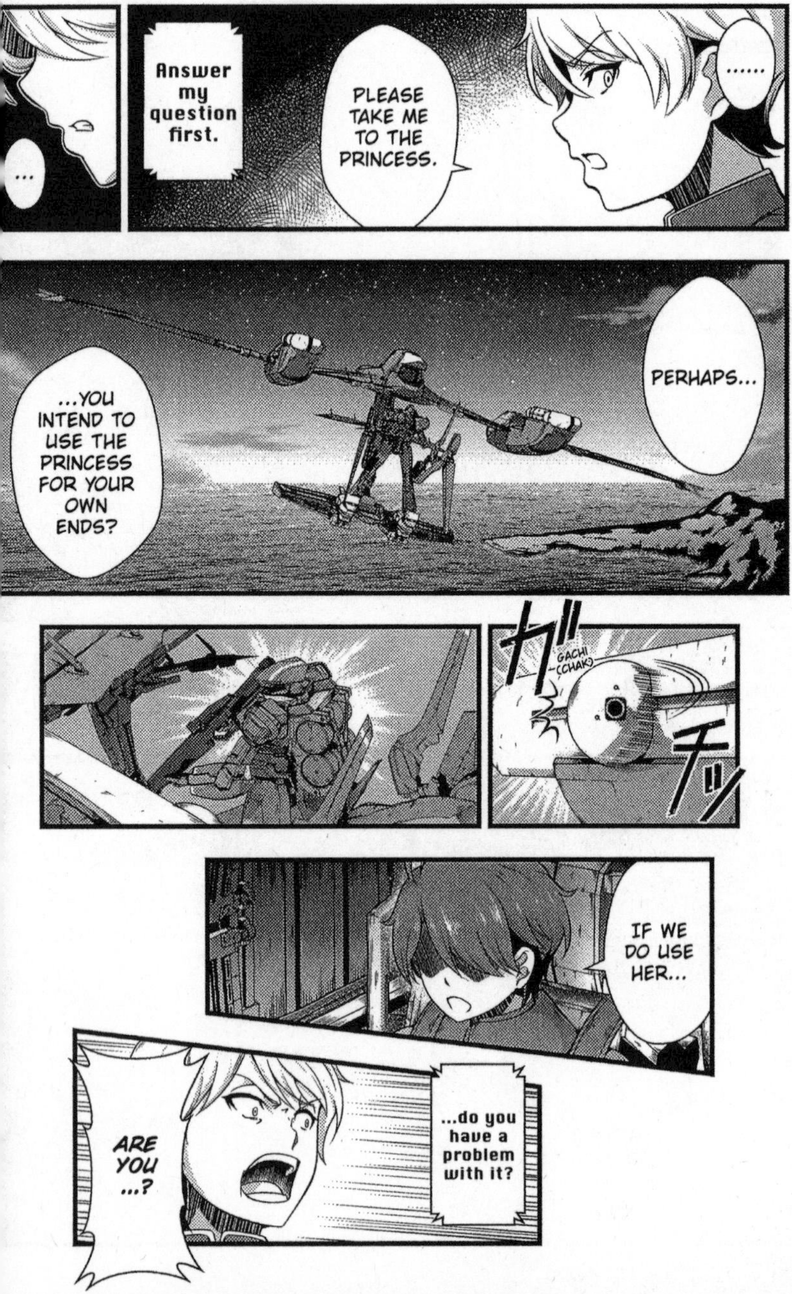
......
PLEASE TAKE ME TO THE PRINCESS.
Answer my question first.
...
PERHAPS...
...YOU INTEND TO USE THE PRINCESS FOR YOUR OWN ENDS?
GACHI (CHAK)
IF WE DO USE HER...
...do you have a problem with it?
ARE YOU ...?

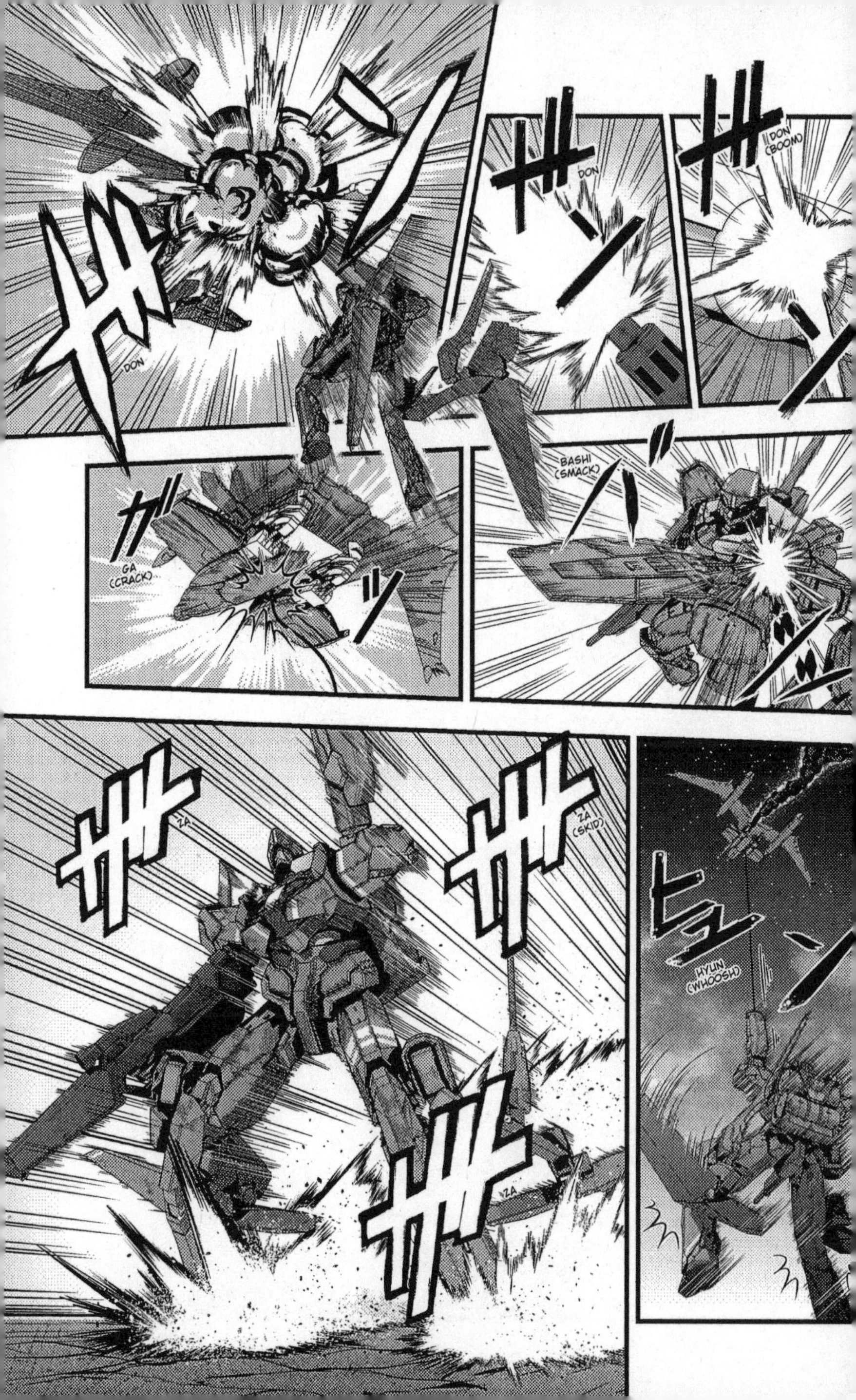
DON (BOOM)
DON
DON
BASHI (SMACK)
GA (CRACK)
HYUN (WHOOSH)
ZA (SKID)
ZA
ZA

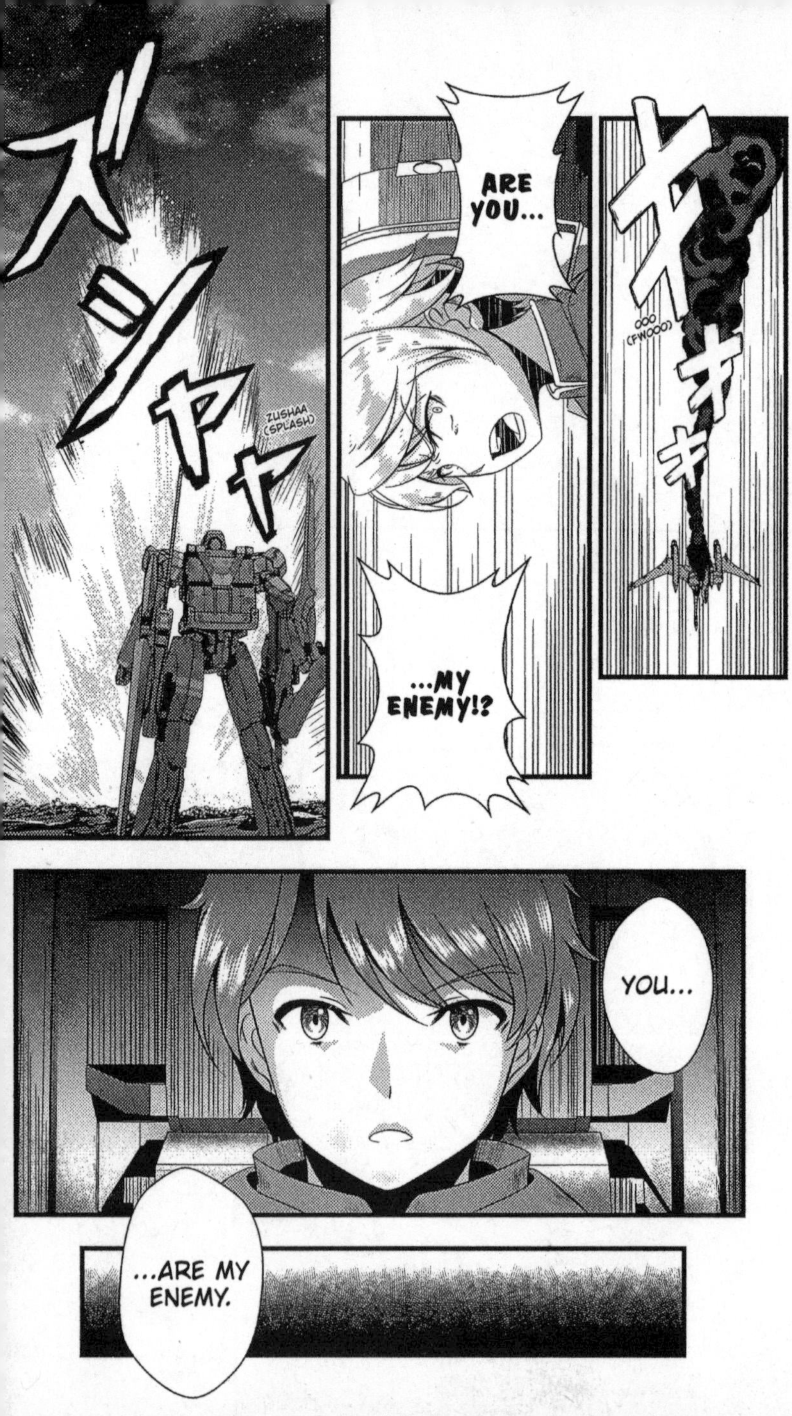
OOO (FWOOO)
ARE YOU...
...MY ENEMY!?
ZUSHAA (SPLASH)
YOU...
...ARE MY ENEMY.

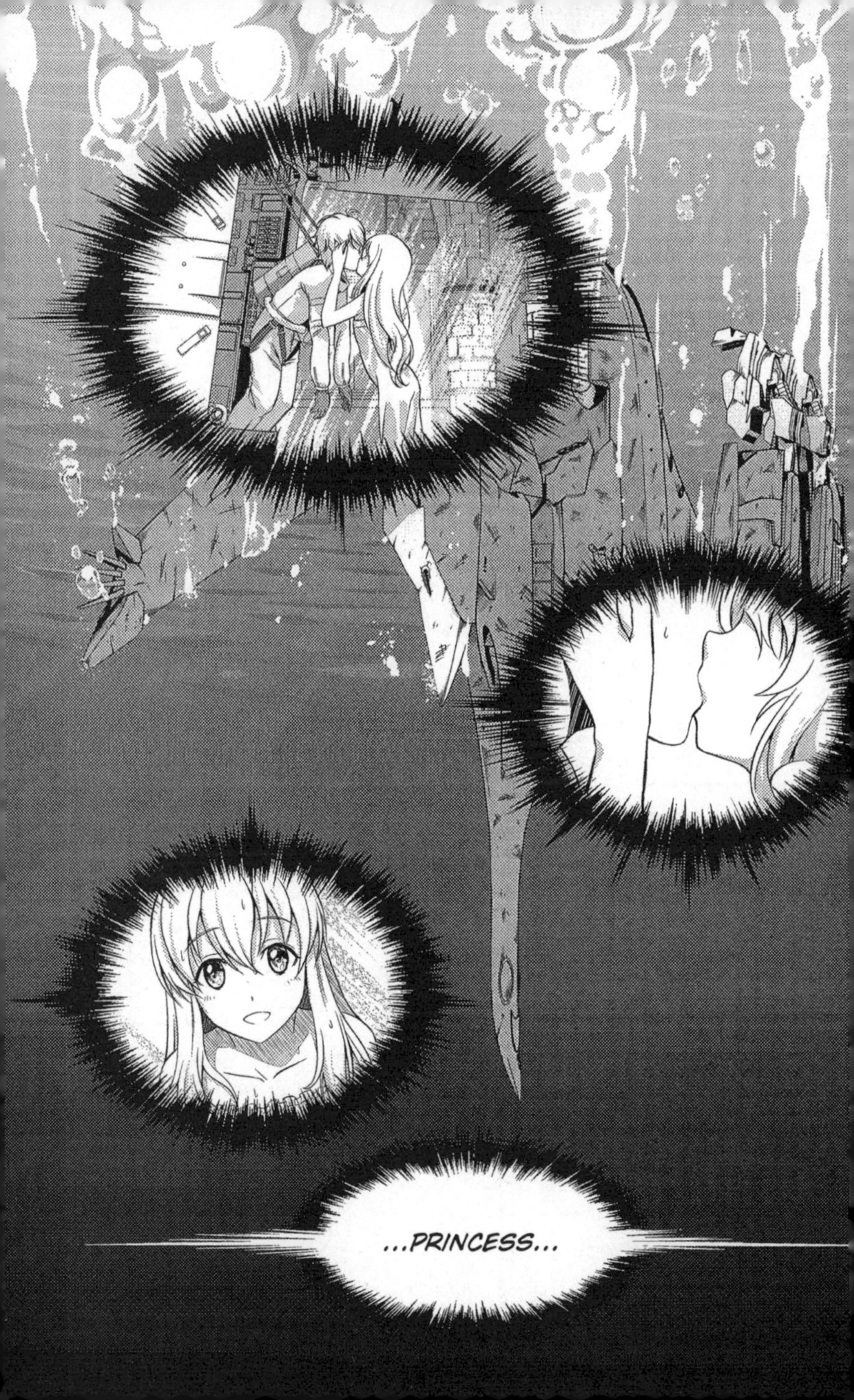
...PRINCESS...

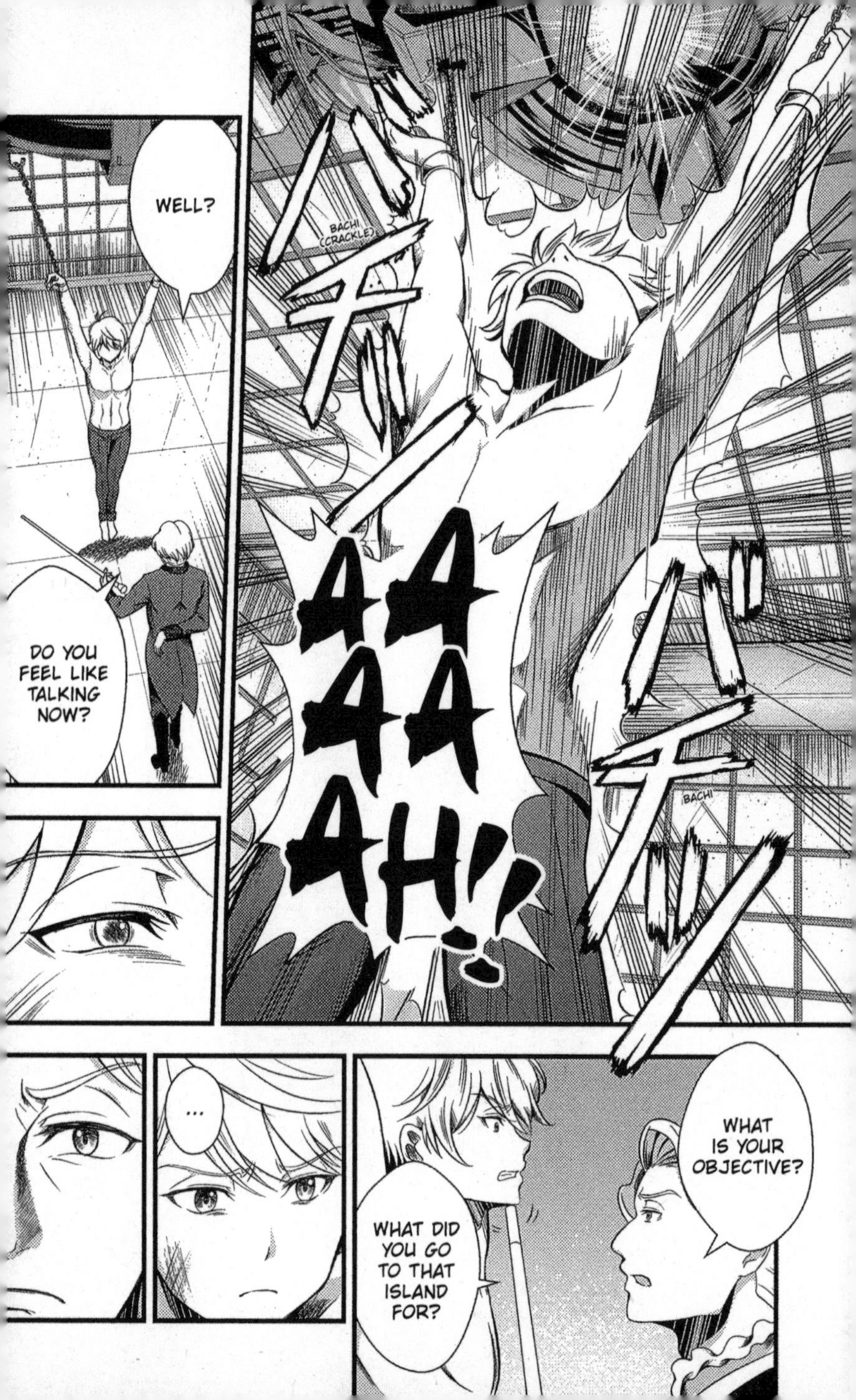
BACHI (CRACKLE)
AAAAAAH!!
BACHI
WELL?
DO YOU FEEL LIKE TALKING NOW?
WHAT IS YOUR OBJECTIVE?
WHAT DID YOU GO TO THAT ISLAND FOR?
...

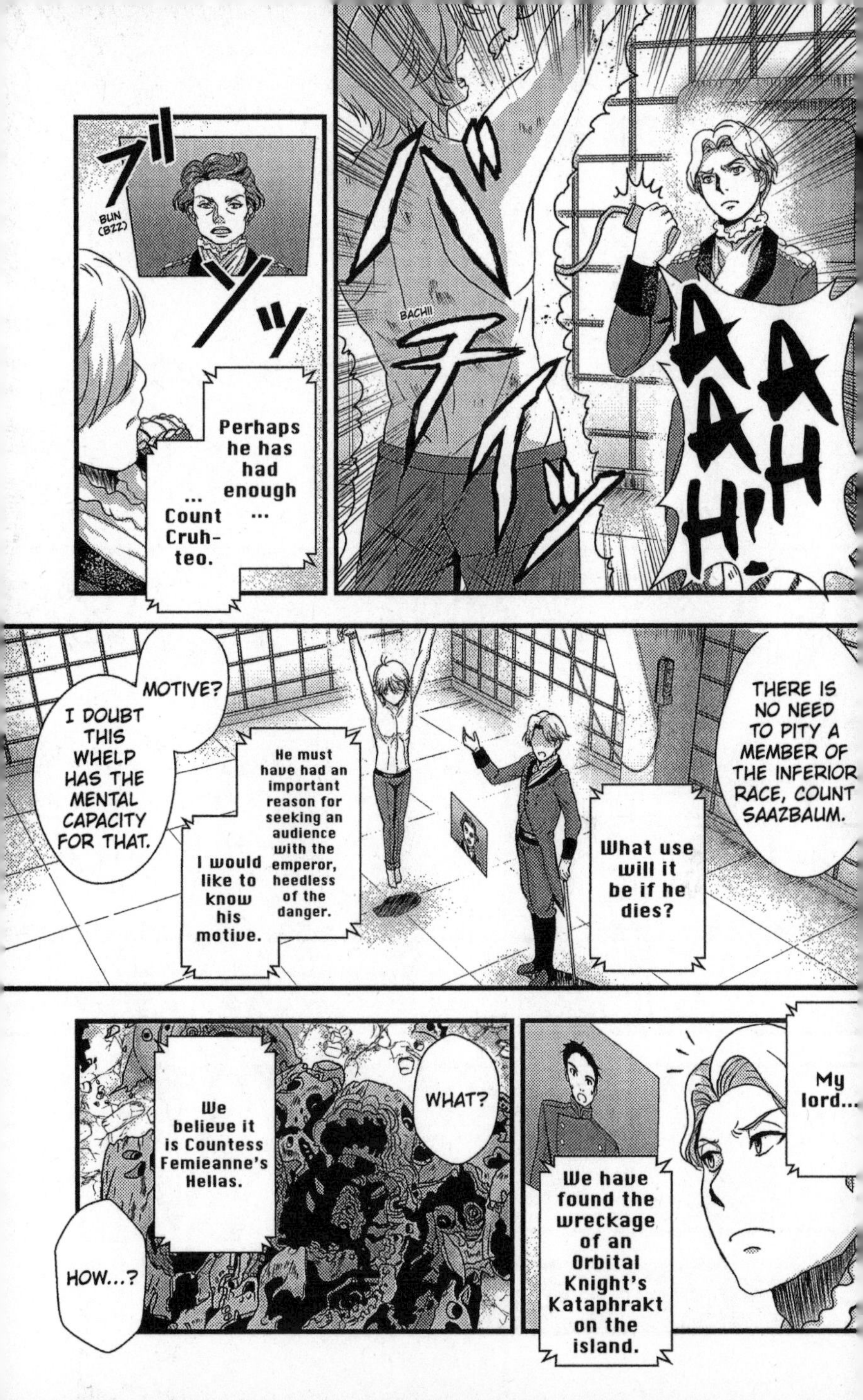
AAAHH!!
BACHII
BUN (BZZ)
Perhaps he has had enough... ...Count Cruhteo.
THERE IS NO NEED TO PITY A MEMBER OF THE INFERIOR RACE, COUNT SAAZBAUM.
What use will it be if he dies?
He must have had an important reason for seeking an audience with the emperor, heedless of the danger.
I would like to know his motive.
MOTIVE?
I DOUBT THIS WHELP HAS THE MENTAL CAPACITY FOR THAT.
My lord...
We have found the wreckage of an Orbital Knight's Kataphrakt on the island.
WHAT?
We believe it is Countess Femieanne's Hellas.
HOW...?

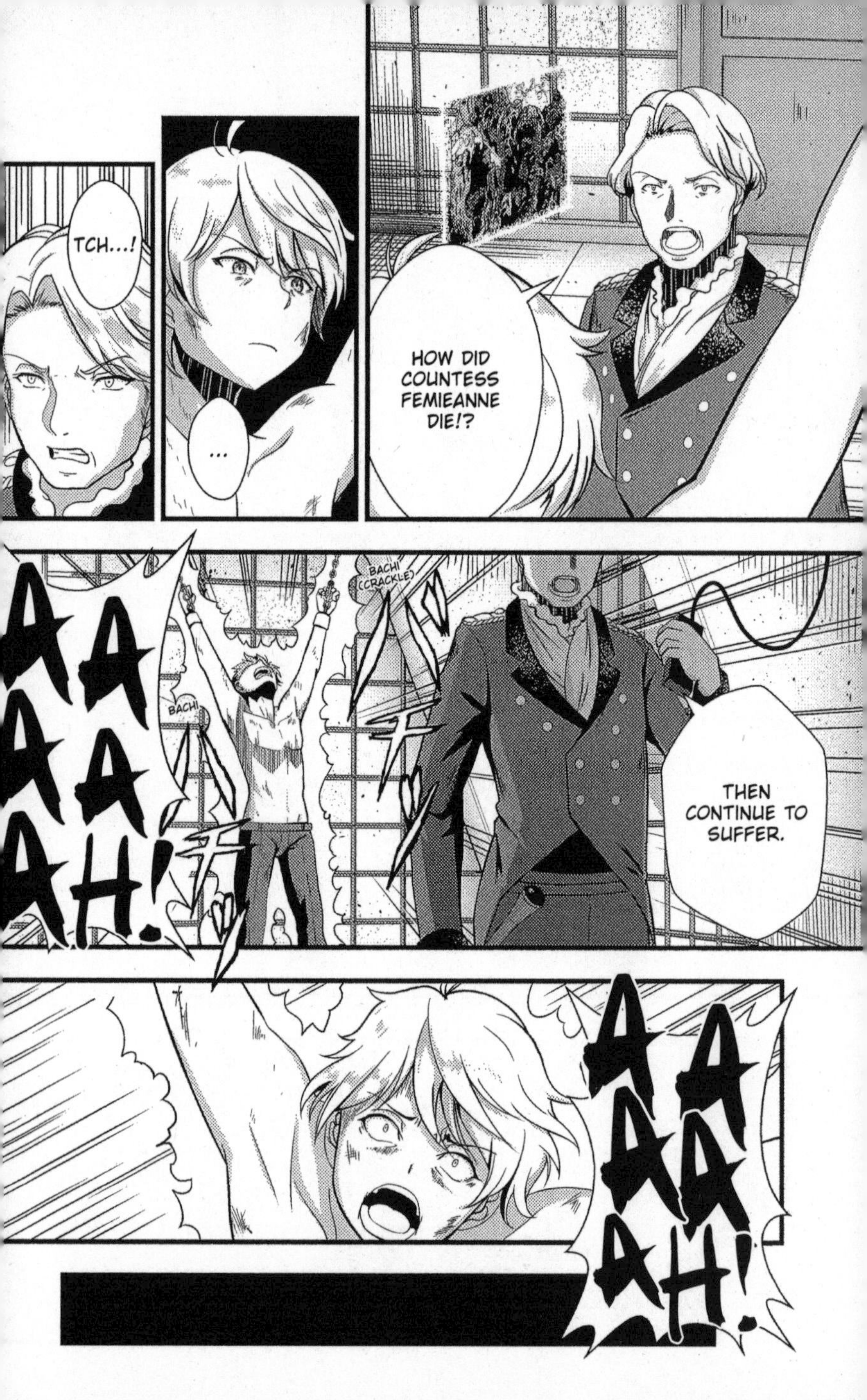
HOW DID COUNTESS FEMIEANNE DIE!?
...
TCH...!
THEN CONTINUE TO SUFFER.
BACHI (CRACKLE)
BACHI
AAAAAAH!
AAAAAAH!

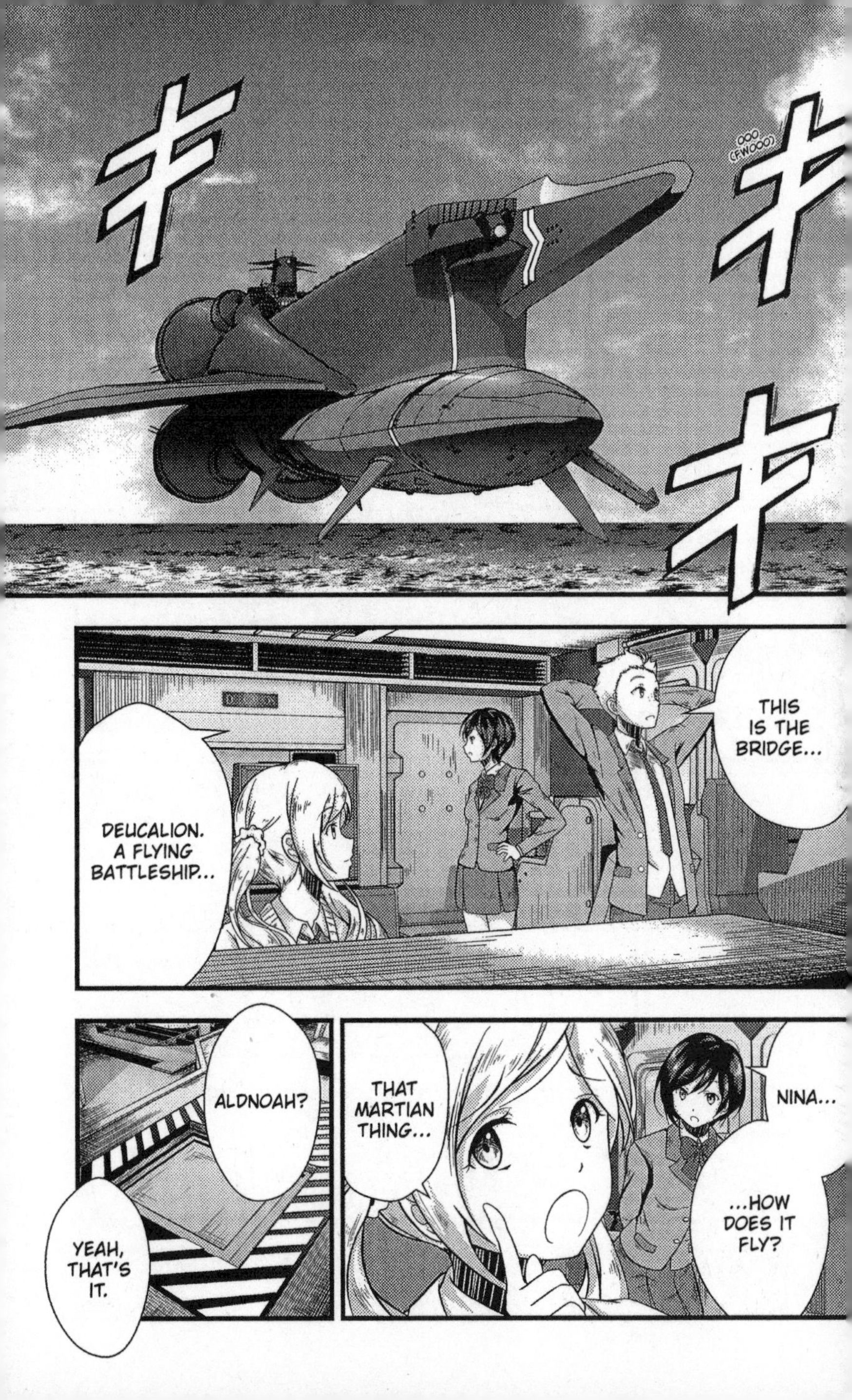
OOO (FWOOO)
THIS IS THE BRIDGE...
DEUCALION. A FLYING BATTLESHIP...
NINA...
...HOW DOES IT FLY?
THAT MARTIAN THING...
ALDNOAH?
YEAH, THAT'S IT.

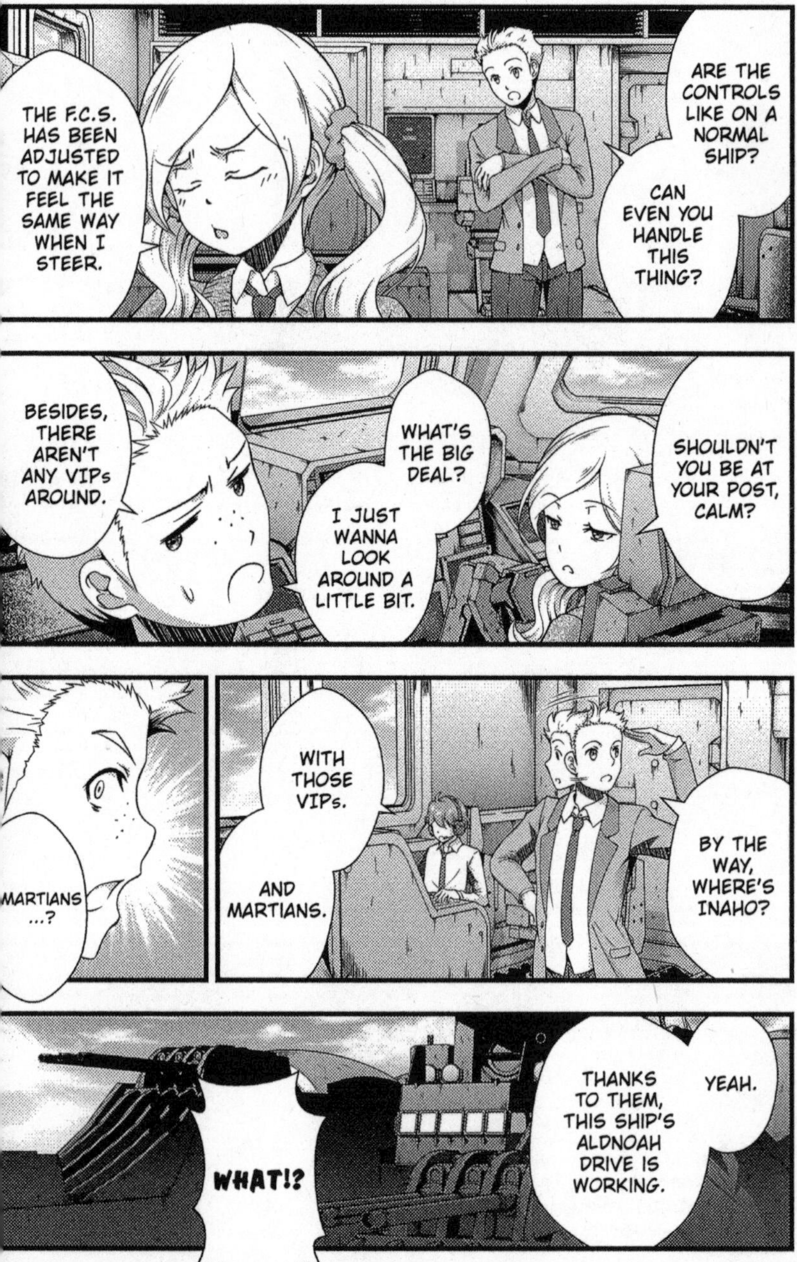
ARE THE CONTROLS LIKE ON A NORMAL SHIP?
CAN EVEN YOU HANDLE THIS THING?
THE F.C.S. HAS BEEN ADJUSTED TO MAKE IT FEEL THE SAME WAY WHEN I STEER.
SHOULDN'T YOU BE AT YOUR POST, CALM?
WHAT'S THE BIG DEAL?
I JUST WANNA LOOK AROUND A LITTLE BIT.
BESIDES, THERE AREN'T ANY VIPs AROUND.
BY THE WAY, WHERE'S INAHO?
WITH THOSE VIPs.
AND MARTIANS.
MARTIANS ...?
YEAH.
THANKS TO THEM, THIS SHIP'S ALDNOAH DRIVE IS WORKING.
WHAT!?

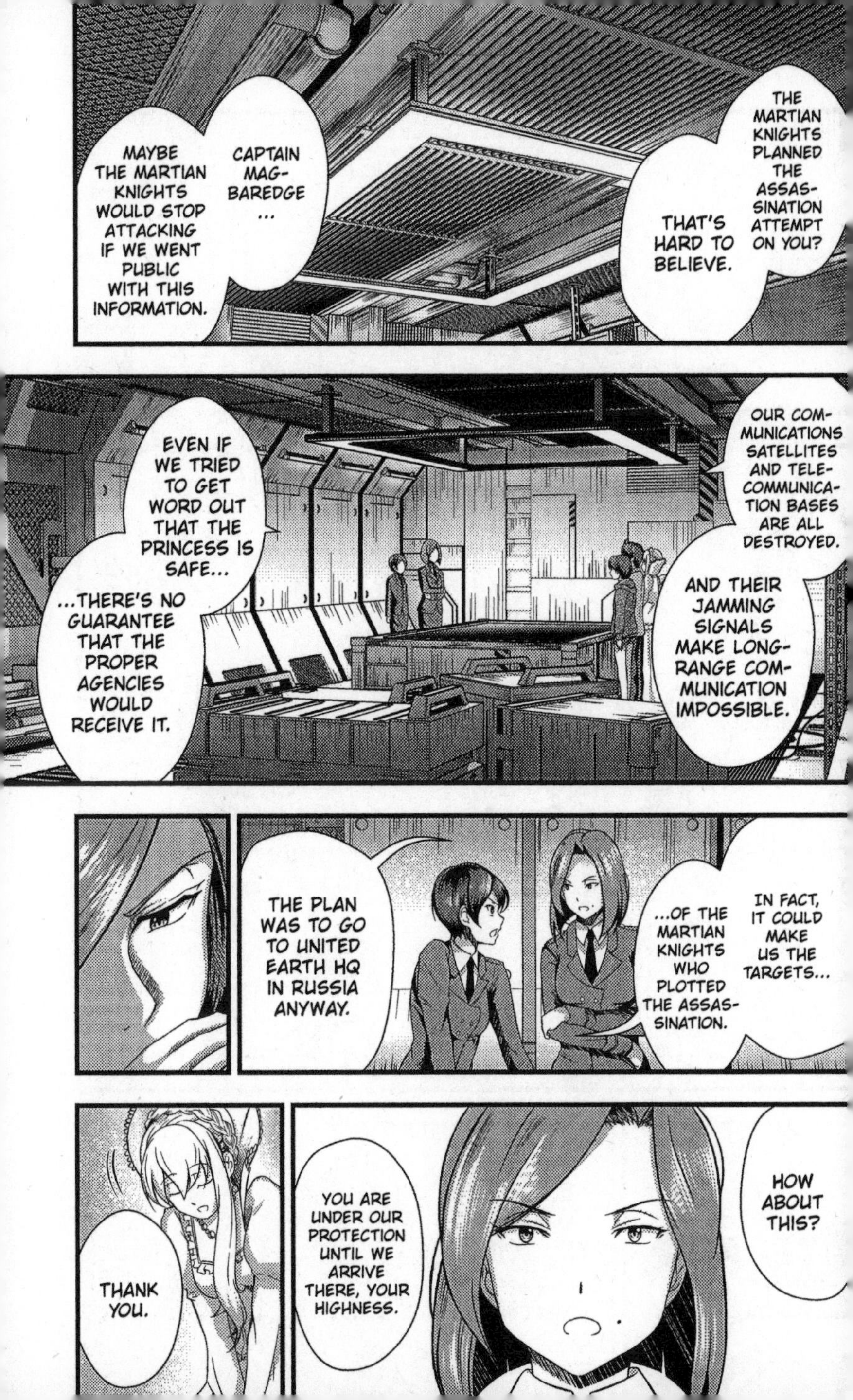
THE MARTIAN KNIGHTS PLANNED THE ASSASSINATION ATTEMPT ON YOU?
THAT'S HARD TO BELIEVE.
CAPTAIN MAGBAREDGE...
MAYBE THE MARTIAN KNIGHTS WOULD STOP ATTACKING IF WE WENT PUBLIC WITH THIS INFORMATION.
OUR COMMUNICATIONS SATELLITES AND TELECOMMUNICATION BASES ARE ALL DESTROYED.
AND THEIR JAMMING SIGNALS MAKE LONG-RANGE COMMUNICATION IMPOSSIBLE.
EVEN IF WE TRIED TO GET WORD OUT THAT THE PRINCESS IS SAFE...
...THERE'S NO GUARANTEE THAT THE PROPER AGENCIES WOULD RECEIVE IT.
IN FACT, IT COULD MAKE US THE TARGETS...
...OF THE MARTIAN KNIGHTS WHO PLOTTED THE ASSASSINATION.
THE PLAN WAS TO GO TO UNITED EARTH HQ IN RUSSIA ANYWAY.
HOW ABOUT THIS?
YOU ARE UNDER OUR PROTECTION UNTIL WE ARRIVE THERE, YOUR HIGHNESS.
THANK YOU.

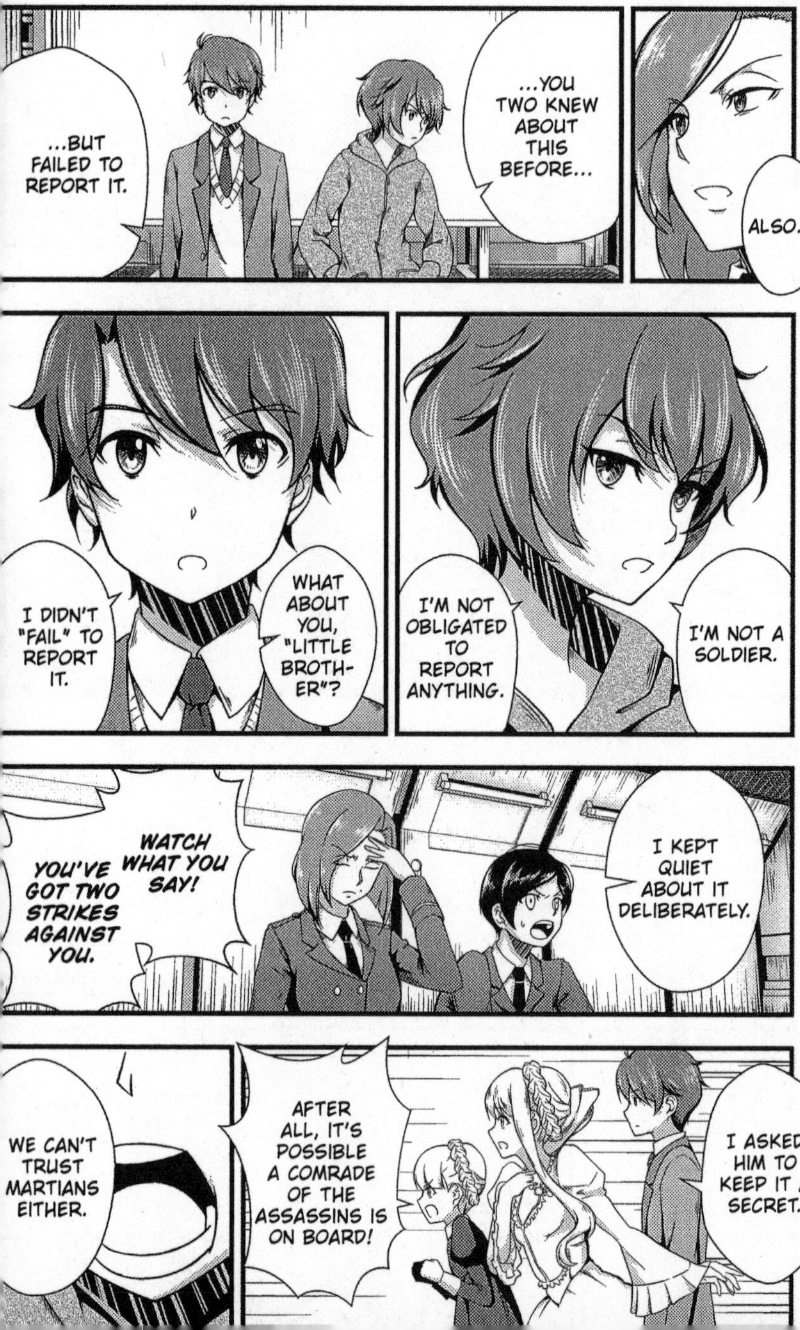
ALSO...
...YOU TWO KNEW ABOUT THIS BEFORE...
...BUT FAILED TO REPORT IT.
I'M NOT A SOLDIER.
I'M NOT OBLIGATED TO REPORT ANYTHING.
WHAT ABOUT YOU, "LITTLE BROTHER"?
I DIDN'T "FAIL" TO REPORT IT.
I KEPT QUIET ABOUT IT DELIBERATELY.
WATCH WHAT YOU SAY!
YOU'VE GOT TWO STRIKES AGAINST YOU.
I ASKED HIM TO KEEP IT A SECRET.
AFTER ALL, IT'S POSSIBLE A COMRADE OF THE ASSASSINS IS ON BOARD!
WE CAN'T TRUST MARTIANS EITHER.

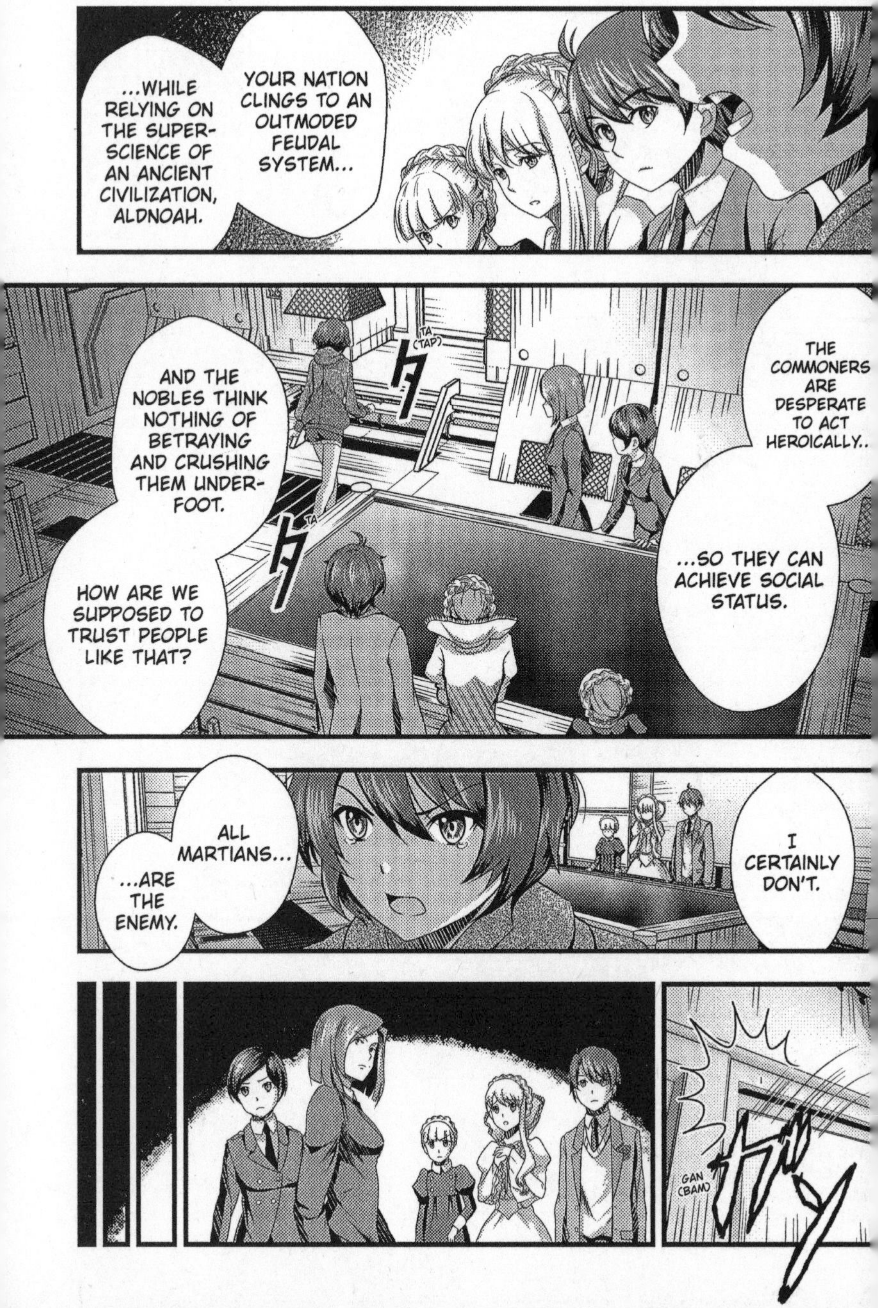
YOUR NATION CLINGS TO AN OUTMODED FEUDAL SYSTEM...
...WHILE RELYING ON THE SUPER-SCIENCE OF AN ANCIENT CIVILIZATION, ALDNOAH.
THE COMMONERS ARE DESPERATE TO ACT HEROICALLY..
...SO THEY CAN ACHIEVE SOCIAL STATUS.
TA (TAP)
AND THE NOBLES THINK NOTHING OF BETRAYING AND CRUSHING THEM UNDER-FOOT.
TA
HOW ARE WE SUPPOSED TO TRUST PEOPLE LIKE THAT?
I CERTAINLY DON'T.
ALL MARTIANS...
...ARE THE ENEMY.
GAN (BAM)

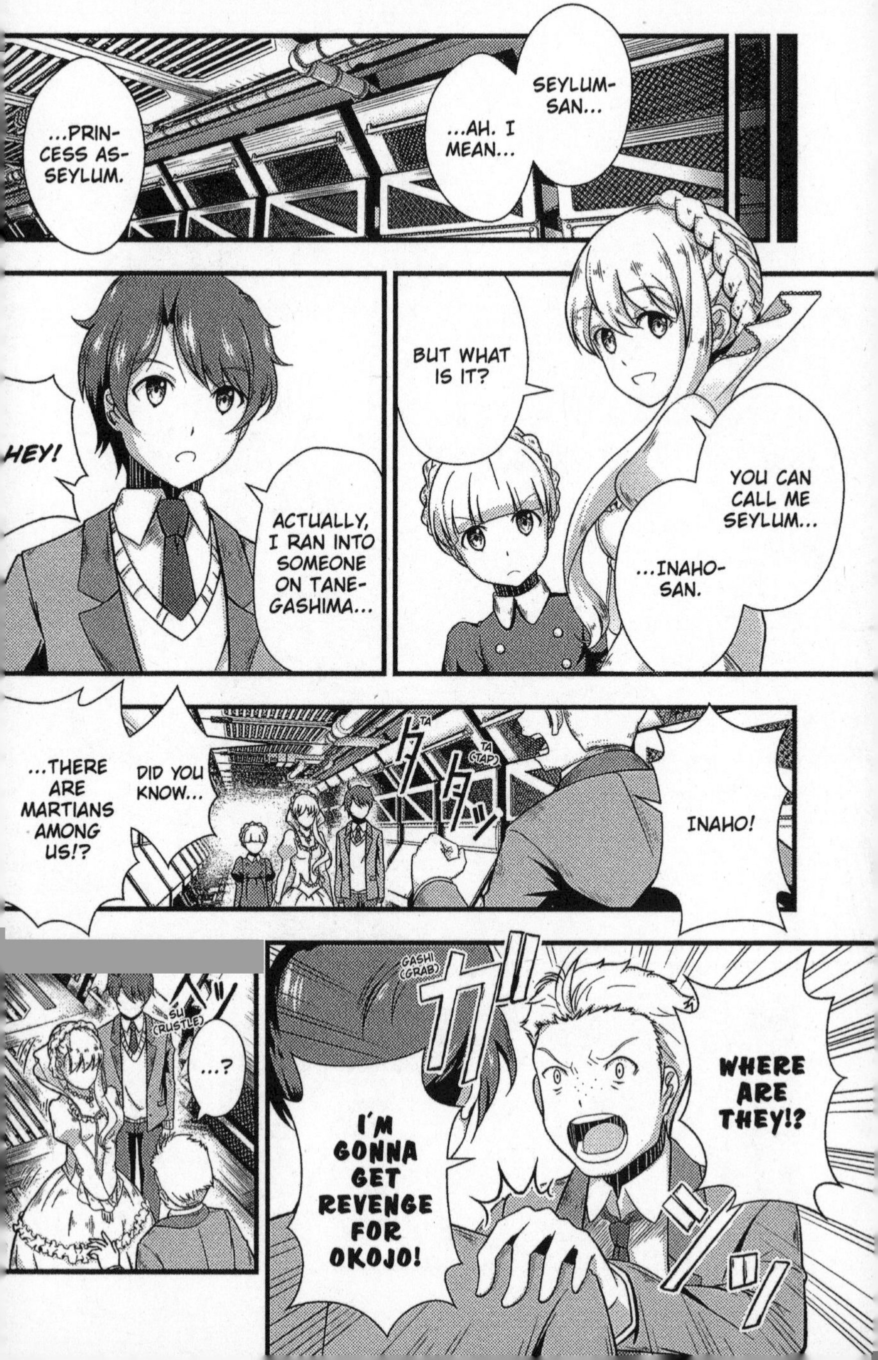
SEYLUM-SAN...
...AH. I MEAN...
...PRINCESS AS-SEYLUM.
YOU CAN CALL ME SEYLUM...
...INAHO-SAN.
BUT WHAT IS IT?
ACTUALLY, I RAN INTO SOMEONE ON TANEGASHIMA...
HEY!
INAHO!
TA
TA (TAP)
DID YOU KNOW...
...THERE ARE MARTIANS AMONG US!?
GASHI (GRAB)
WHERE ARE THEY!?
I'M GONNA GET REVENGE FOR OKOJO!
SU (RUSTLE)
...?

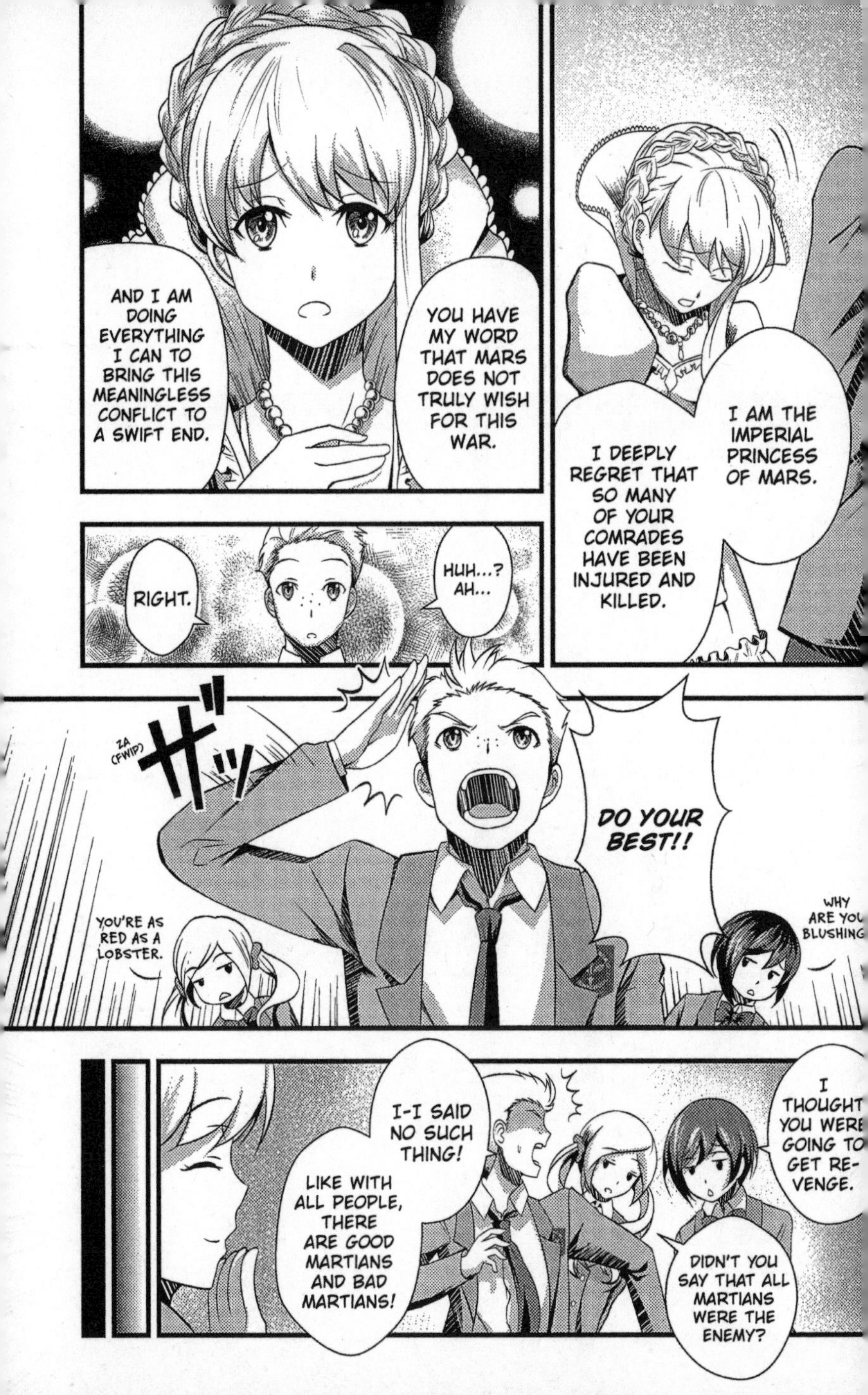
I AM THE IMPERIAL PRINCESS OF MARS.
I DEEPLY REGRET THAT SO MANY OF YOUR COMRADES HAVE BEEN INJURED AND KILLED.
YOU HAVE MY WORD THAT MARS DOES NOT TRULY WISH FOR THIS WAR.
AND I AM DOING EVERYTHING I CAN TO BRING THIS MEANINGLESS CONFLICT TO A SWIFT END.
HUH...? AH...
RIGHT.
DO YOUR BEST!!
ZA (FWIP)
WHY ARE YOU BLUSHING
YOU'RE AS RED AS A LOBSTER.
I THOUGHT YOU WERE GOING TO GET RE-VENGE.
DIDN'T YOU SAY THAT ALL MARTIANS WERE THE ENEMY?
I-I SAID NO SUCH THING!
LIKE WITH ALL PEOPLE, THERE ARE GOOD MARTIANS AND BAD MARTIANS!

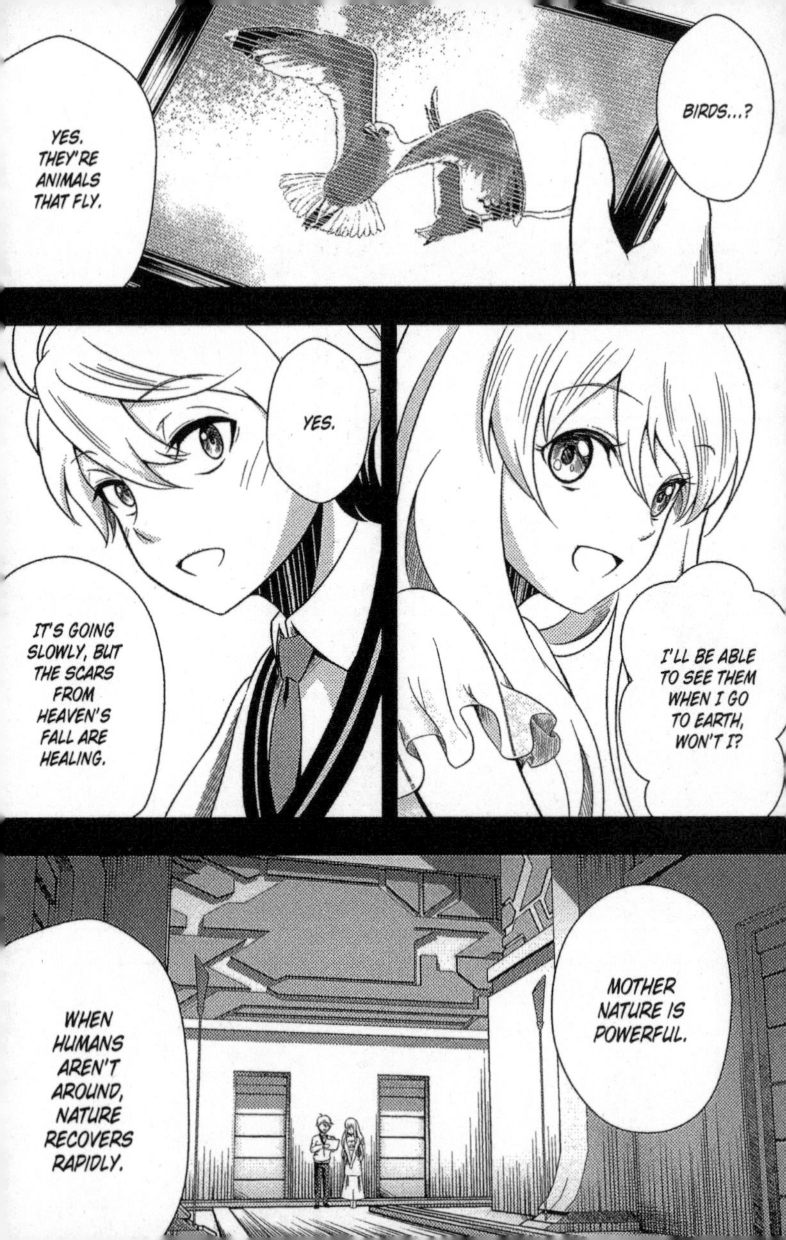
BIRDS...?
YES. THEY'RE ANIMALS THAT FLY.
I'LL BE ABLE TO SEE THEM WHEN I GO TO EARTH, WON'T I?
YES.
IT'S GOING SLOWLY, BUT THE SCARS FROM HEAVEN'S FALL ARE HEALING.
MOTHER NATURE IS POWERFUL.
WHEN HUMANS AREN'T AROUND, NATURE RECOVERS RAPIDLY.

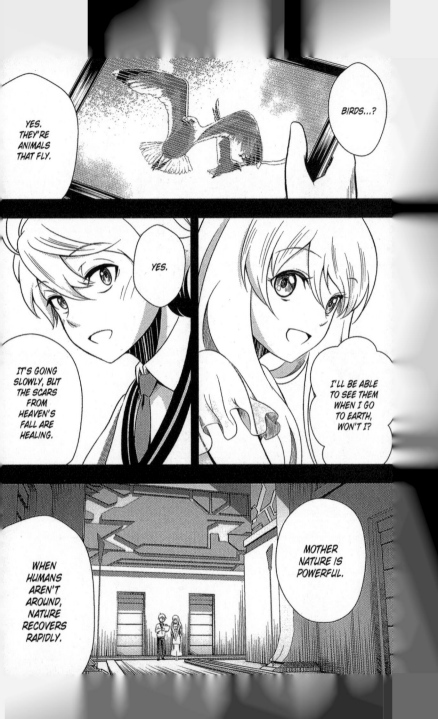

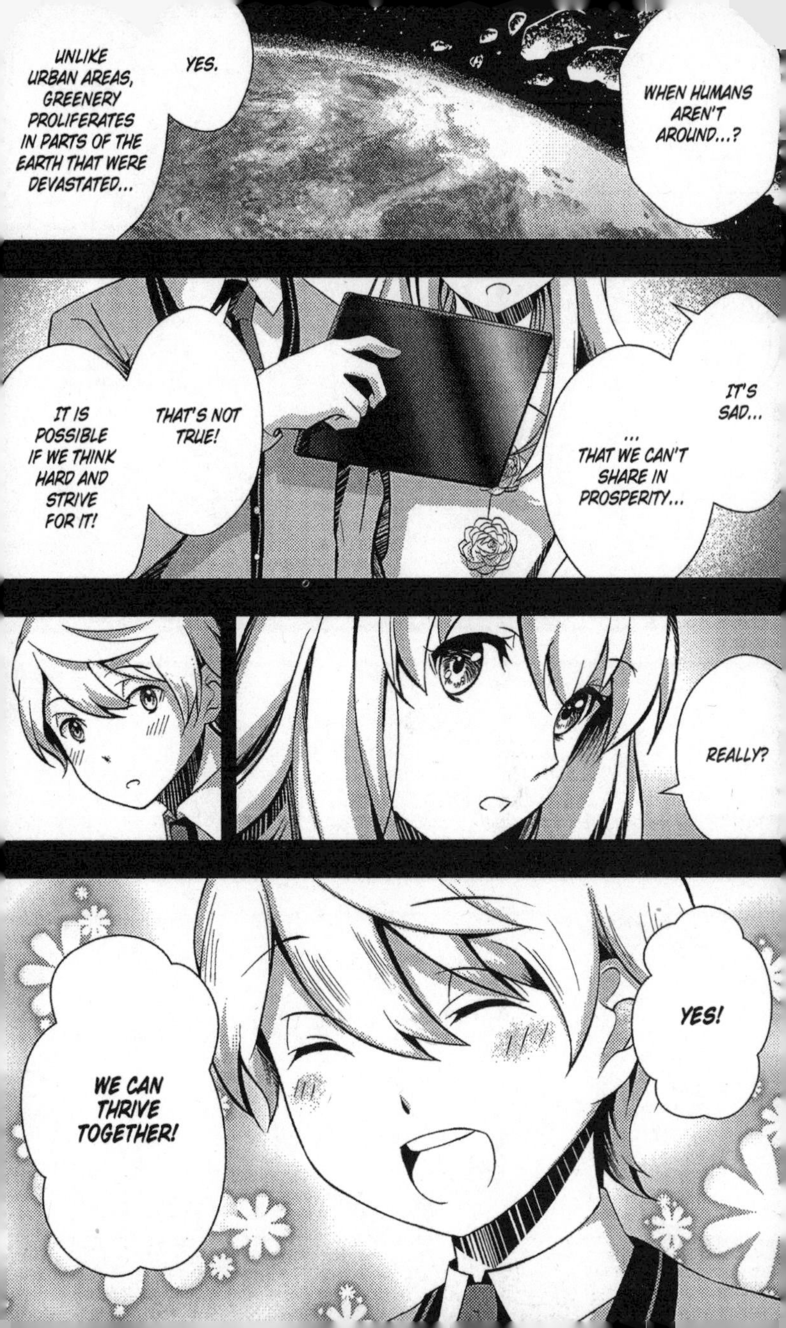
WHEN HUMANS AREN'T AROUND...?
YES.
UNLIKE URBAN AREAS, GREENERY PROLIFERATES IN PARTS OF THE EARTH THAT WERE DEVASTATED...
IT'S SAD...
...THAT WE CAN'T SHARE IN PROSPERITY...
THAT'S NOT TRUE!
IT IS POSSIBLE IF WE THINK HARD AND STRIVE FOR IT!
REALLY?
YES!
WE CAN THRIVE TOGETHER!

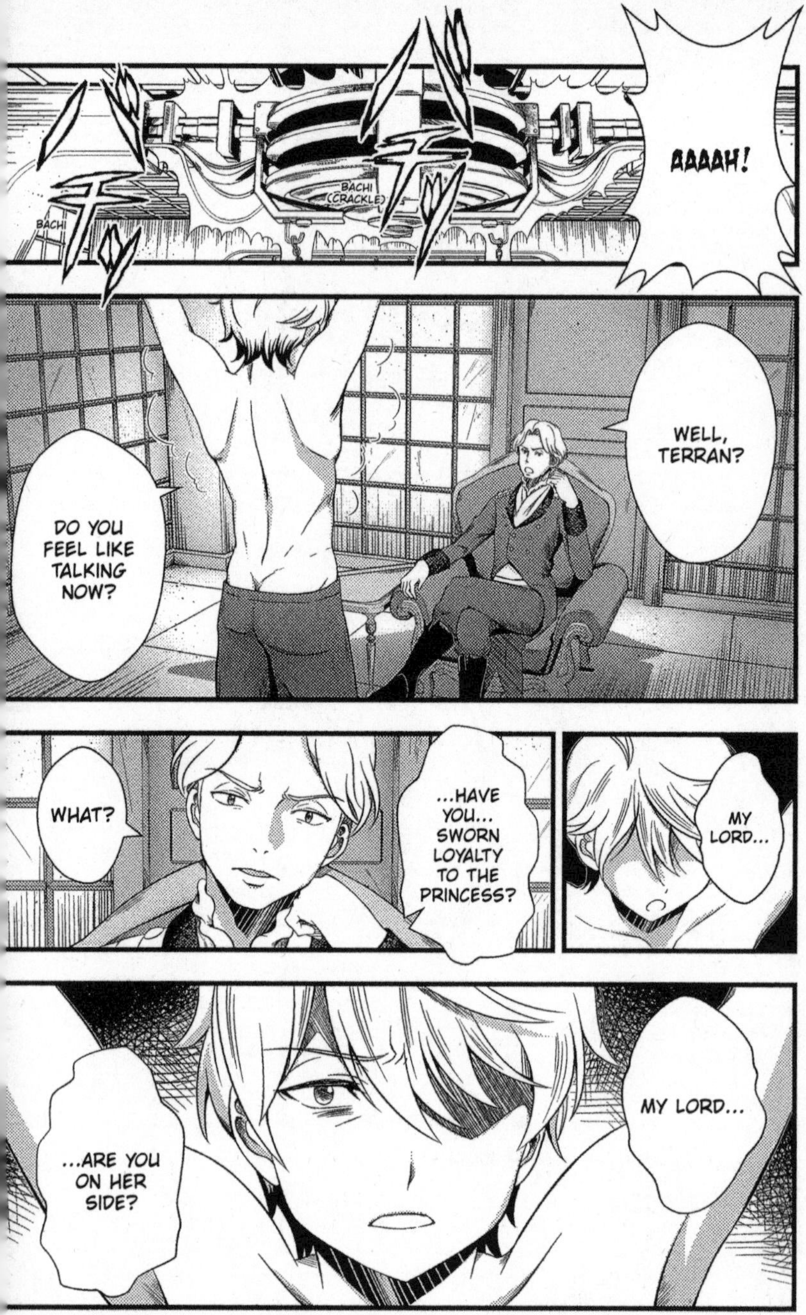
AAAAH!
BACHI (CRACKLE)
BACHI
WELL, TERRAN?
DO YOU FEEL LIKE TALKING NOW?
MY LORD...
...HAVE YOU... SWORN LOYALTY TO THE PRINCESS?
WHAT?
MY LORD...
...ARE YOU ON HER SIDE?

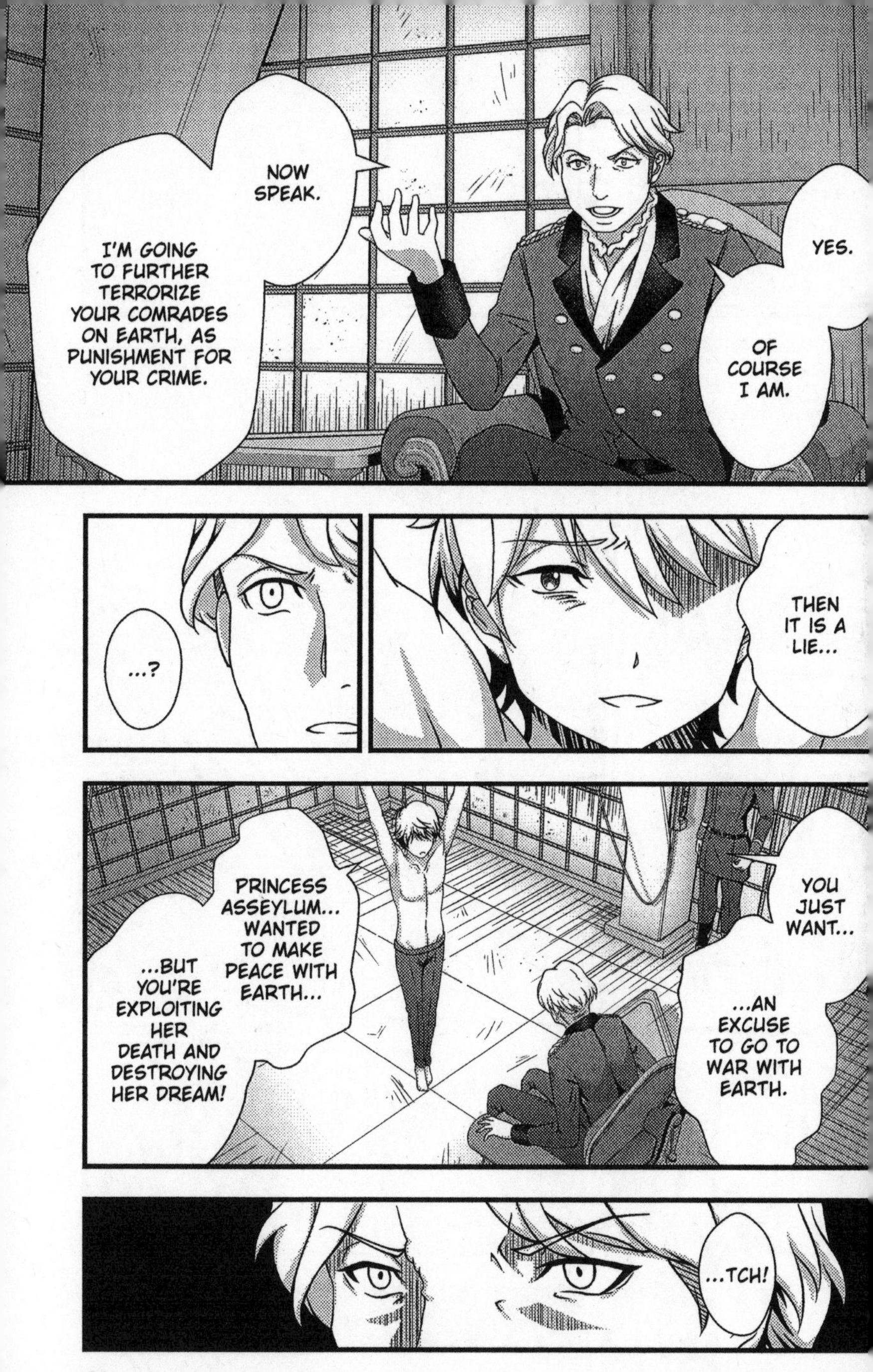
YES.
OF COURSE I AM.
NOW SPEAK.
I'M GOING TO FURTHER TERRORIZE YOUR COMRADES ON EARTH, AS PUNISHMENT FOR YOUR CRIME.
THEN IT IS A LIE...
...?
YOU JUST WANT...
...AN EXCUSE TO GO TO WAR WITH EARTH.
PRINCESS ASSEYLUM... WANTED TO MAKE PEACE WITH EARTH...
...BUT YOU'RE EXPLOITING HER DEATH AND DESTROYING HER DREAM!
...TCH!

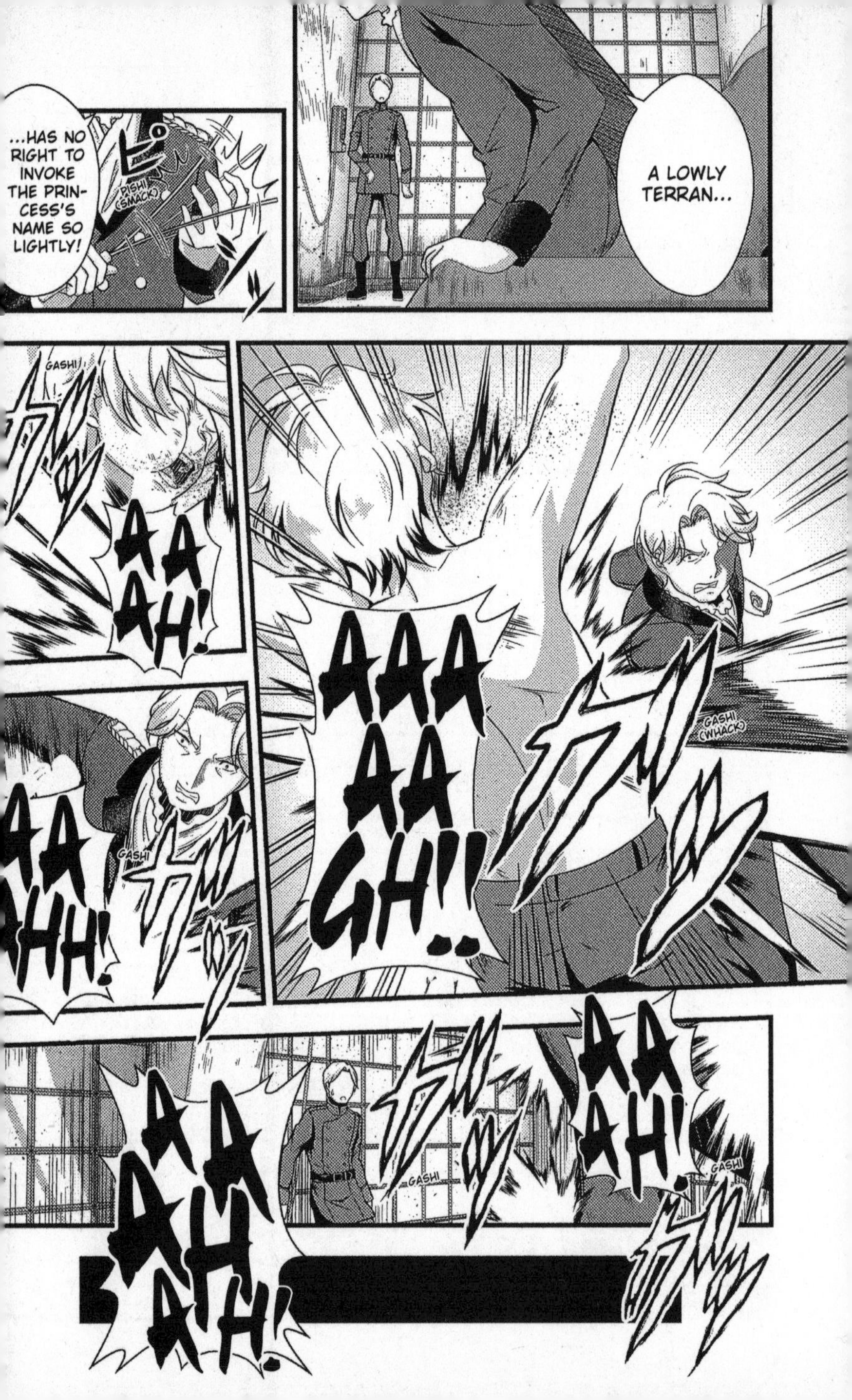
A LOWLY TERRAN...
PISHI (SMACK)
...HAS NO RIGHT TO INVOKE THE PRIN-CESS'S NAME SO LIGHTLY!
GASHI (WHACK)
AAAAAAGH!!
GASHI
AAAAH!
GASHI
AAAAHH!
GASHI
AAAAH!
GASHI
AAAAAH!

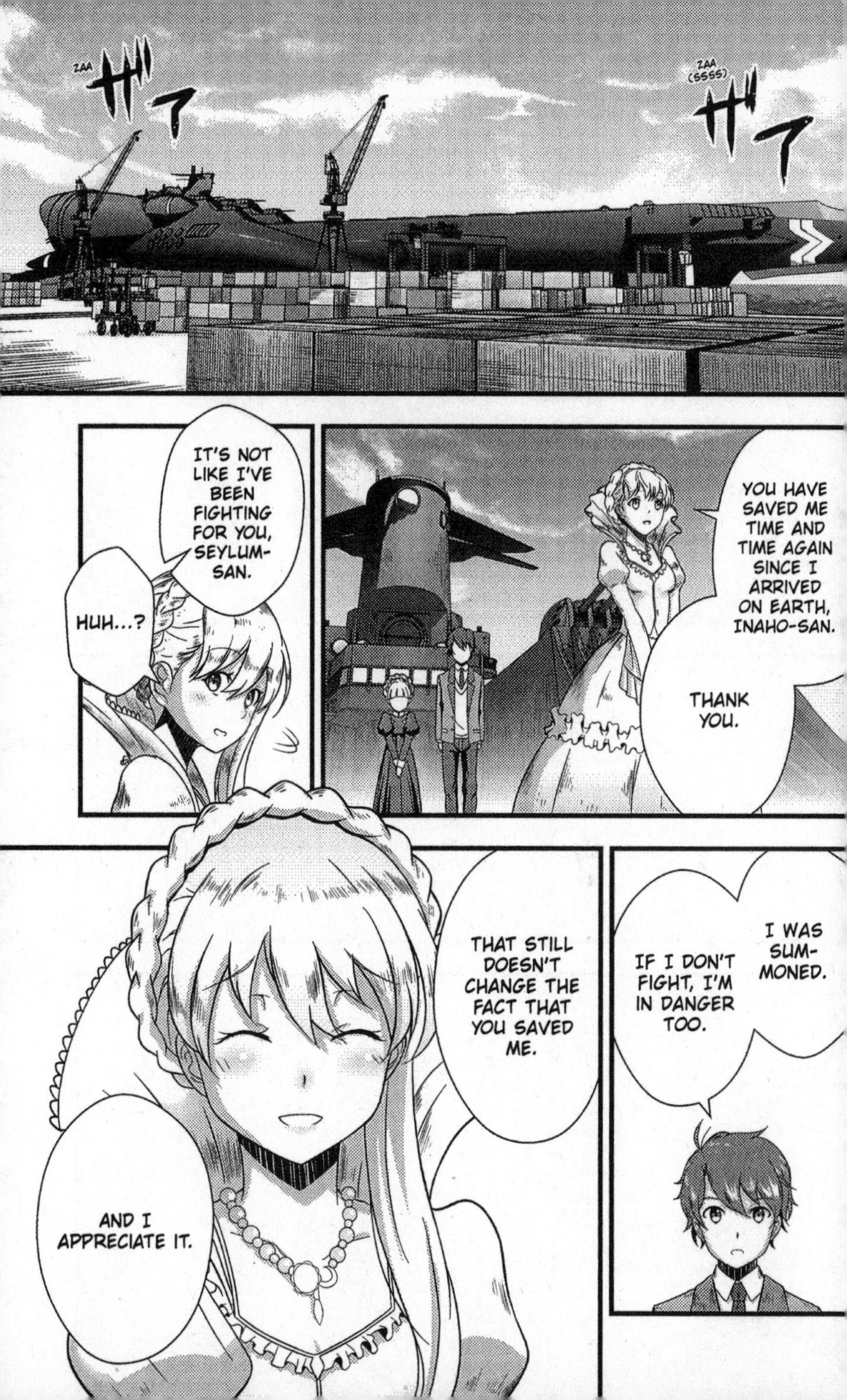
ZAA (SSSS)
ザア
ZAA
ザア
YOU HAVE SAVED ME TIME AND TIME AGAIN SINCE I ARRIVED ON EARTH, INAHO-SAN.
THANK YOU.
IT'S NOT LIKE I'VE BEEN FIGHTING FOR YOU, SEYLUM-SAN.
HUH...?
I WAS SUMMONED.
IF I DON'T FIGHT, I'M IN DANGER TOO.
THAT STILL DOESN'T CHANGE THE FACT THAT YOU SAVED ME.
AND I APPRECIATE IT.

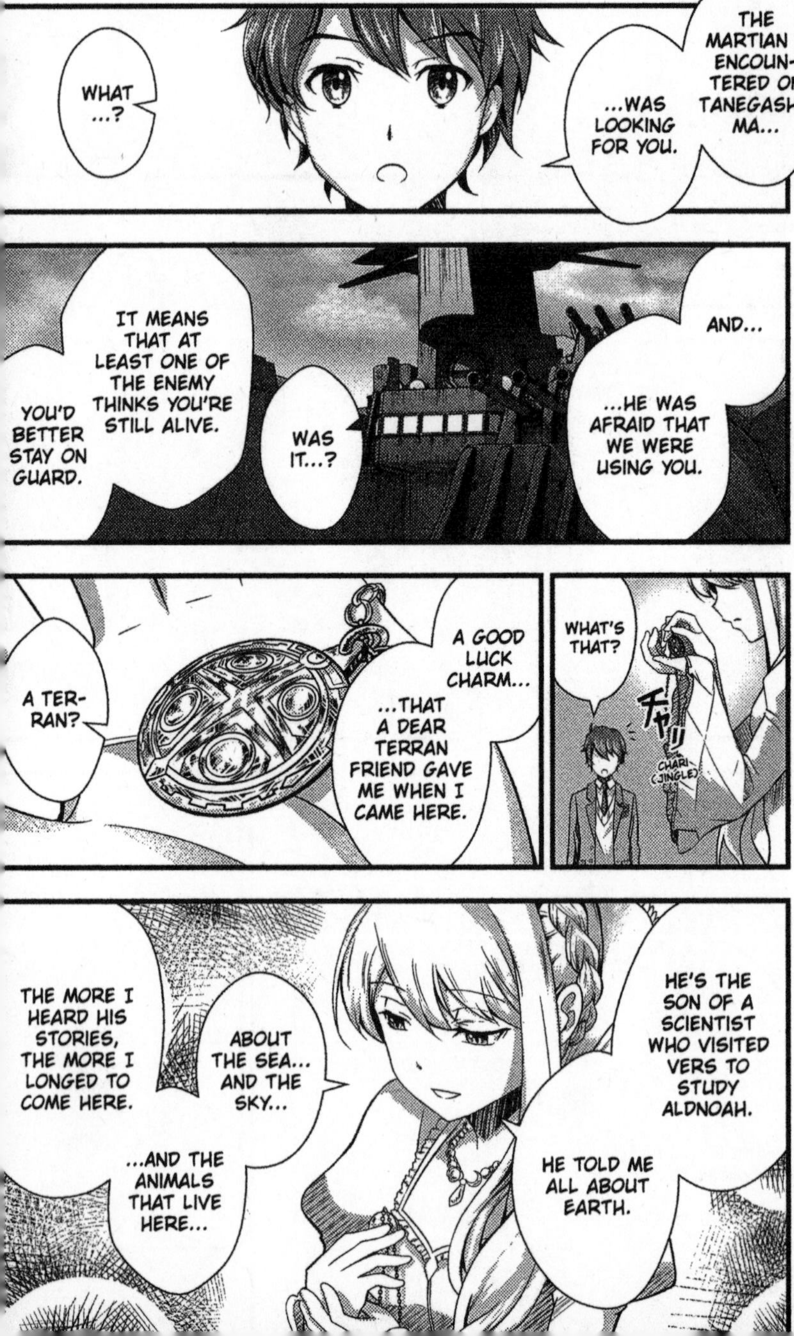
THE MARTIAN I ENCOUNTERED ON TANEGASHIMA...
...WAS LOOKING FOR YOU.
WHAT ...?
AND...
...HE WAS AFRAID THAT WE WERE USING YOU.
WAS IT...?
IT MEANS THAT AT LEAST ONE OF THE ENEMY THINKS YOU'RE STILL ALIVE.
YOU'D BETTER STAY ON GUARD.
WHAT'S THAT?
チャリ
CHARI (JINGLE)
A GOOD LUCK CHARM...
...THAT A DEAR TERRAN FRIEND GAVE ME WHEN I CAME HERE.
A TERRAN?
HE'S THE SON OF A SCIENTIST WHO VISITED VERS TO STUDY ALDNOAH.
HE TOLD ME ALL ABOUT EARTH.
ABOUT THE SEA... AND THE SKY...
...AND THE ANIMALS THAT LIVE HERE...
THE MORE I HEARD HIS STORIES, THE MORE I LONGED TO COME HERE.

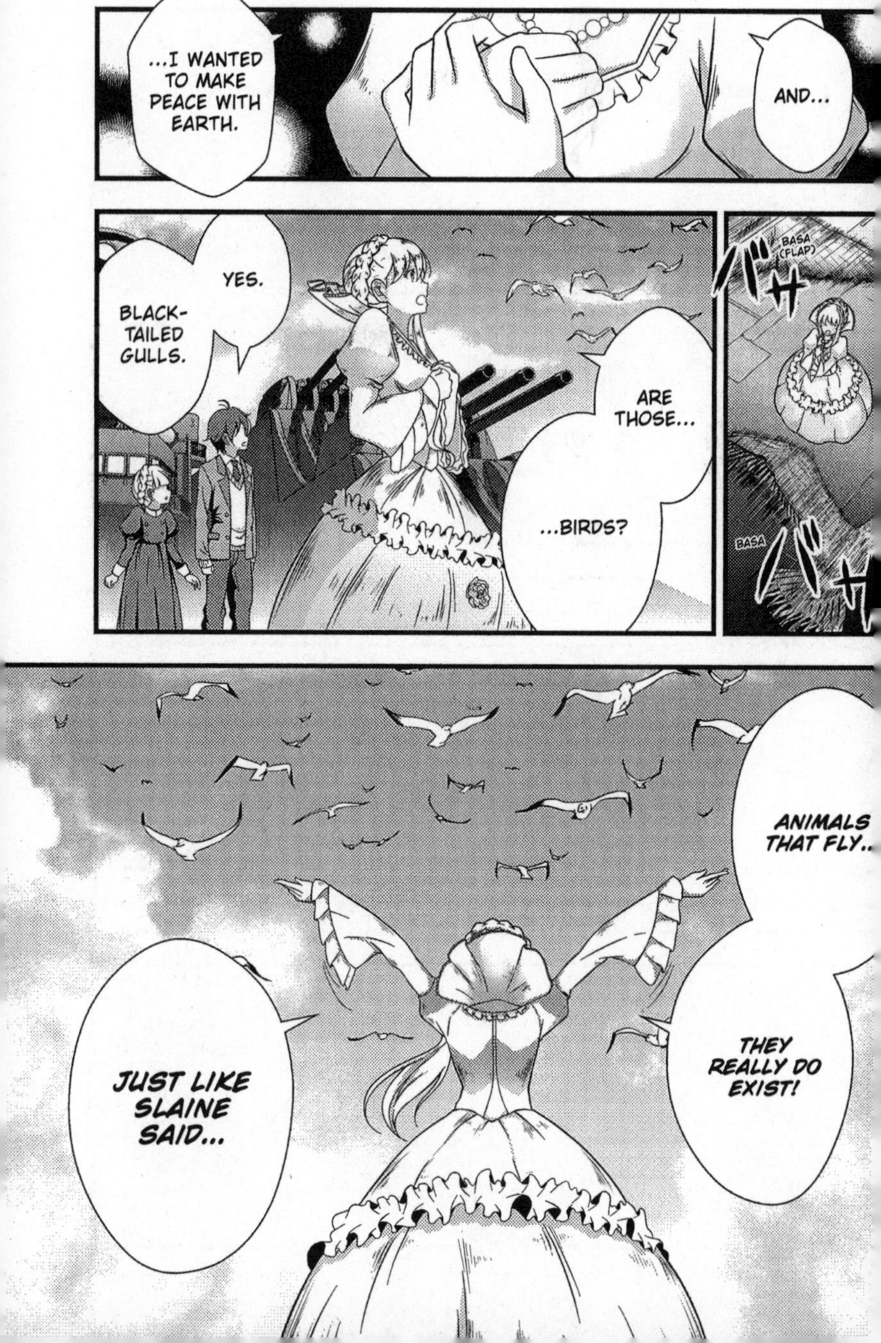
AND...
...I WANTED TO MAKE PEACE WITH EARTH.
BASA (FLAP)
BASA
ARE THOSE...
...BIRDS?
YES.
BLACK-TAILED GULLS.
ANIMALS THAT FLY..
THEY REALLY DO EXIST!
JUST LIKE SLAINE SAID...

PRINCESS ASSEYLUM SAVED MY LIFE THAT DAY...

IF SHE HADN'T BEEN THERE, I WOULDN'T BE ALIVE RIGHT NOW...

SO THIS TIME...

...I'M GOING TO PROTECT THE PRINCESS!

I CAN'T REVEAL THAT SHE'S ALIVE...

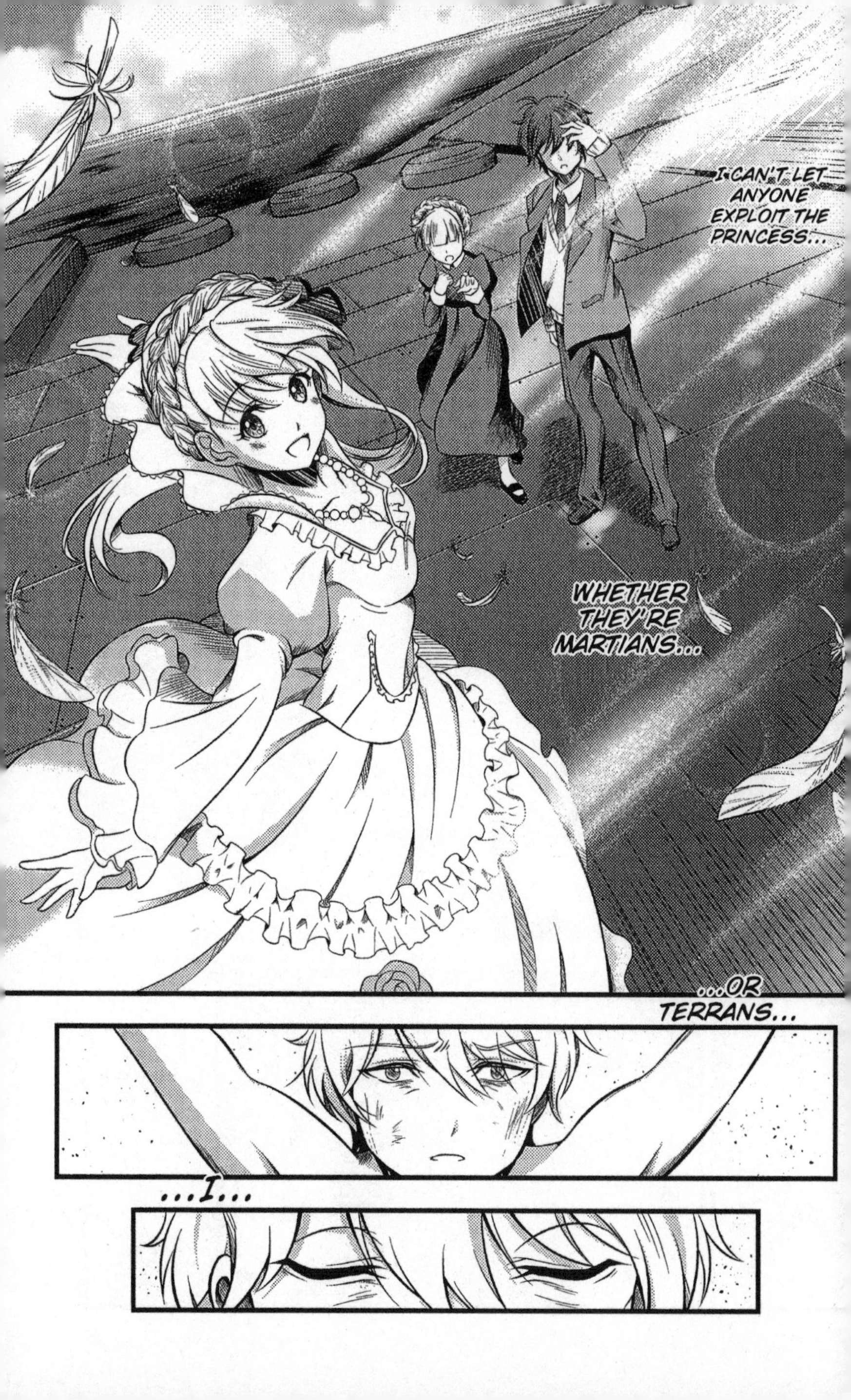
I CAN'T LET ANYONE EXPLOIT THE PRINCESS...
WHETHER THEY'RE MARTIANS...
...OR TERRANS...
...I...

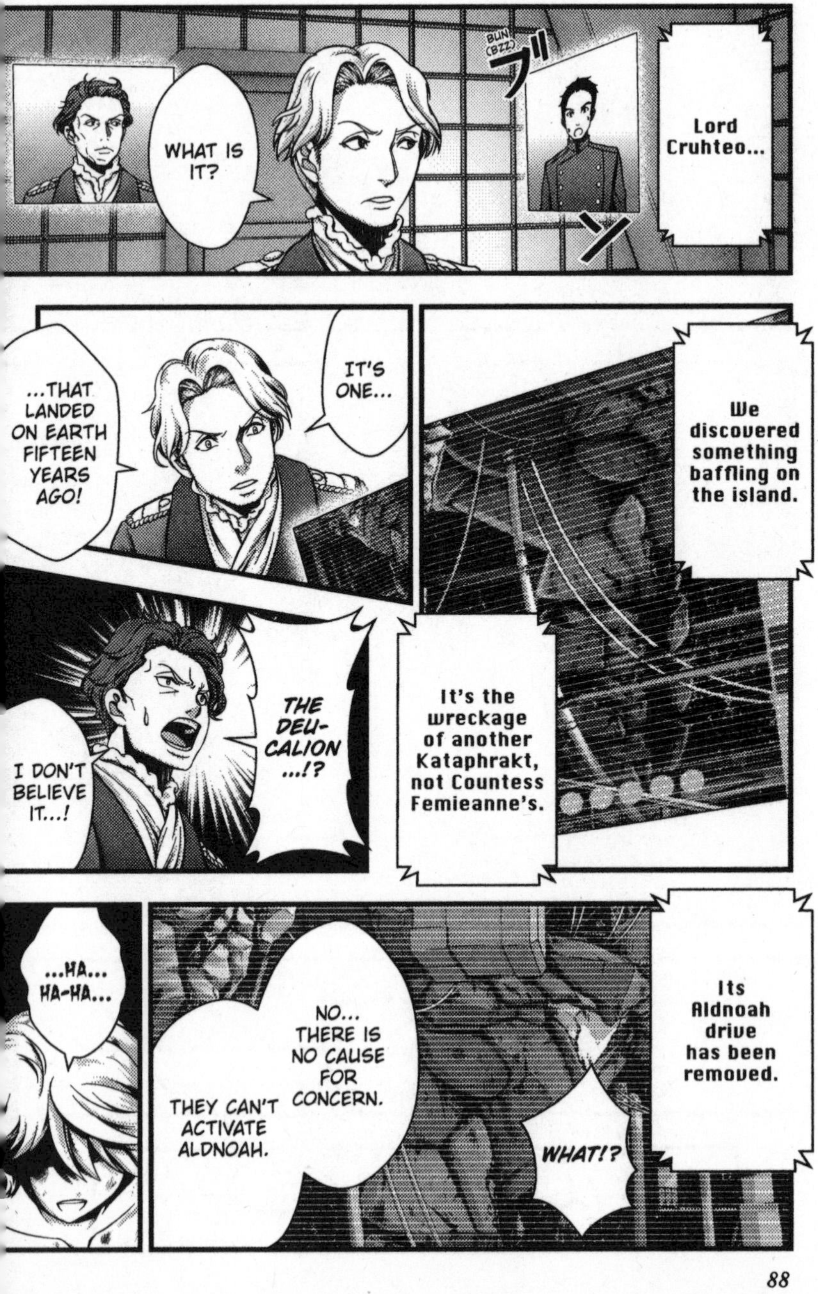
Lord Cruhteo...
BUN (BZZ)
WHAT IS IT?
We discovered something baffling on the island.
It's the wreckage of another Kataphrakt, not Countess Femieanne's.
IT'S ONE...
...THAT LANDED ON EARTH FIFTEEN YEARS AGO!
THE DEUCALION ...!?
I DON'T BELIEVE IT...!
Its Aldnoah drive has been removed.
WHAT!?
NO... THERE IS NO CAUSE FOR CONCERN.
THEY CAN'T ACTIVATE ALDNOAH.
...HA... HA-HA...

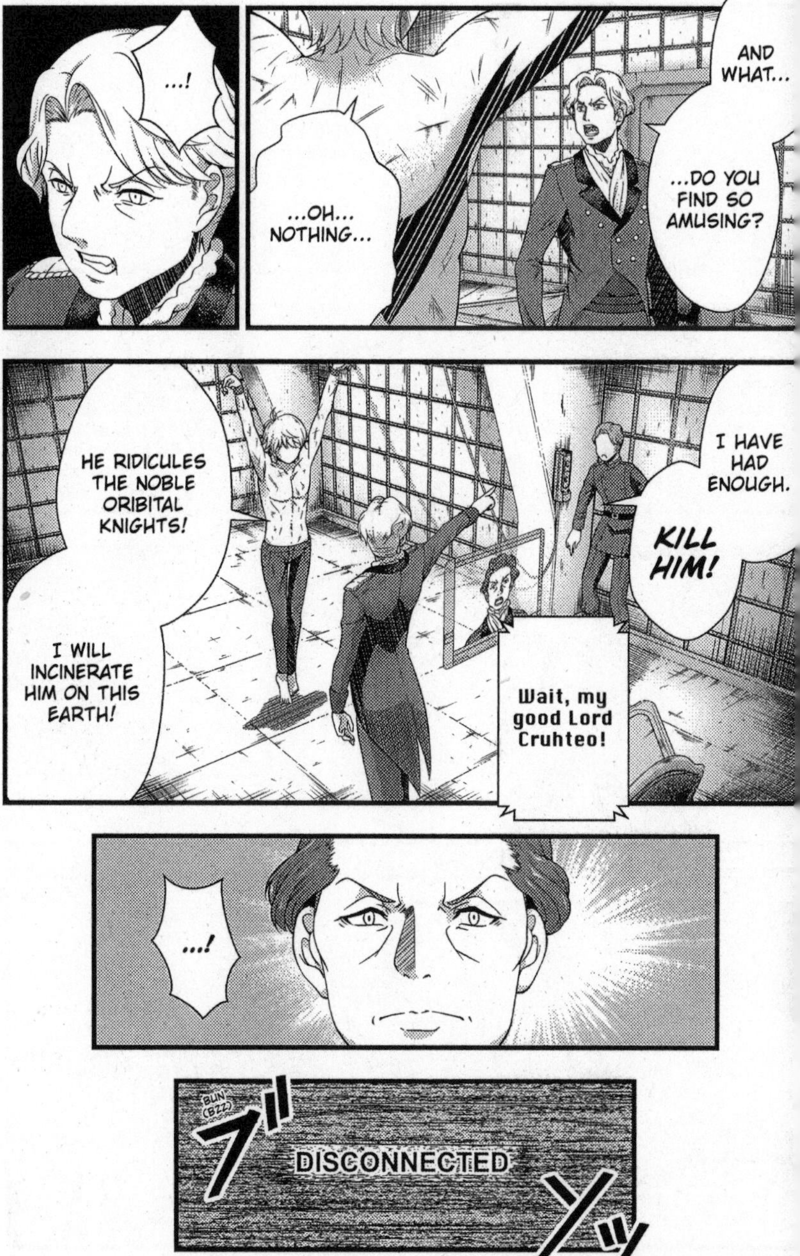
AND WHAT...
...DO YOU FIND SO AMUSING?
...OH... NOTHING...
...!
I HAVE HAD ENOUGH.
KILL HIM!
HE RIDICULES THE NOBLE ORIBITAL KNIGHTS!
I WILL INCINERATE HIM ON THIS EARTH!
Wait, my good Lord Cruhteo!
...!
BUN (BZZ)
DISCONNECTED

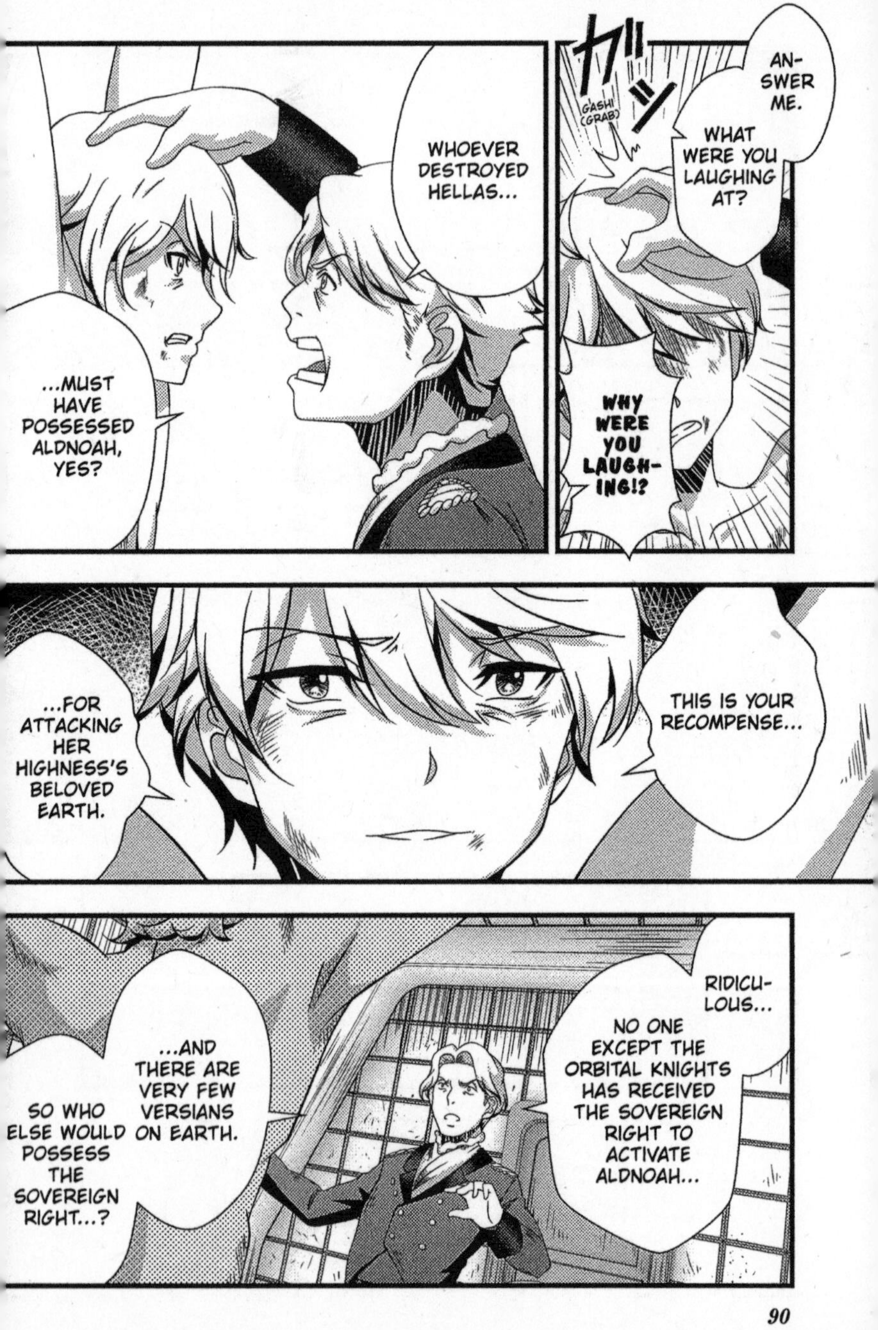
ANSWER ME.
WHAT WERE YOU LAUGHING AT?
GASHI (GRAB)
WHY WERE YOU LAUGHING!?
WHOEVER DESTROYED HELLAS...
...MUST HAVE POSSESSED ALDNOAH, YES?
THIS IS YOUR RECOMPENSE...
...FOR ATTACKING HER HIGHNESS'S BELOVED EARTH.
RIDICULOUS...
NO ONE EXCEPT THE ORBITAL KNIGHTS HAS RECEIVED THE SOVEREIGN RIGHT TO ACTIVATE ALDNOAH...
...AND THERE ARE VERY FEW VERSIANS ON EARTH.
SO WHO ELSE WOULD POSSESS THE SOVEREIGN RIGHT...?

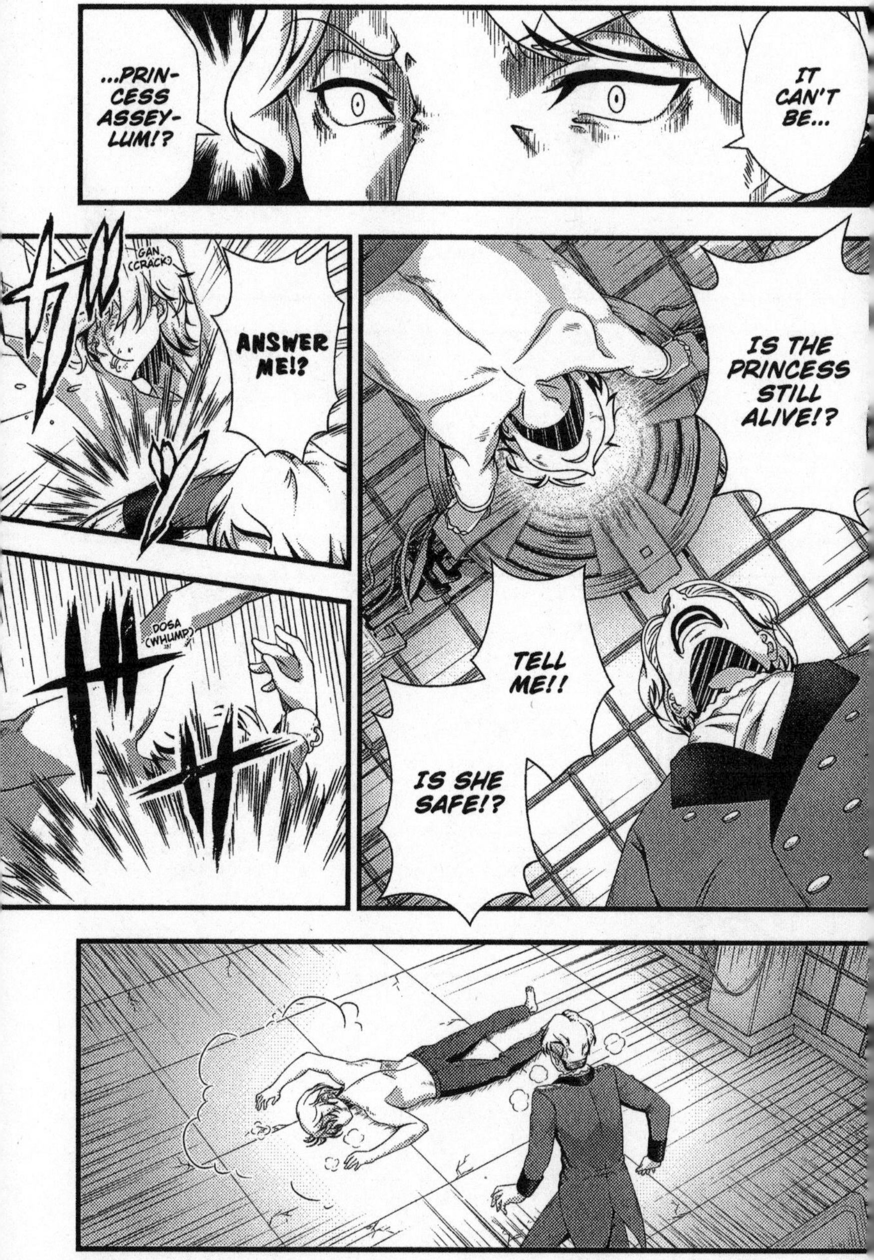
IT CAN'T BE...
...PRINCESS ASSEYLUM!?
IS THE PRINCESS STILL ALIVE!?
TELL ME!!
IS SHE SAFE!?
ANSWER ME!?
GAN (CRACK)
DOSA (WHUMP)

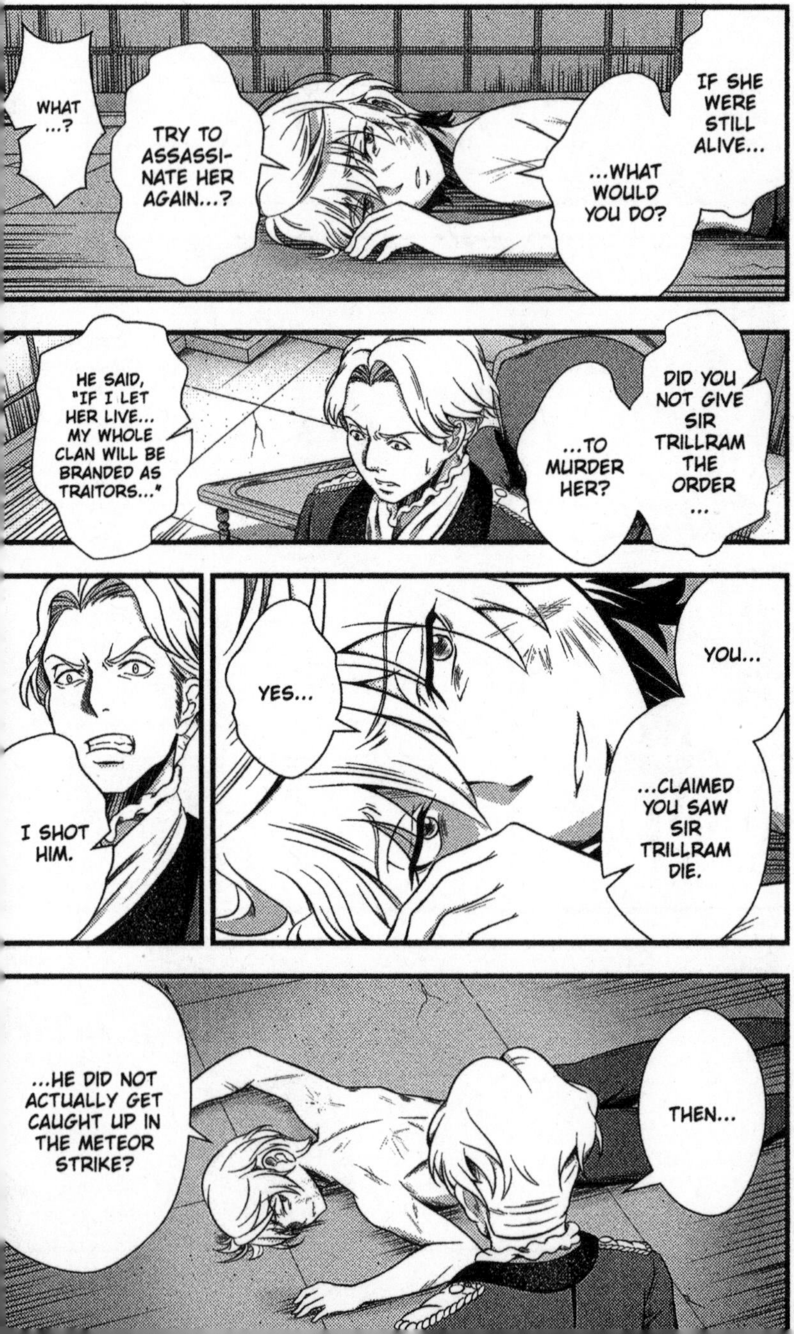
IF SHE WERE STILL ALIVE...
...WHAT WOULD YOU DO?
TRY TO ASSASSI-NATE HER AGAIN...?
WHAT ...?
DID YOU NOT GIVE SIR TRILLRAM THE ORDER ...
...TO MURDER HER?
HE SAID, "IF I LET HER LIVE... MY WHOLE CLAN WILL BE BRANDED AS TRAITORS..."
YOU...
...CLAIMED YOU SAW SIR TRILLRAM DIE.
YES...
I SHOT HIM.
THEN...
...HE DID NOT ACTUALLY GET CAUGHT UP IN THE METEOR STRIKE?

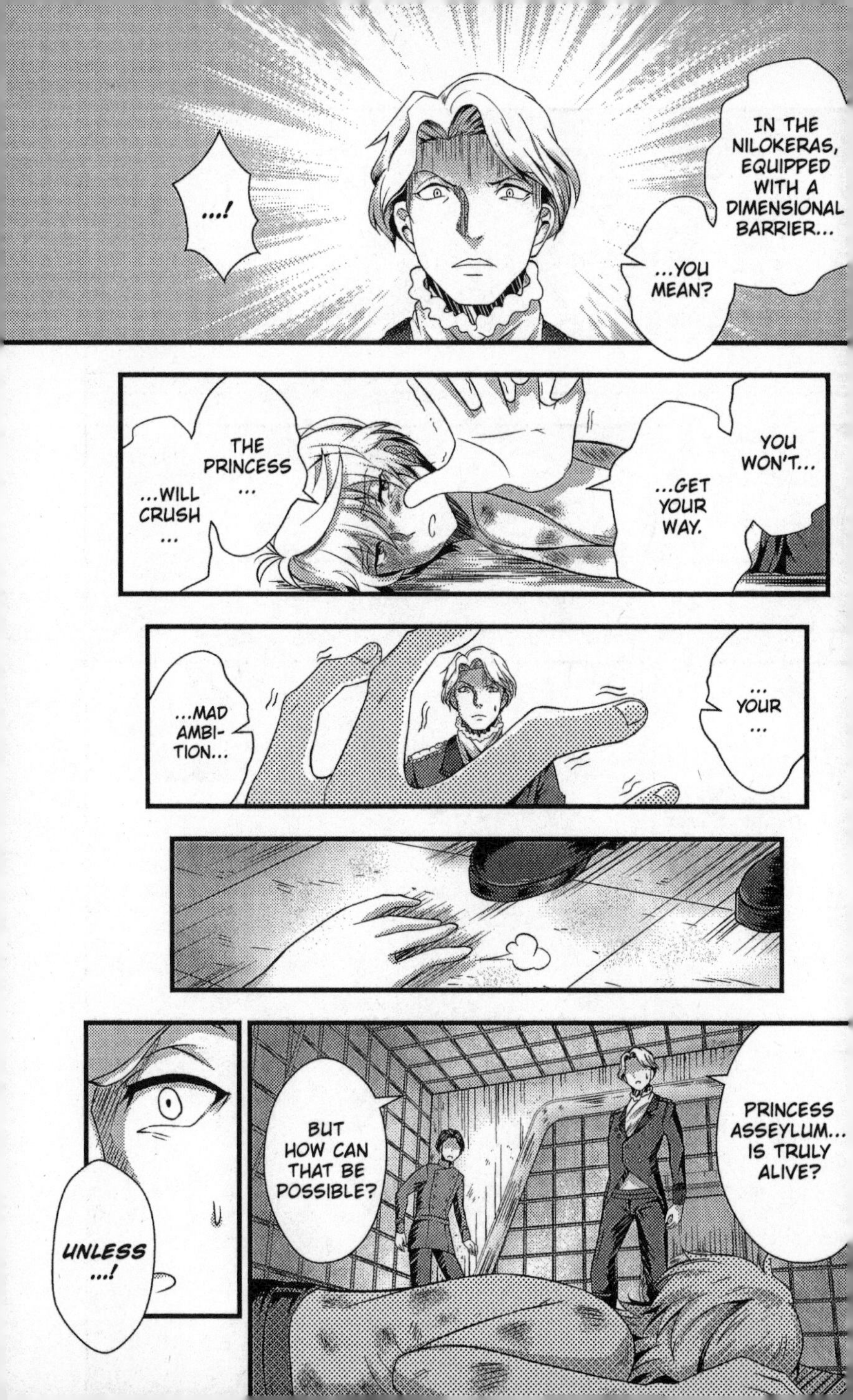
IN THE NILOKERAS, EQUIPPED WITH A DIMENSIONAL BARRIER...
...YOU MEAN?
...!
YOU WON'T...
...GET YOUR WAY.
THE PRINCESS ...
...WILL CRUSH ...
... YOUR ...
...MAD AMBITION...
PRINCESS ASSEYLUM... IS TRULY ALIVE?
BUT HOW CAN THAT BE POSSIBLE?
UNLESS ...!

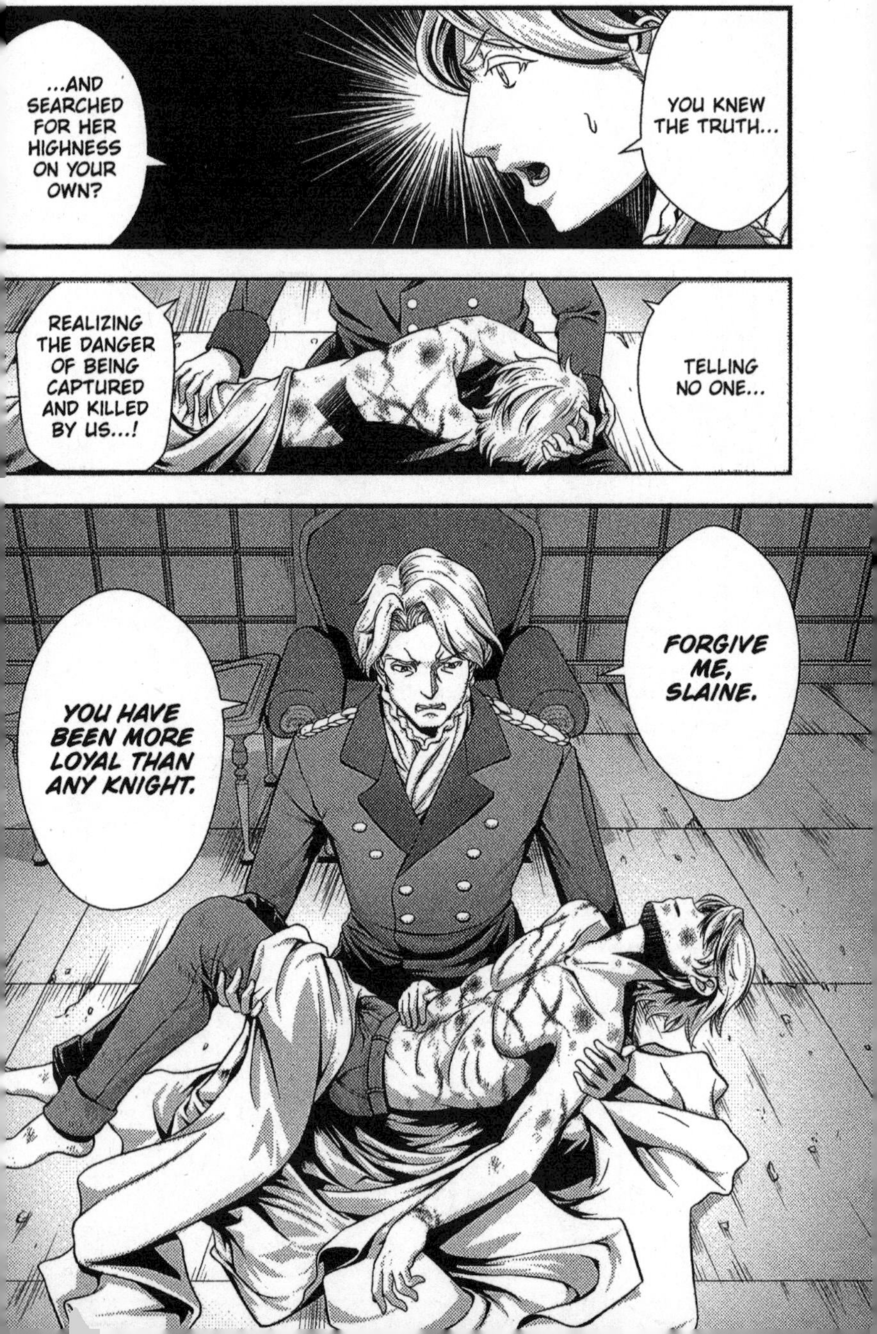
YOU KNEW THE TRUTH...
...AND SEARCHED FOR HER HIGHNESS ON YOUR OWN?
TELLING NO ONE...
REALIZING THE DANGER OF BEING CAPTURED AND KILLED BY US...!
FORGIVE ME, SLAINE.
YOU HAVE BEEN MORE LOYAL THAN ANY KNIGHT.

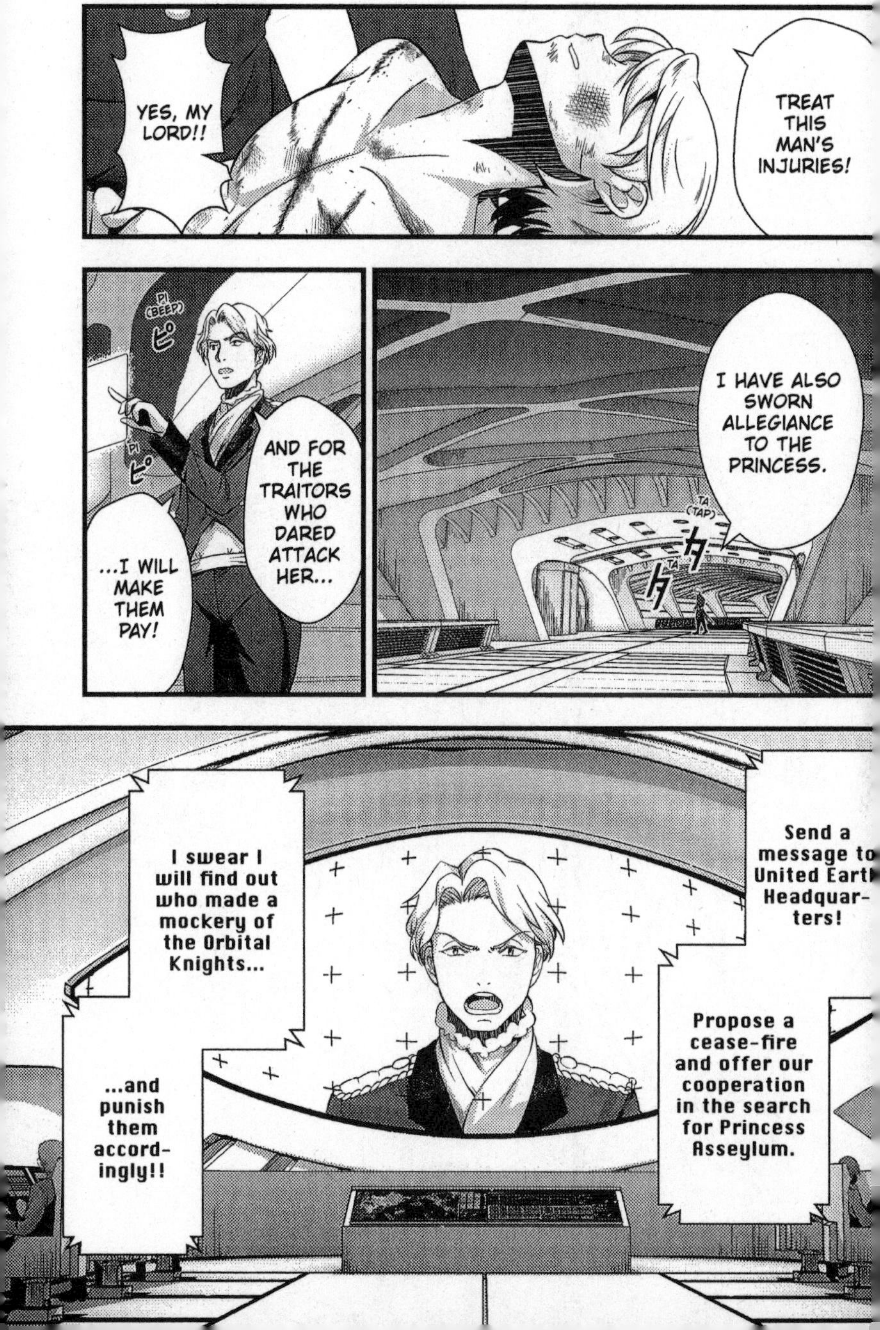
TREAT THIS MAN'S INJURIES!
YES, MY LORD!!
I HAVE ALSO SWORN ALLEGIANCE TO THE PRINCESS.
TA (TAP) タ
TA タ
PI (BEEP) ピ
AND FOR THE TRAITORS WHO DARED ATTACK HER...
PI ピ
...I WILL MAKE THEM PAY!
Send a message to United Eart Headquar- ters!
Propose a cease-fire and offer our cooperation in the search for Princess Asseylum.
I swear I will find out who made a mockery of the Orbital Knights...
...and punish them accord- ingly!!

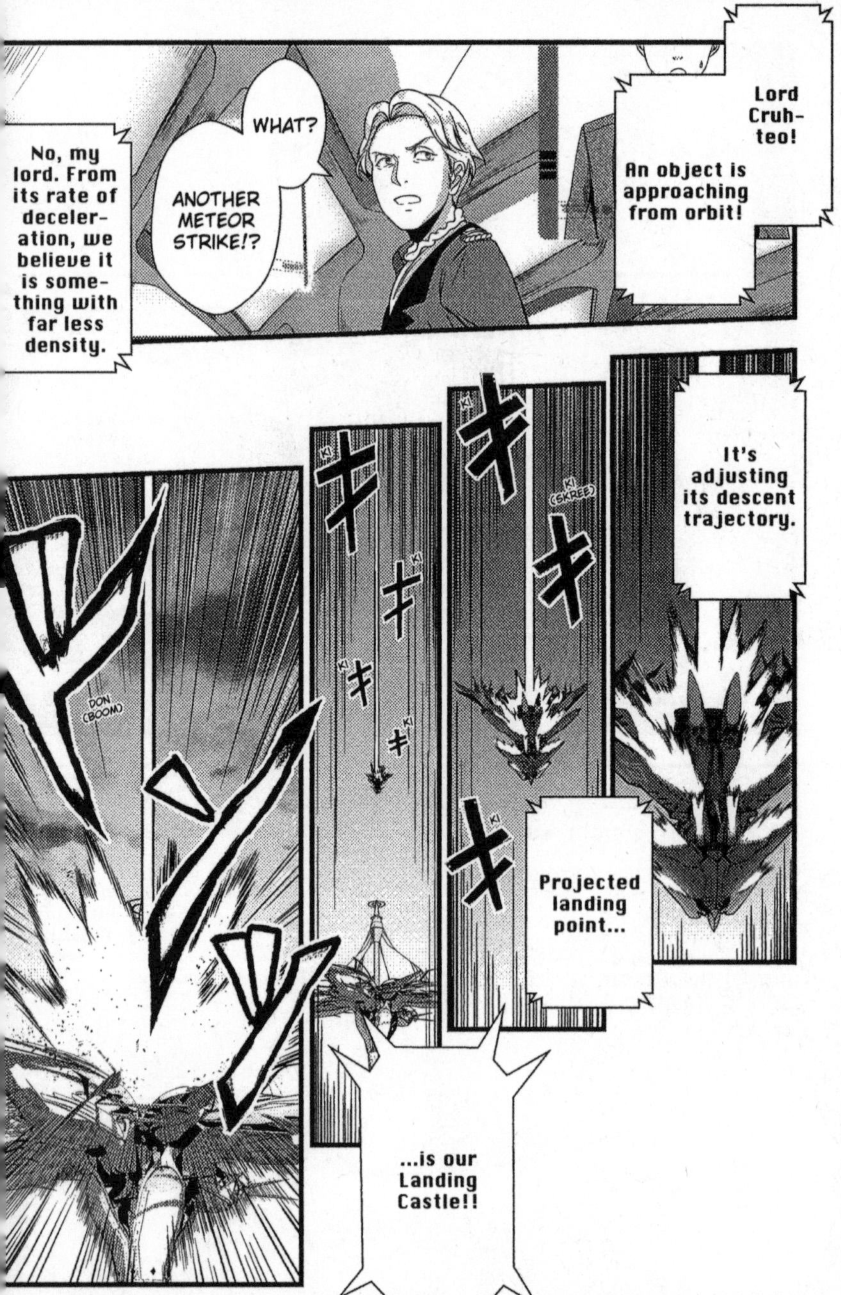
Lord Cruh-teo!
An object is approaching from orbit!
WHAT?
ANOTHER METEOR STRIKE!?
No, my lord. From its rate of deceler-ation, we believe it is some-thing with far less density.
It's adjusting its descent trajectory.
KI
KI (SKREE)
KI
Projected landing point...
KI
KI
KI
KI
DON (BOOM)
...is our Landing Castle!!

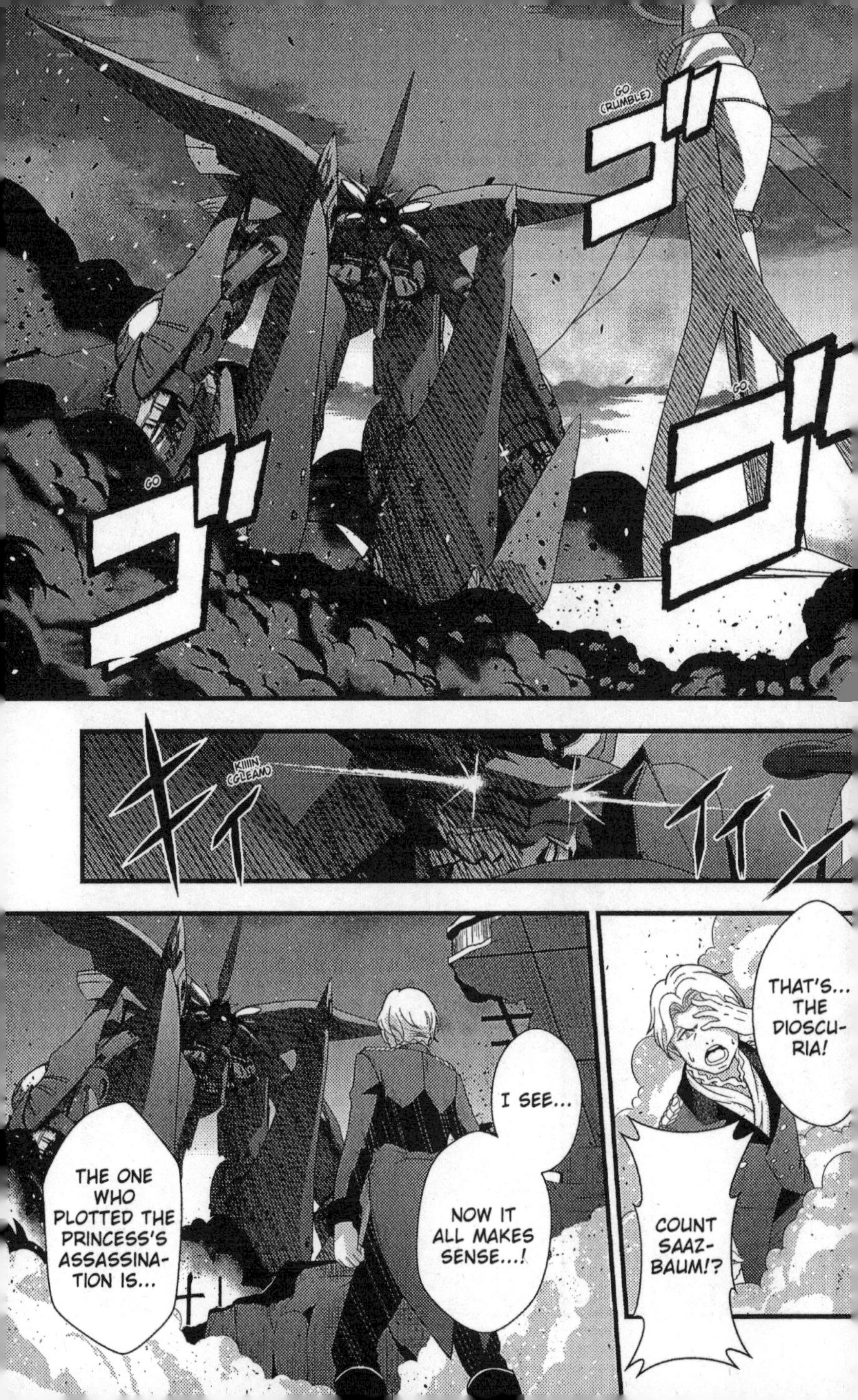
GO (RUMBLE)
GO
GO
KIIIN (GLEAM)
THAT'S... THE DIOSCU-RIA!
COUNT SAAZ-BAUM!?
I SEE...
NOW IT ALL MAKES SENSE...!
THE ONE WHO PLOTTED THE PRINCESS'S ASSASSINA-TION IS...

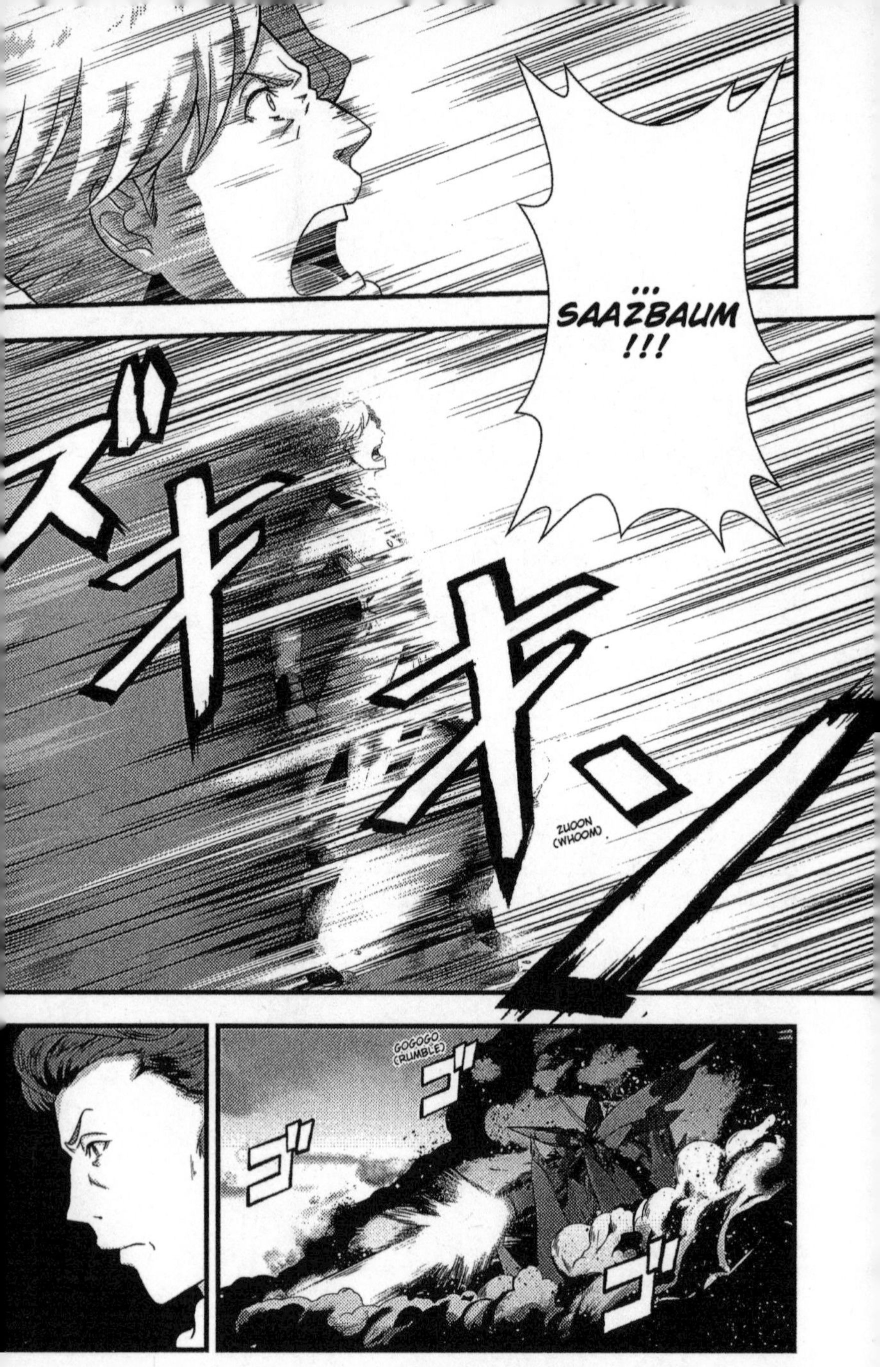
... SAAZBAUM !!!
ZUOON (WHOOM)
GOGOGO (RUMBLE)
ゴ
ゴ
ゴ

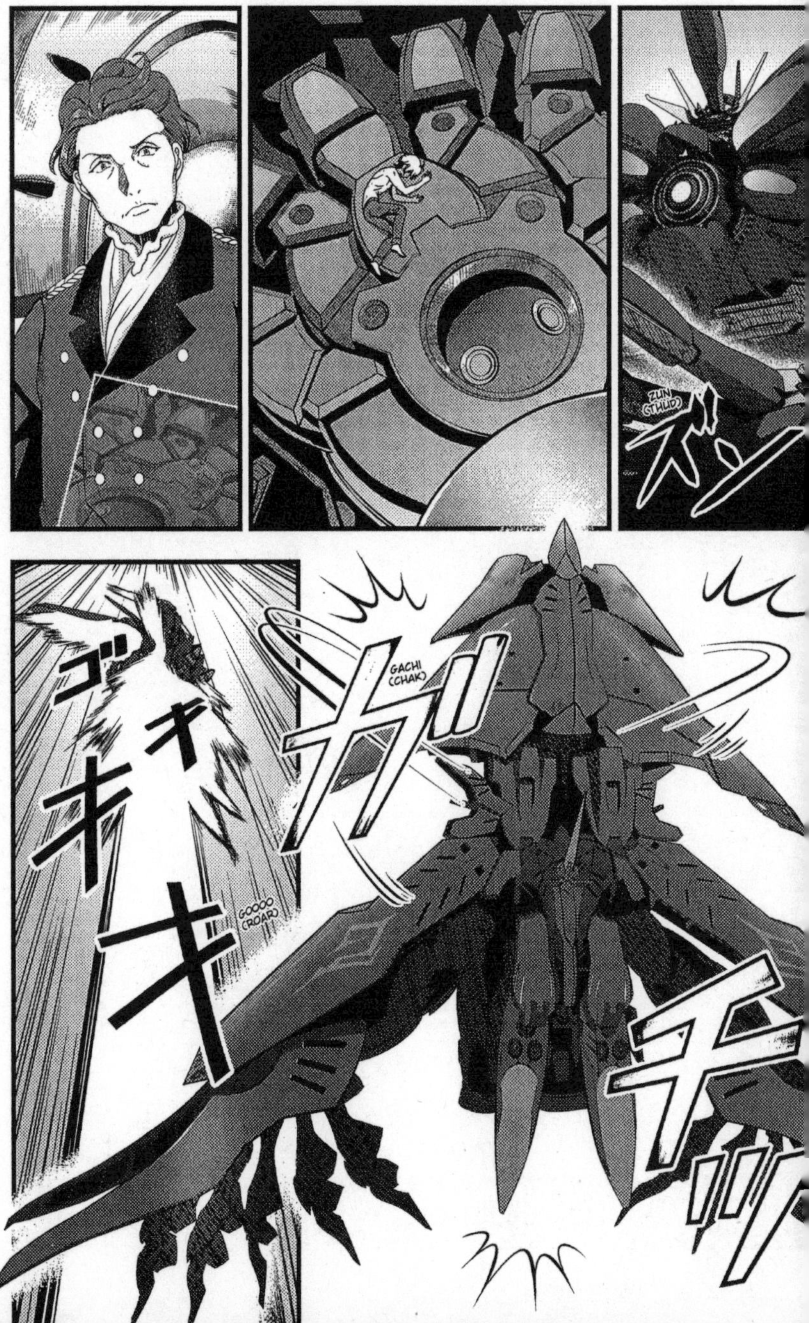
ZUN (THUD)
GACHI (CHAK)
GOOOO (ROAR)

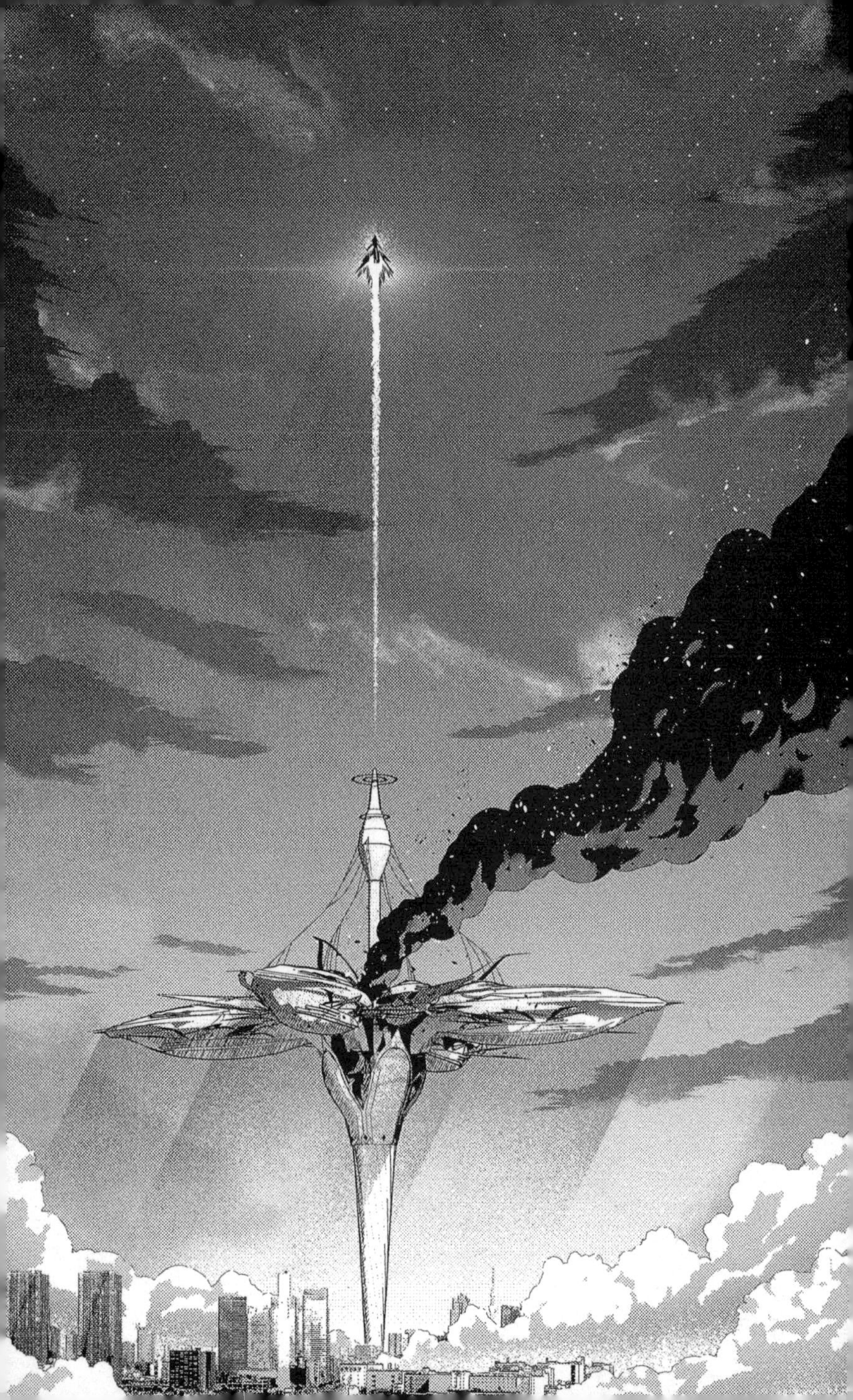

# EP09 Recall Device —Darkness Visible—

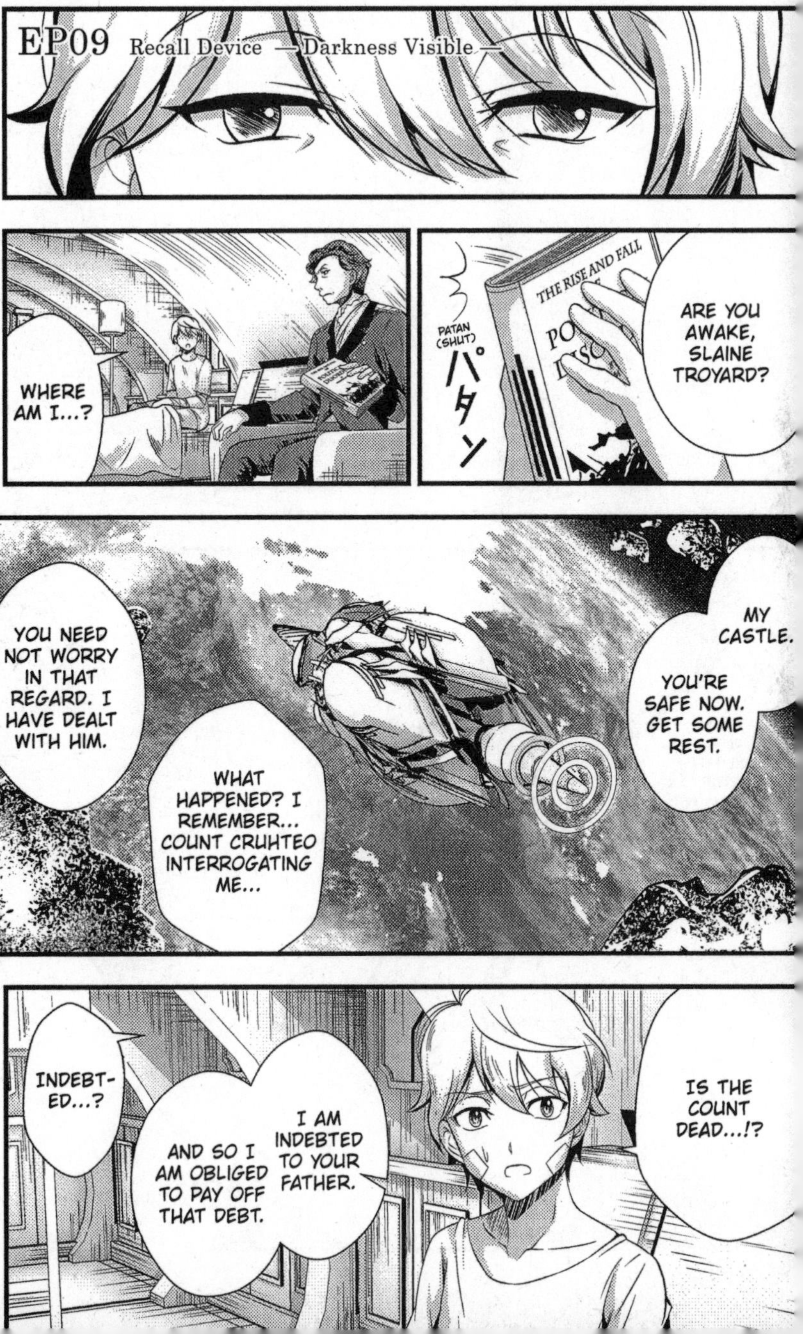

ARE YOU AWAKE, SLAINE TROYARD?
PATAN (SHUT)
パタン
WHERE AM I...?
MY CASTLE.
YOU'RE SAFE NOW. GET SOME REST.
WHAT HAPPENED? I REMEMBER... COUNT CRUHTEO INTERROGATING ME...
YOU NEED NOT WORRY IN THAT REGARD. I HAVE DEALT WITH HIM.
IS THE COUNT DEAD...!?
I AM INDEBTED TO YOUR FATHER.
AND SO I AM OBLIGED TO PAY OFF THAT DEBT.
INDEBT-ED...?

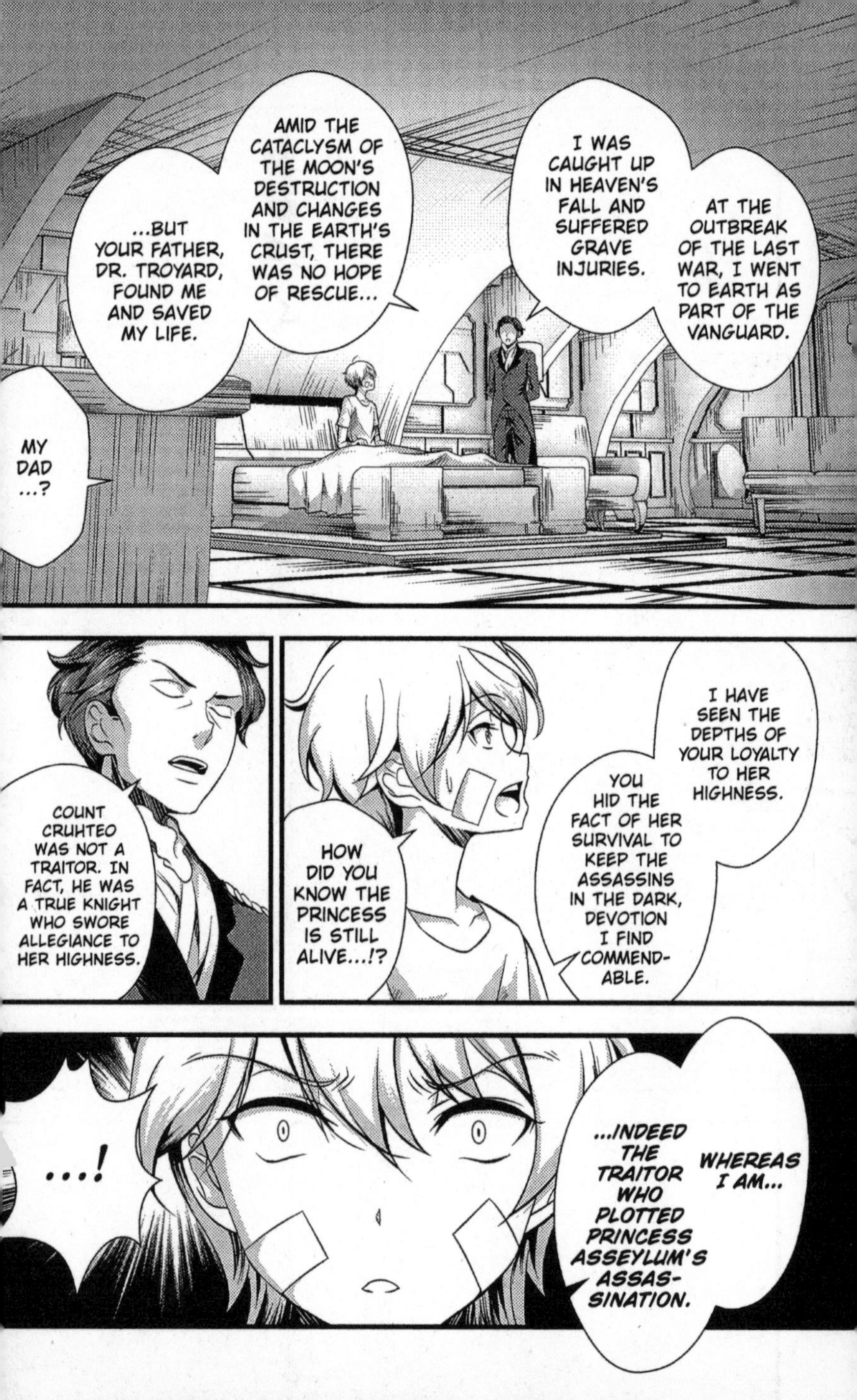
AT THE OUTBREAK OF THE LAST WAR, I WENT TO EARTH AS PART OF THE VANGUARD.
I WAS CAUGHT UP IN HEAVEN'S FALL AND SUFFERED GRAVE INJURIES.
AMID THE CATACLYSM OF THE MOON'S DESTRUCTION AND CHANGES IN THE EARTH'S CRUST, THERE WAS NO HOPE OF RESCUE...
...BUT YOUR FATHER, DR. TROYARD, FOUND ME AND SAVED MY LIFE.
MY DAD ...?
I HAVE SEEN THE DEPTHS OF YOUR LOYALTY TO HER HIGHNESS.
YOU HID THE FACT OF HER SURVIVAL TO KEEP THE ASSASSINS IN THE DARK, DEVOTION I FIND COMMEND-ABLE.
HOW DID YOU KNOW THE PRINCESS IS STILL ALIVE...!?
COUNT CRUHTEO WAS NOT A TRAITOR. IN FACT, HE WAS A TRUE KNIGHT WHO SWORE ALLEGIANCE TO HER HIGHNESS.
WHEREAS I AM...
...INDEED THE TRAITOR WHO PLOTTED PRINCESS ASSEYLUM'S ASSAS-SINATION.
...!

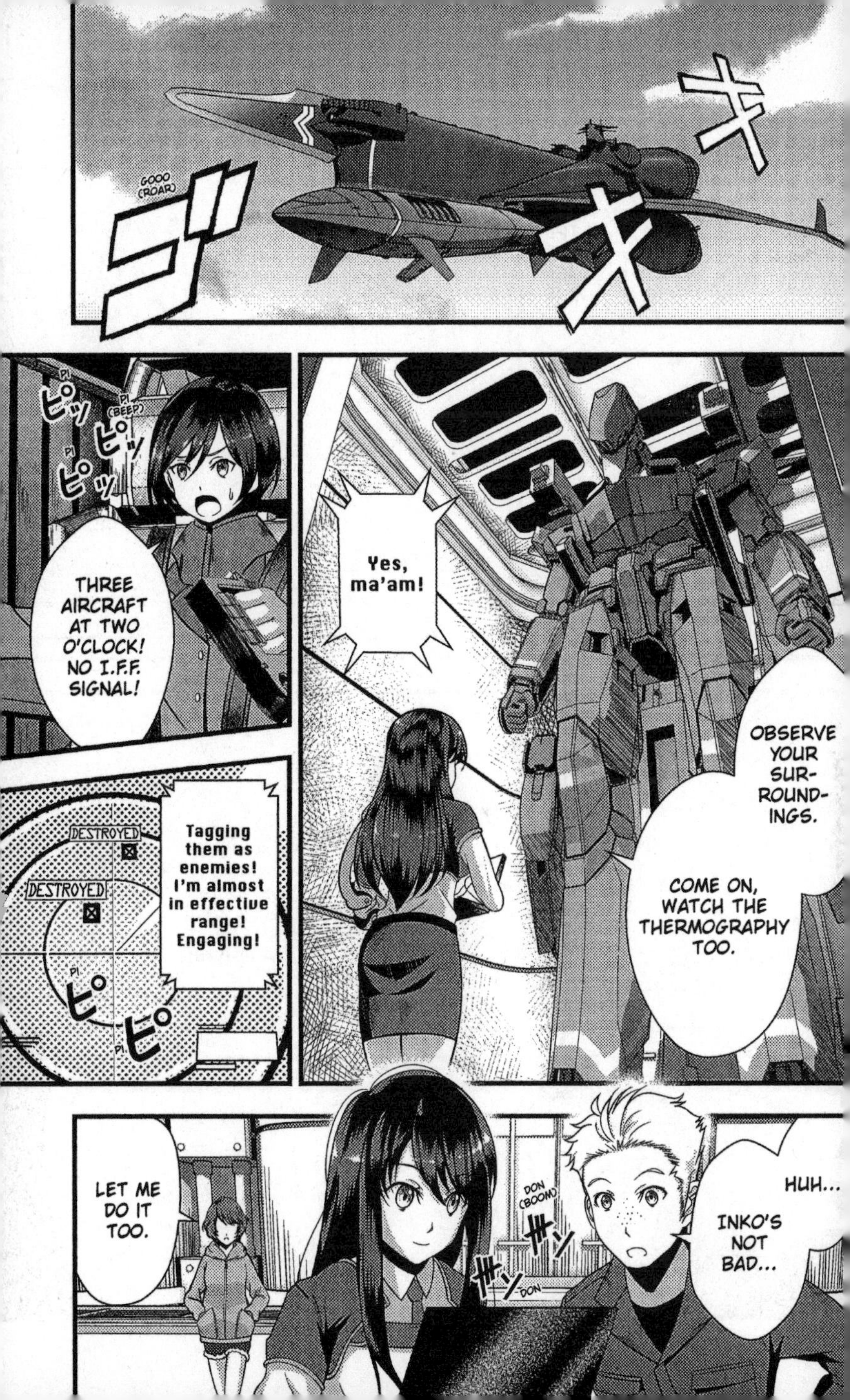
GOOO (ROAR)
Yes, ma'am!
OBSERVE YOUR SUR-ROUNDINGS.
COME ON, WATCH THE THERMOGRAPHY TOO.
PI
PI (BEEP)
PI
THREE AIRCRAFT AT TWO O'CLOCK! NO I.F.F. SIGNAL!
Tagging them as enemies! I'm almost in effective range! Engaging!
DESTROYED
DESTROYED
PI
PI
HUH...
INKO'S NOT BAD...
DON (BOOM)
DON
LET ME DO IT TOO.

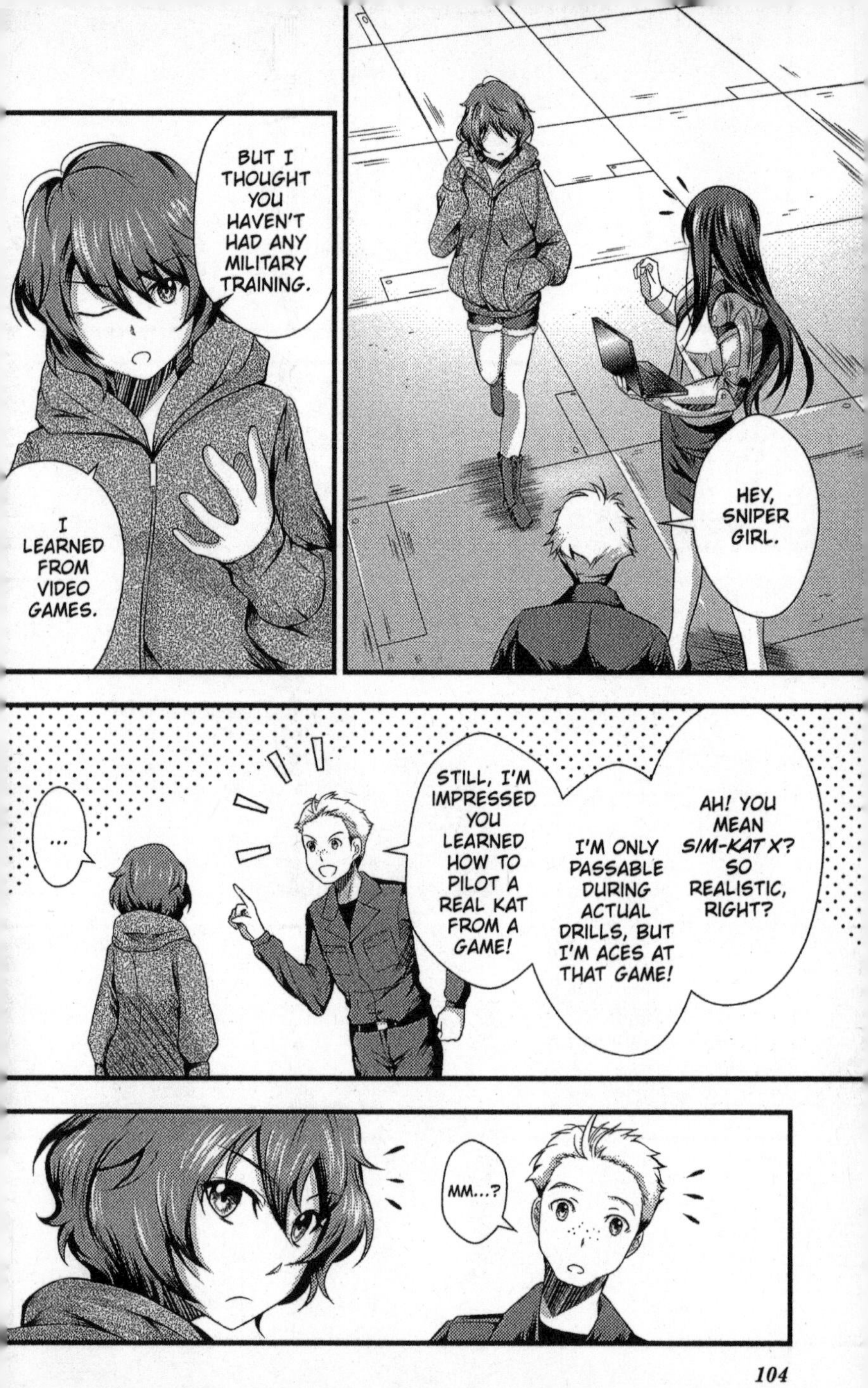
HEY, SNIPER GIRL.
BUT I THOUGHT YOU HAVEN'T HAD ANY MILITARY TRAINING.
I LEARNED FROM VIDEO GAMES.
AH! YOU MEAN *SIM-KAT X*? SO REALISTIC, RIGHT?
I'M ONLY PASSABLE DURING ACTUAL DRILLS, BUT I'M ACES AT THAT GAME!
STILL, I'M IMPRESSED YOU LEARNED HOW TO PILOT A REAL KAT FROM A GAME!
...
MM...?

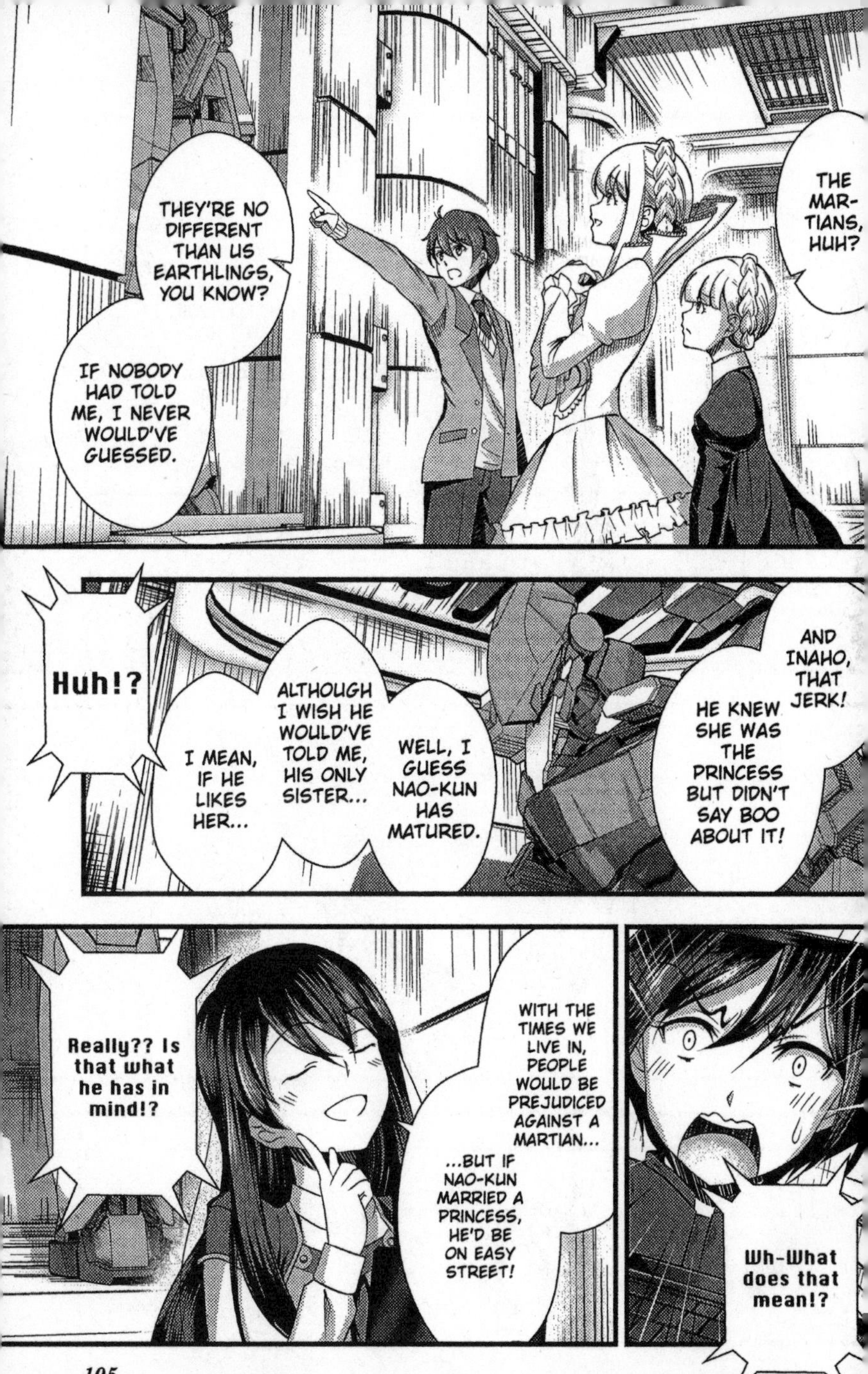
THE MAR-TIANS, HUH?
THEY'RE NO DIFFERENT THAN US EARTHLINGS, YOU KNOW?
IF NOBODY HAD TOLD ME, I NEVER WOULD'VE GUESSED.
AND INAHO, THAT JERK!
HE KNEW SHE WAS THE PRINCESS BUT DIDN'T SAY BOO ABOUT IT!
WELL, I GUESS NAO-KUN HAS MATURED.
ALTHOUGH I WISH HE WOULD'VE TOLD ME, HIS ONLY SISTER...
I MEAN, IF HE LIKES HER...
Huh!?
Wh-What does that mean!?
WITH THE TIMES WE LIVE IN, PEOPLE WOULD BE PREJUDICED AGAINST A MARTIAN...
...BUT IF NAO-KUN MARRIED A PRINCESS, HE'D BE ON EASY STREET!
Really?? Is that what he has in mind!?

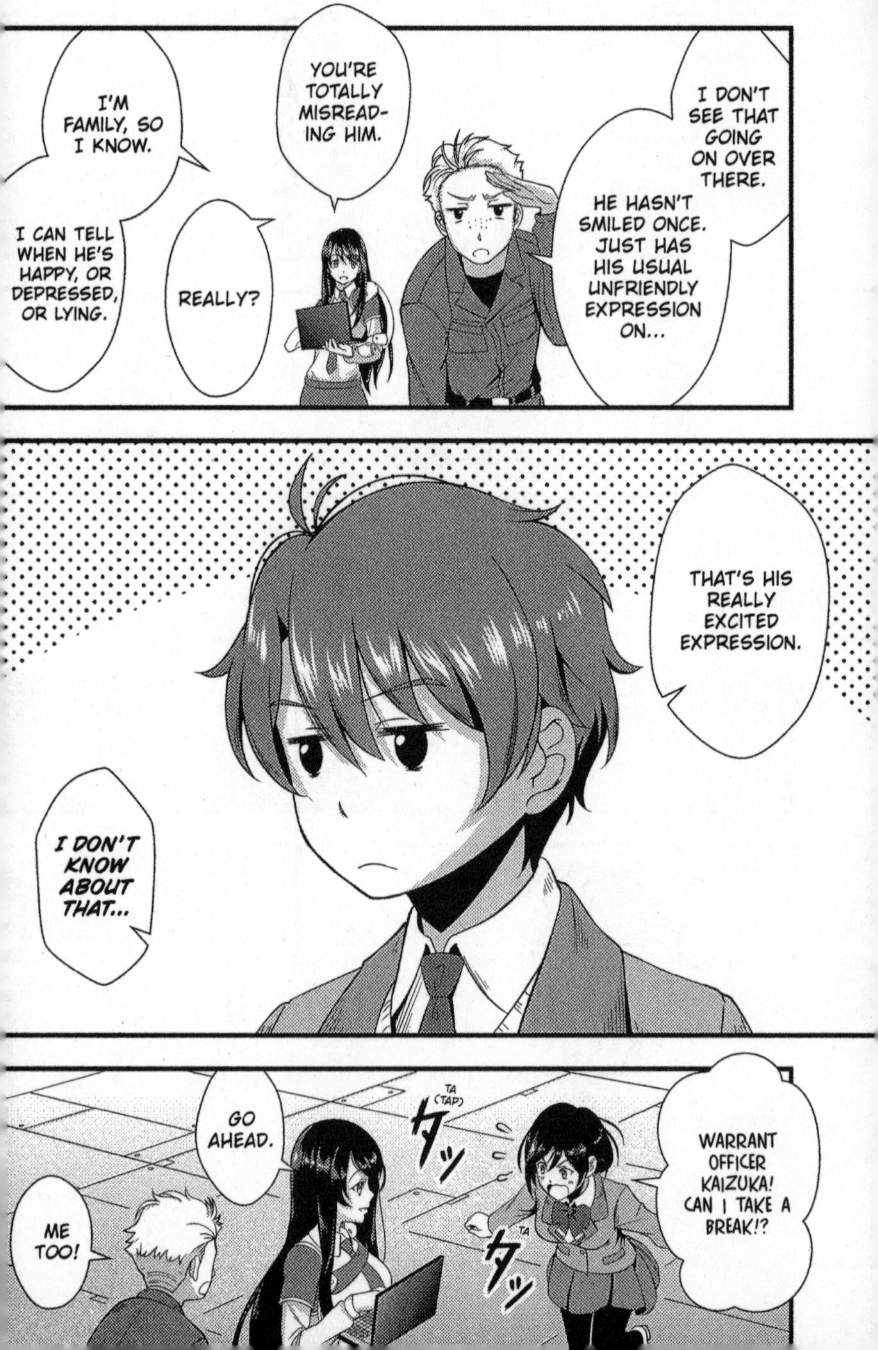
I DON'T SEE THAT GOING ON OVER THERE.
HE HASN'T SMILED ONCE. JUST HAS HIS USUAL UNFRIENDLY EXPRESSION ON...
YOU'RE TOTALLY MISREADING HIM.
I'M FAMILY, SO I KNOW.
REALLY?
I CAN TELL WHEN HE'S HAPPY, OR DEPRESSED, OR LYING.
THAT'S HIS REALLY EXCITED EXPRESSION.
I DON'T KNOW ABOUT THAT...
WARRANT OFFICER KAIZUKA! CAN I TAKE A BREAK!?
TA (TAP)
TA
GO AHEAD.
ME TOO!

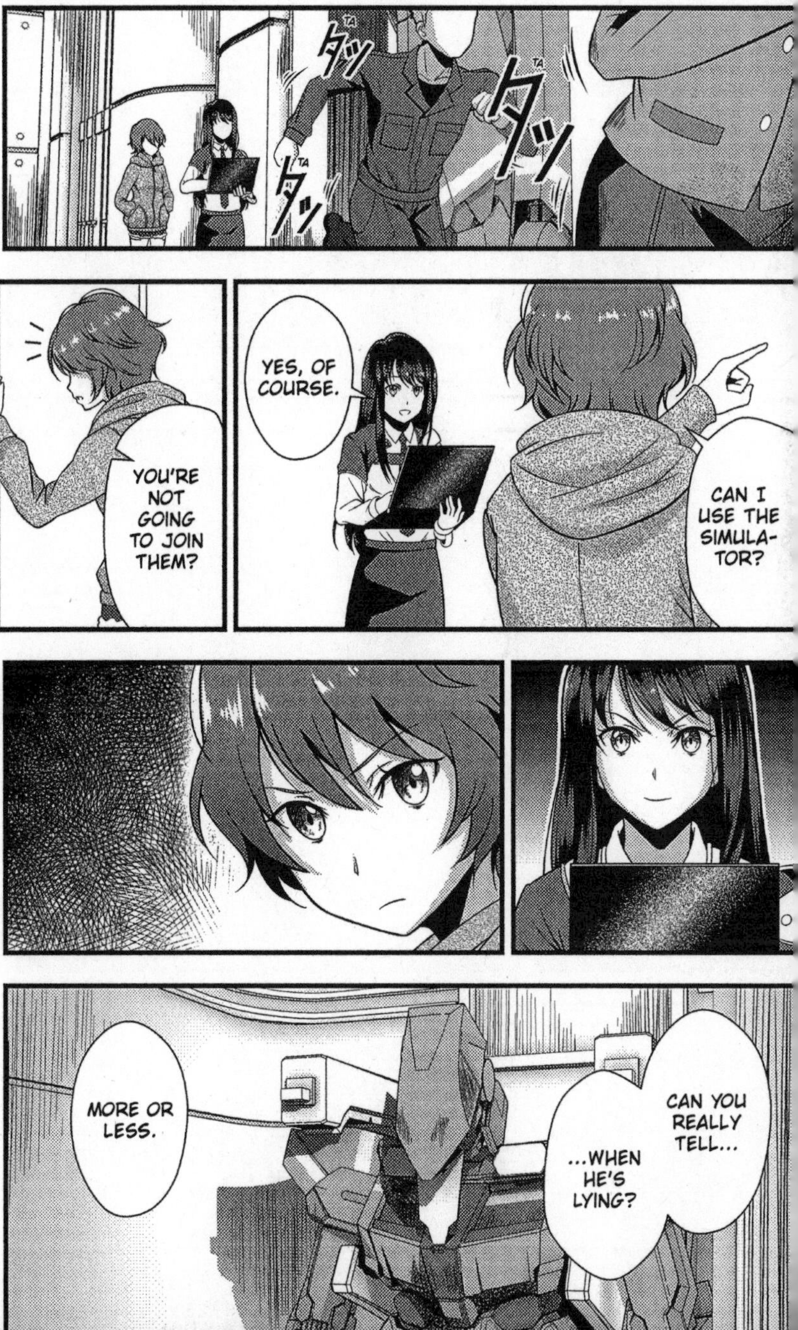
タッ
TA
タッ
TA
タッ
TA
CAN I USE THE SIMULATOR?
YES, OF COURSE.
YOU'RE NOT GOING TO JOIN THEM?
CAN YOU REALLY TELL...
...WHEN HE'S LYING?
MORE OR LESS.

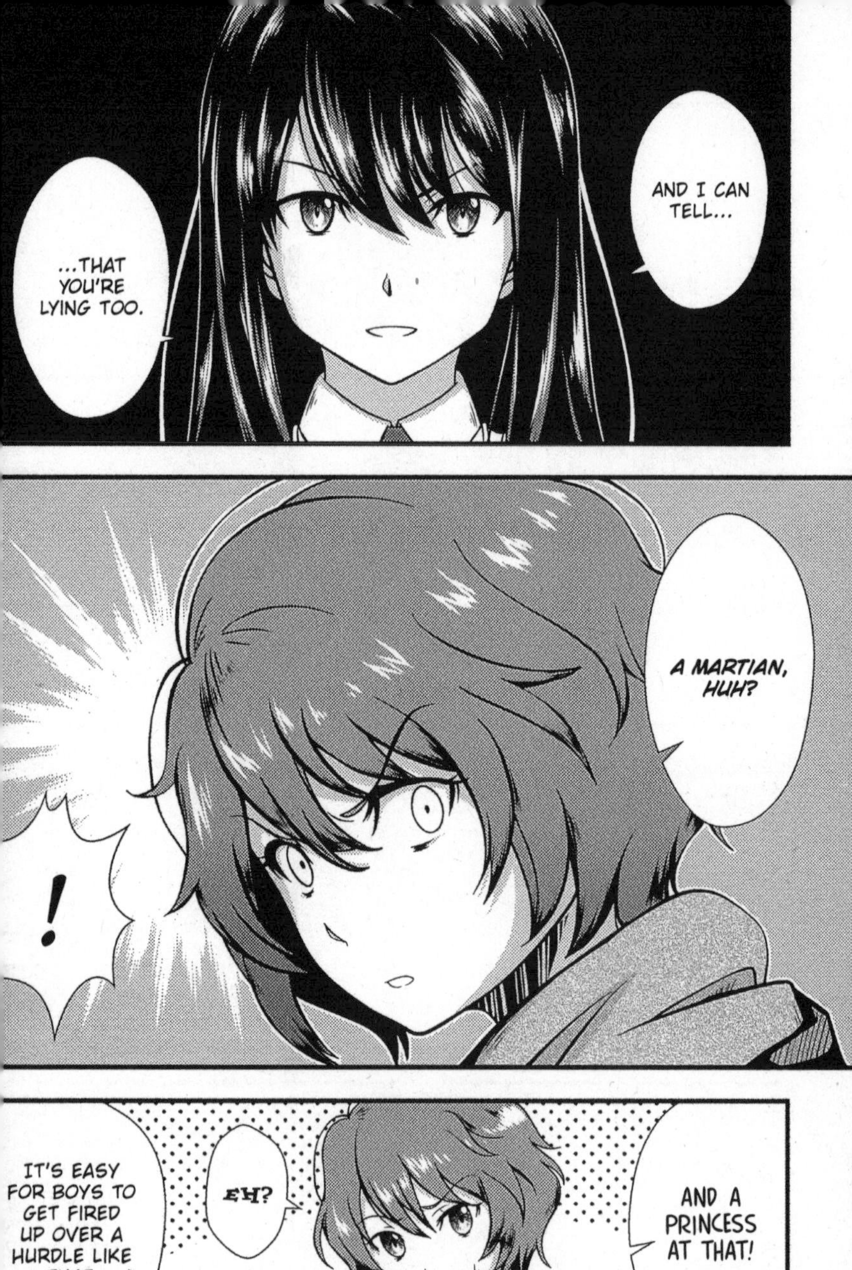
AND I CAN TELL...
...THAT YOU'RE LYING TOO.
A MARTIAN, HUH?
!
AND A PRINCESS AT THAT!
EH?
IT'S EASY FOR BOYS TO GET FIRED UP OVER A HURDLE LIKE THAT.

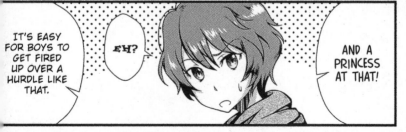

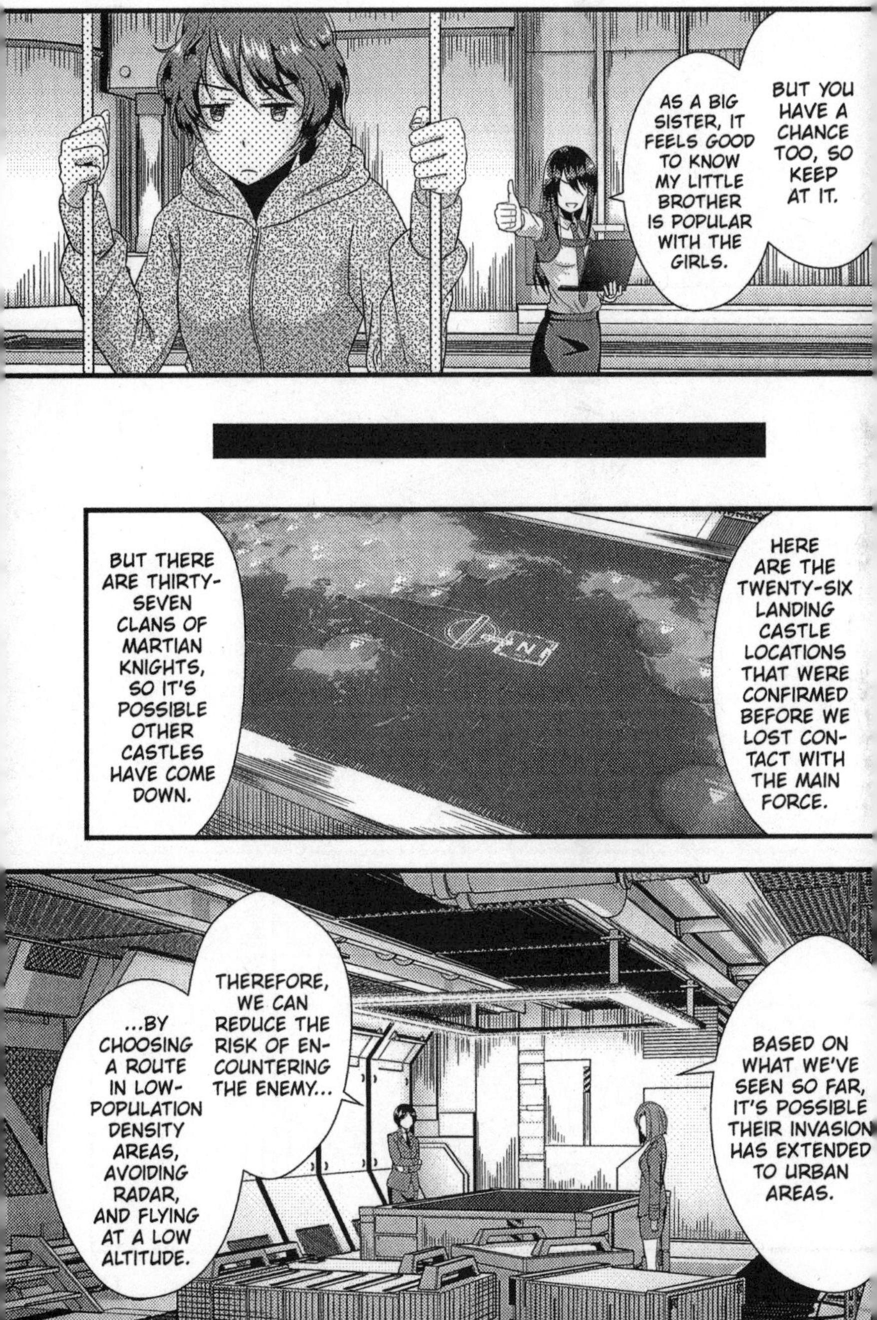
BUT YOU HAVE A CHANCE TOO, SO KEEP AT IT.
AS A BIG SISTER, IT FEELS GOOD TO KNOW MY LITTLE BROTHER IS POPULAR WITH THE GIRLS.
[redacted]
HERE ARE THE TWENTY-SIX LANDING CASTLE LOCATIONS THAT WERE CONFIRMED BEFORE WE LOST CON-TACT WITH THE MAIN FORCE.
BUT THERE ARE THIRTY-SEVEN CLANS OF MARTIAN KNIGHTS, SO IT'S POSSIBLE OTHER CASTLES HAVE COME DOWN.
BASED ON WHAT WE'VE SEEN SO FAR, IT'S POSSIBLE THEIR INVASION HAS EXTENDED TO URBAN AREAS.
THEREFORE, WE CAN REDUCE THE RISK OF EN-COUNTERING THE ENEMY...
...BY CHOOSING A ROUTE IN LOW-POPULATION DENSITY AREAS, AVOIDING RADAR, AND FLYING AT A LOW ALTITUDE.

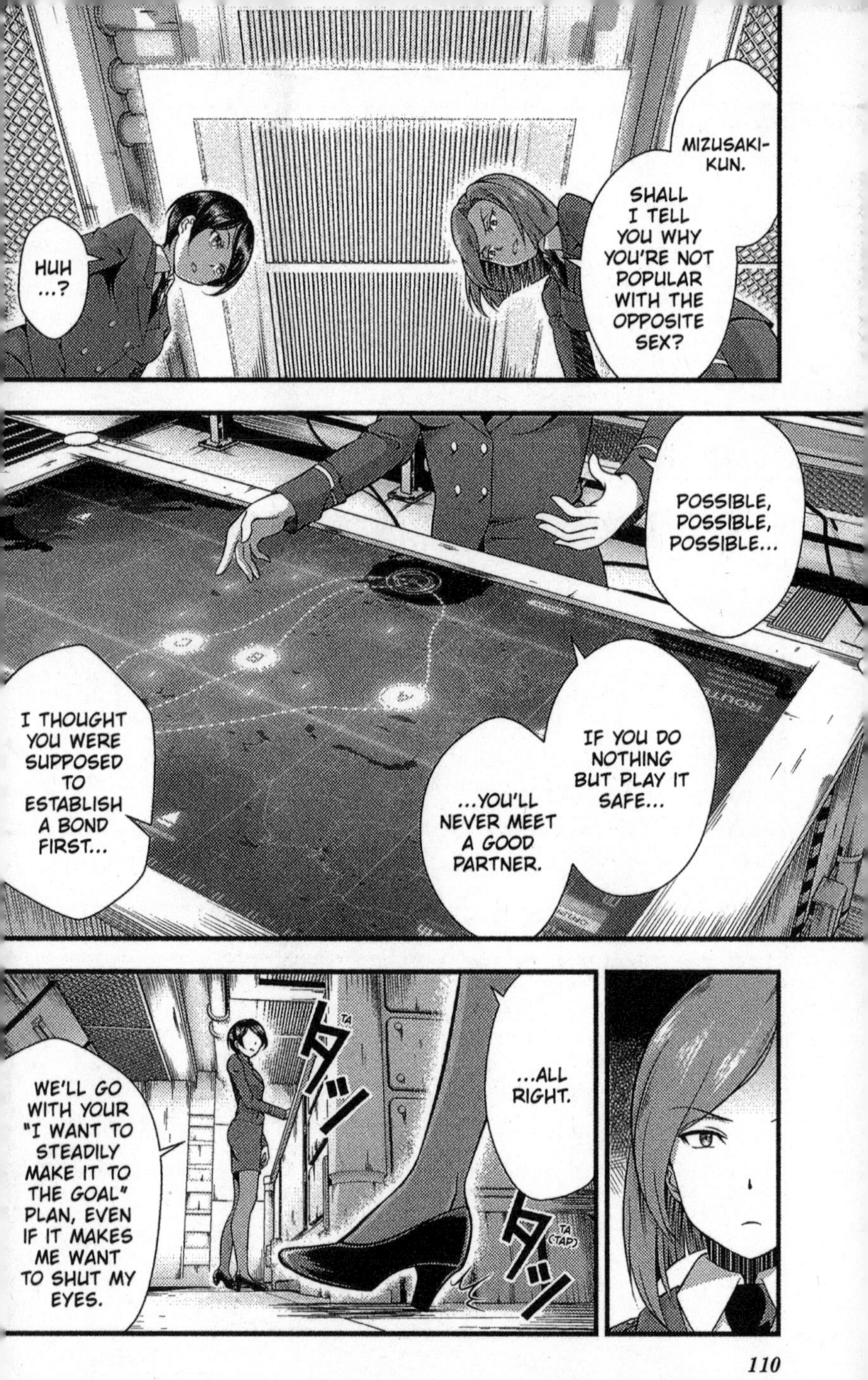
MIZUSAKI-KUN.
SHALL I TELL YOU WHY YOU'RE NOT POPULAR WITH THE OPPOSITE SEX?
HUH ...?
POSSIBLE, POSSIBLE, POSSIBLE...
IF YOU DO NOTHING BUT PLAY IT SAFE...
...YOU'LL NEVER MEET A GOOD PARTNER.
I THOUGHT YOU WERE SUPPOSED TO ESTABLISH A BOND FIRST...
...ALL RIGHT.
TA
TA (TAP)
WE'LL GO WITH YOUR "I WANT TO STEADILY MAKE IT TO THE GOAL" PLAN, EVEN IF IT MAKES ME WANT TO SHUT MY EYES.

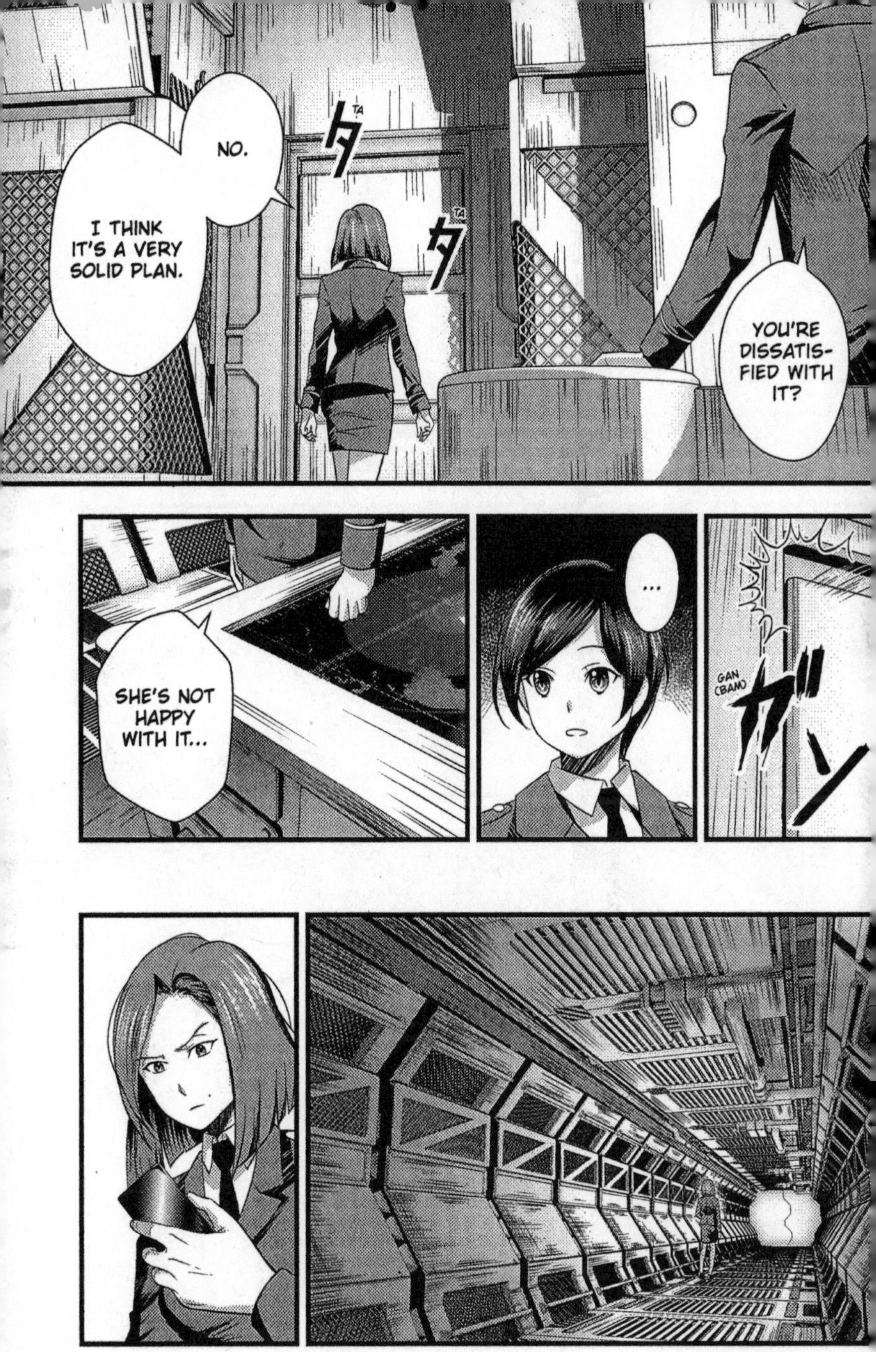
YOU'RE DISSATIS-FIED WITH IT?
タ TA
タ TA
NO.
I THINK IT'S A VERY SOLID PLAN.
ガン
GAN (BAM)
...
SHE'S NOT HAPPY WITH IT...

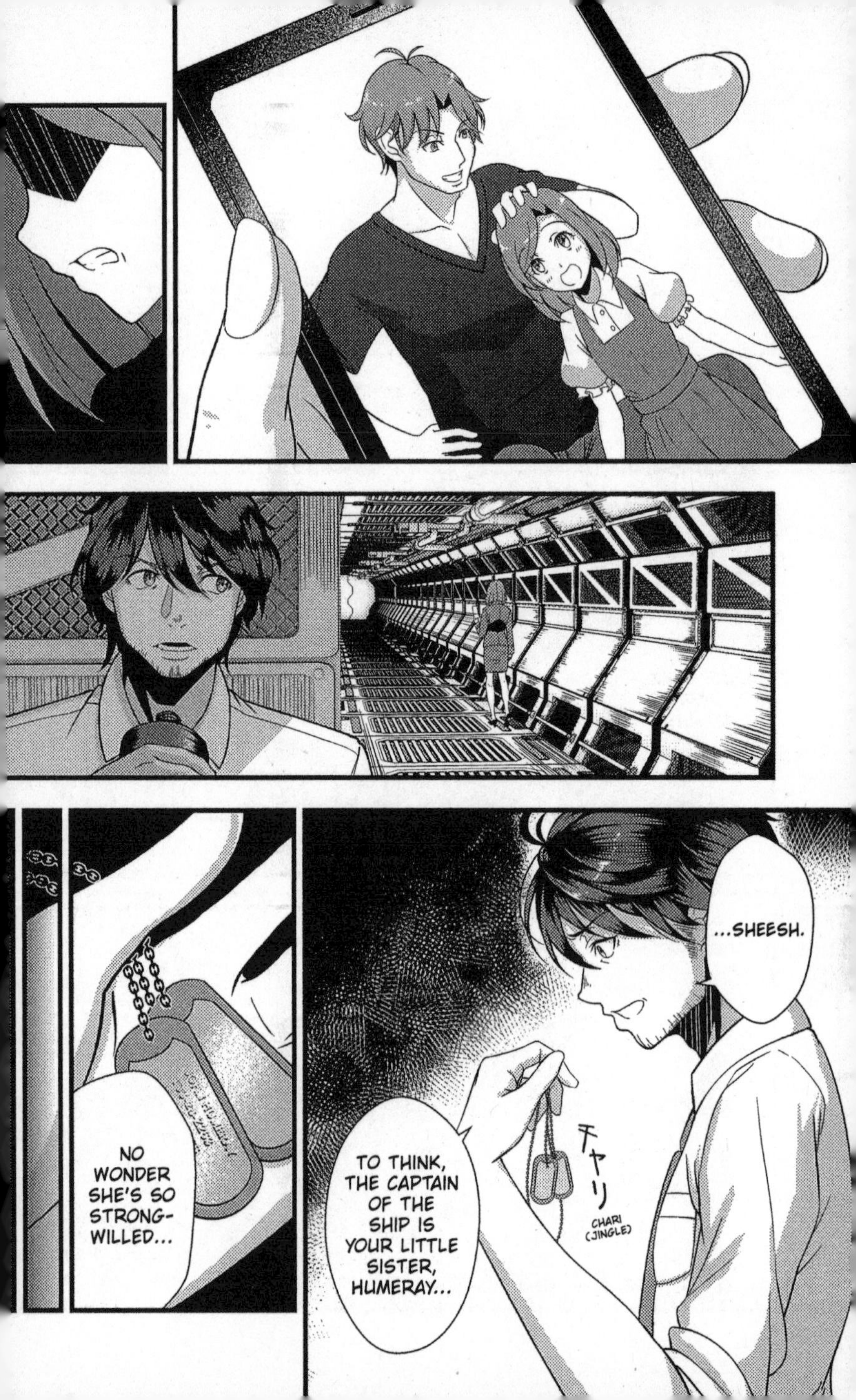
...SHEESH.
TO THINK, THE CAPTAIN OF THE SHIP IS YOUR LITTLE SISTER, HUMERAY...
チャリ
CHARI (JINGLE)
NO WONDER SHE'S SO STRONG-WILLED...

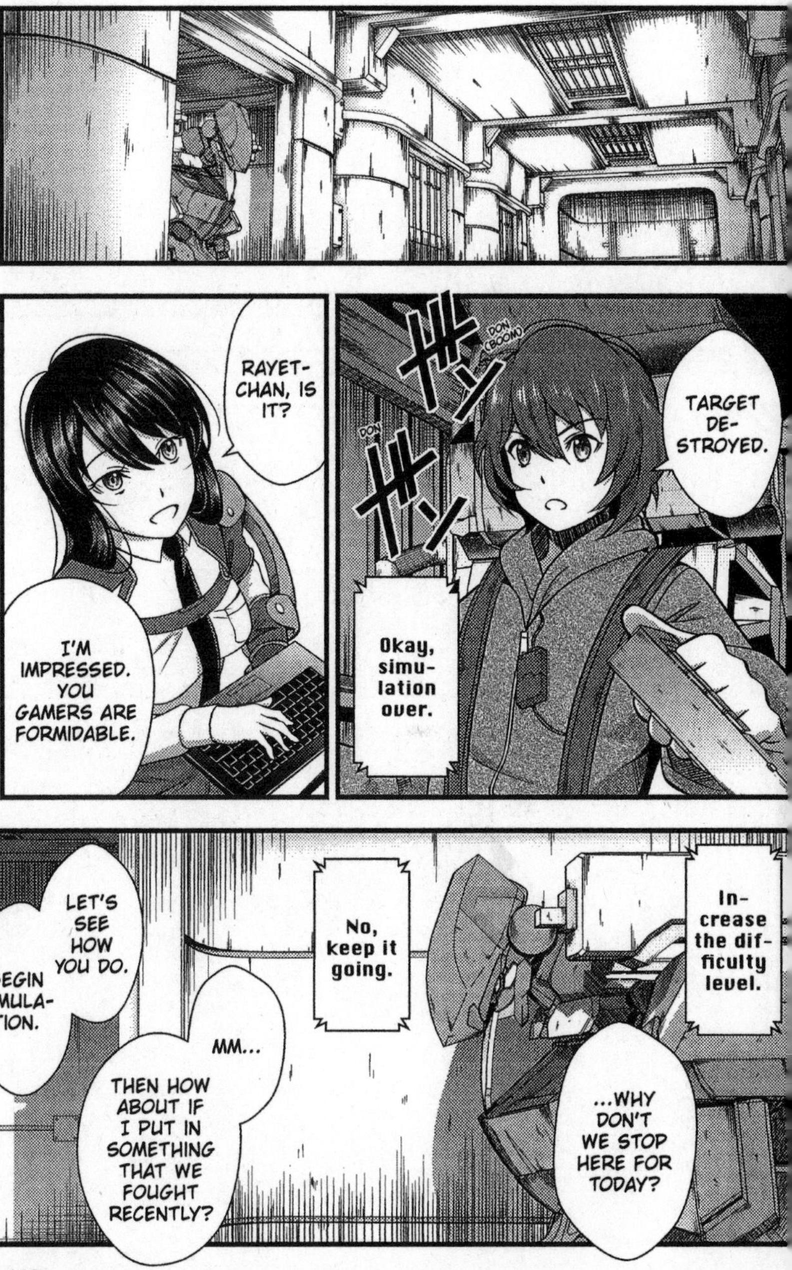
DON (BOOM)
DON
TARGET DE-STROYED.
Okay, simu-lation over.
RAYET-CHAN, IS IT?
I'M IMPRESSED. YOU GAMERS ARE FORMIDABLE.
In-crease the dif-ficulty level.
No, keep it going.
LET'S SEE HOW YOU DO.
BEGIN SIMULA-TION.
MM...
THEN HOW ABOUT IF I PUT IN SOMETHING THAT WE FOUGHT RECENTLY?
...WHY DON'T WE STOP HERE FOR TODAY?

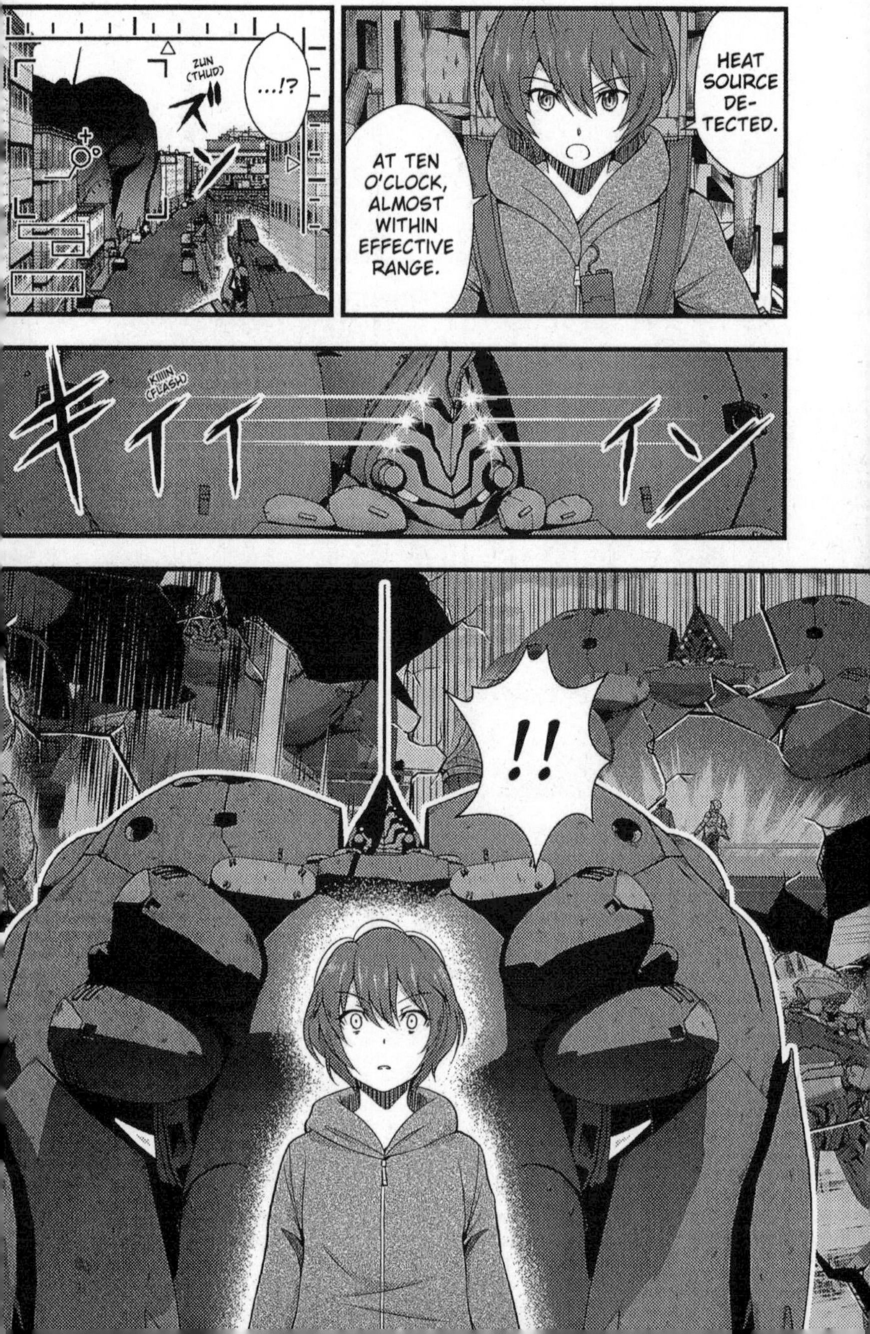
HEAT SOURCE DE-TECTED.
AT TEN O'CLOCK, ALMOST WITHIN EFFECTIVE RANGE.
ZUN (THUD)
ズン
...!?
KIIIN (FLASH)
キイイーイン
!!

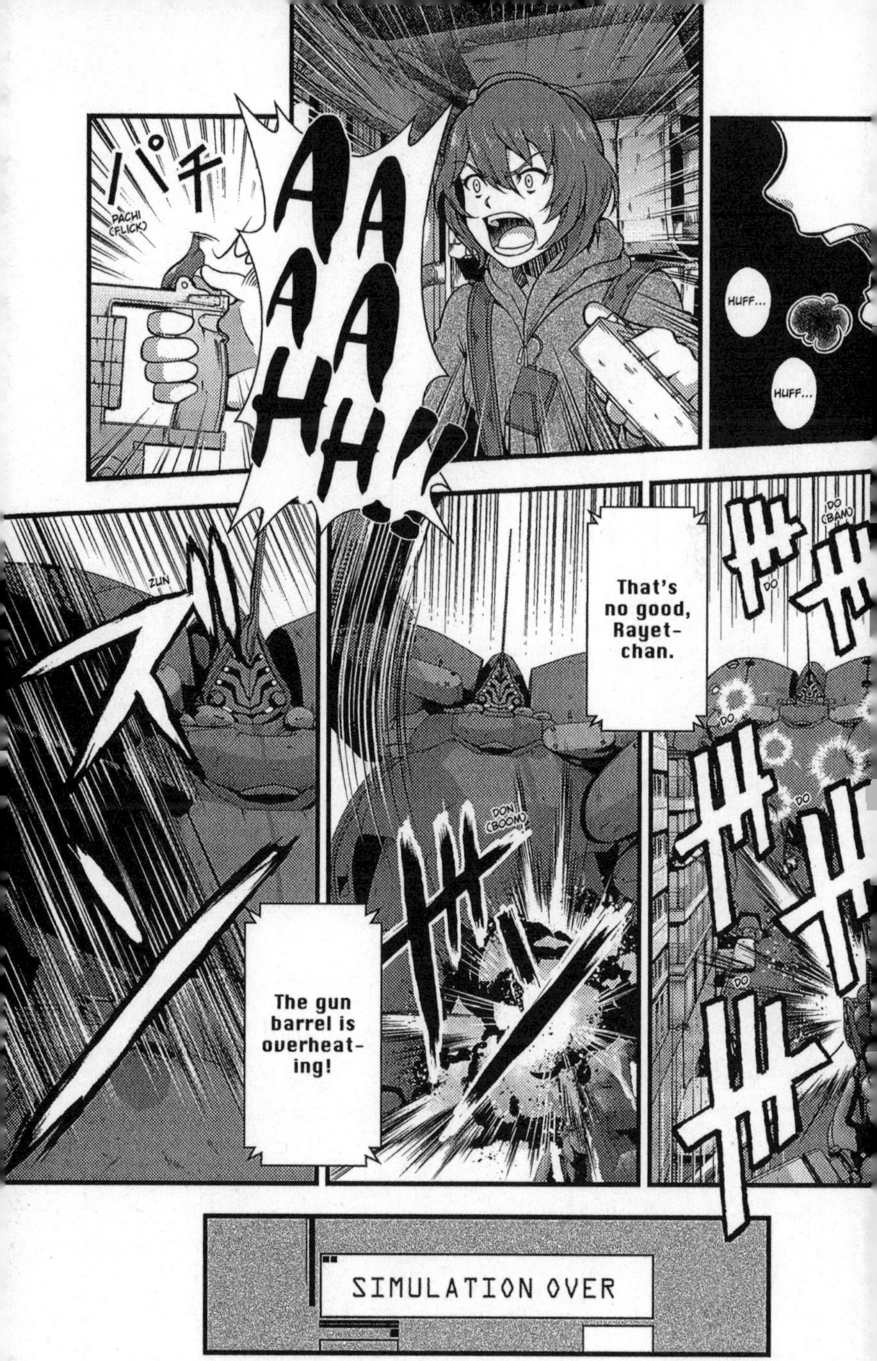
HUFF...
HUFF...
AAAAHH!!
パチ
PACHI (FLICK)
DO (BAM)
DO
DO
DO
DO
That's no good, Rayet-chan.
DON (BOOM)
The gun barrel is overheat-ing!
ZUN
SIMULATION OVER

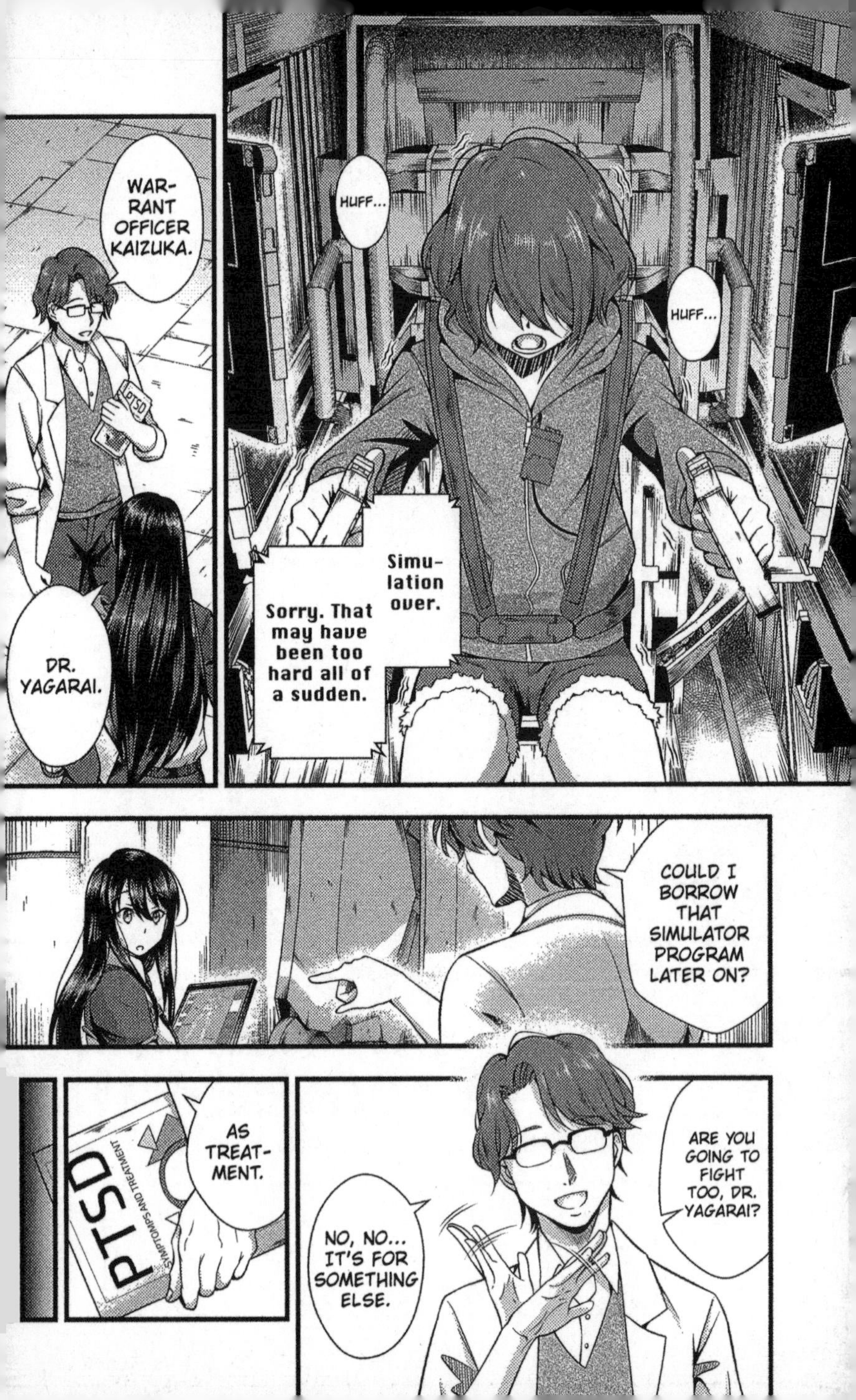
HUFF...
HUFF...
Simulation over.
Sorry. That may have been too hard all of a sudden.
PTSD
WAR-RANT OFFICER KAIZUKA.
DR. YAGARAI.
COULD I BORROW THAT SIMULATOR PROGRAM LATER ON?
ARE YOU GOING TO FIGHT TOO, DR. YAGARAI?
NO, NO... IT'S FOR SOMETHING ELSE.
AS TREAT-MENT.
PTSD
SYMPTOMPS AND TREATMENT

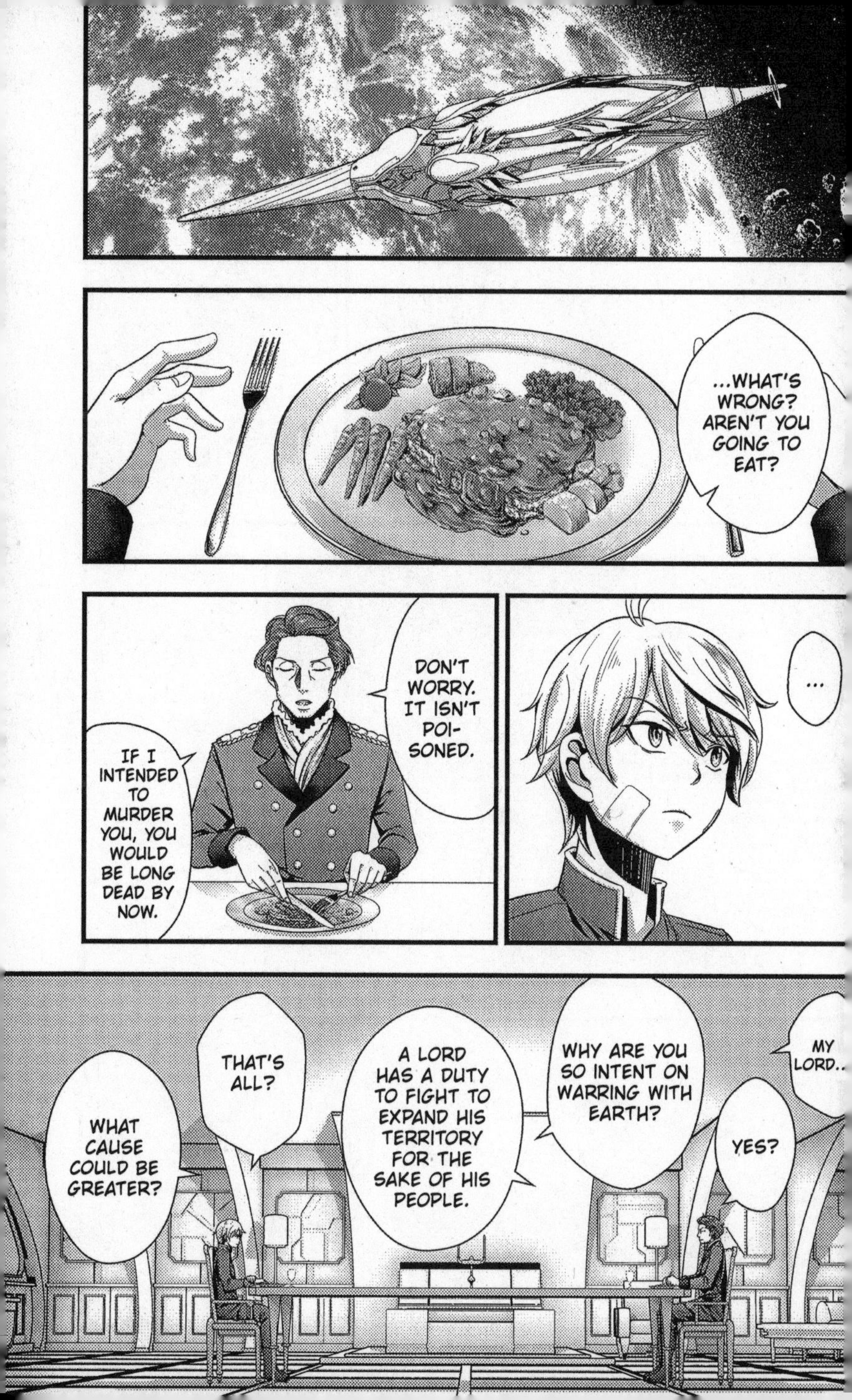
...WHAT'S WRONG? AREN'T YOU GOING TO EAT?
...
DON'T WORRY. IT ISN'T POI-SONED.
IF I INTENDED TO MURDER YOU, YOU WOULD BE LONG DEAD BY NOW.
MY LORD..
YES?
WHY ARE YOU SO INTENT ON WARRING WITH EARTH?
A LORD HAS A DUTY TO FIGHT TO EXPAND HIS TERRITORY FOR THE SAKE OF HIS PEOPLE.
THAT'S ALL?
WHAT CAUSE COULD BE GREATER?

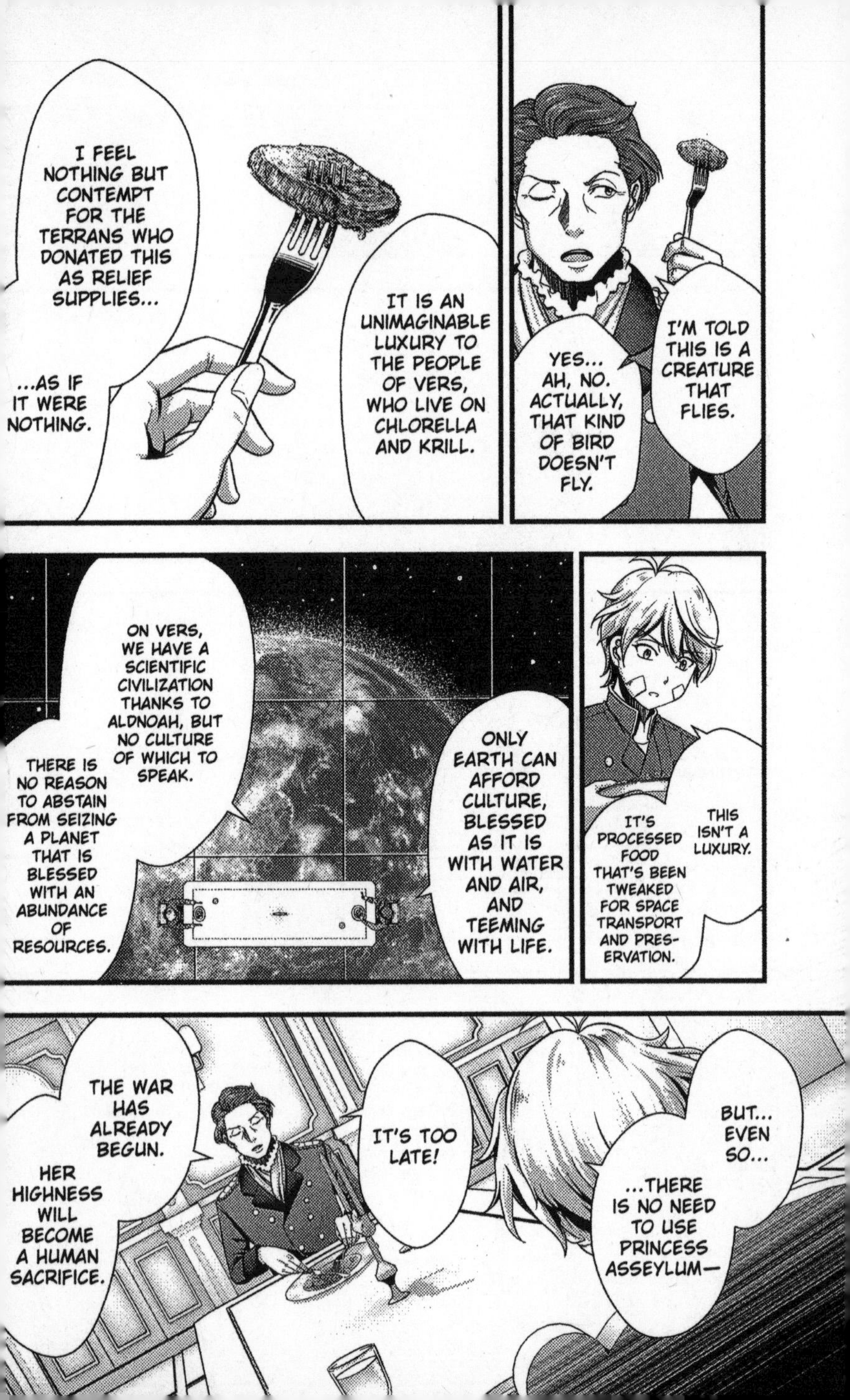

I'M TOLD THIS IS A CREATURE THAT FLIES.
YES... AH, NO. ACTUALLY, THAT KIND OF BIRD DOESN'T FLY.
IT IS AN UNIMAGINABLE LUXURY TO THE PEOPLE OF VERS, WHO LIVE ON CHLORELLA AND KRILL.
I FEEL NOTHING BUT CONTEMPT FOR THE TERRANS WHO DONATED THIS AS RELIEF SUPPLIES...
...AS IF IT WERE NOTHING.
THIS ISN'T A LUXURY.
IT'S PROCESSED FOOD THAT'S BEEN TWEAKED FOR SPACE TRANSPORT AND PRES-ERVATION.
ONLY EARTH CAN AFFORD CULTURE, BLESSED AS IT IS WITH WATER AND AIR, AND TEEMING WITH LIFE.
ON VERS, WE HAVE A SCIENTIFIC CIVILIZATION THANKS TO ALDNOAH, BUT NO CULTURE OF WHICH TO SPEAK.
THERE IS NO REASON TO ABSTAIN FROM SEIZING A PLANET THAT IS BLESSED WITH AN ABUNDANCE OF RESOURCES.
BUT... EVEN SO...
...THERE IS NO NEED TO USE PRINCESS ASSEYLUM—
IT'S TOO LATE!
THE WAR HAS ALREADY BEGUN.
HER HIGHNESS WILL BECOME A HUMAN SACRIFICE.

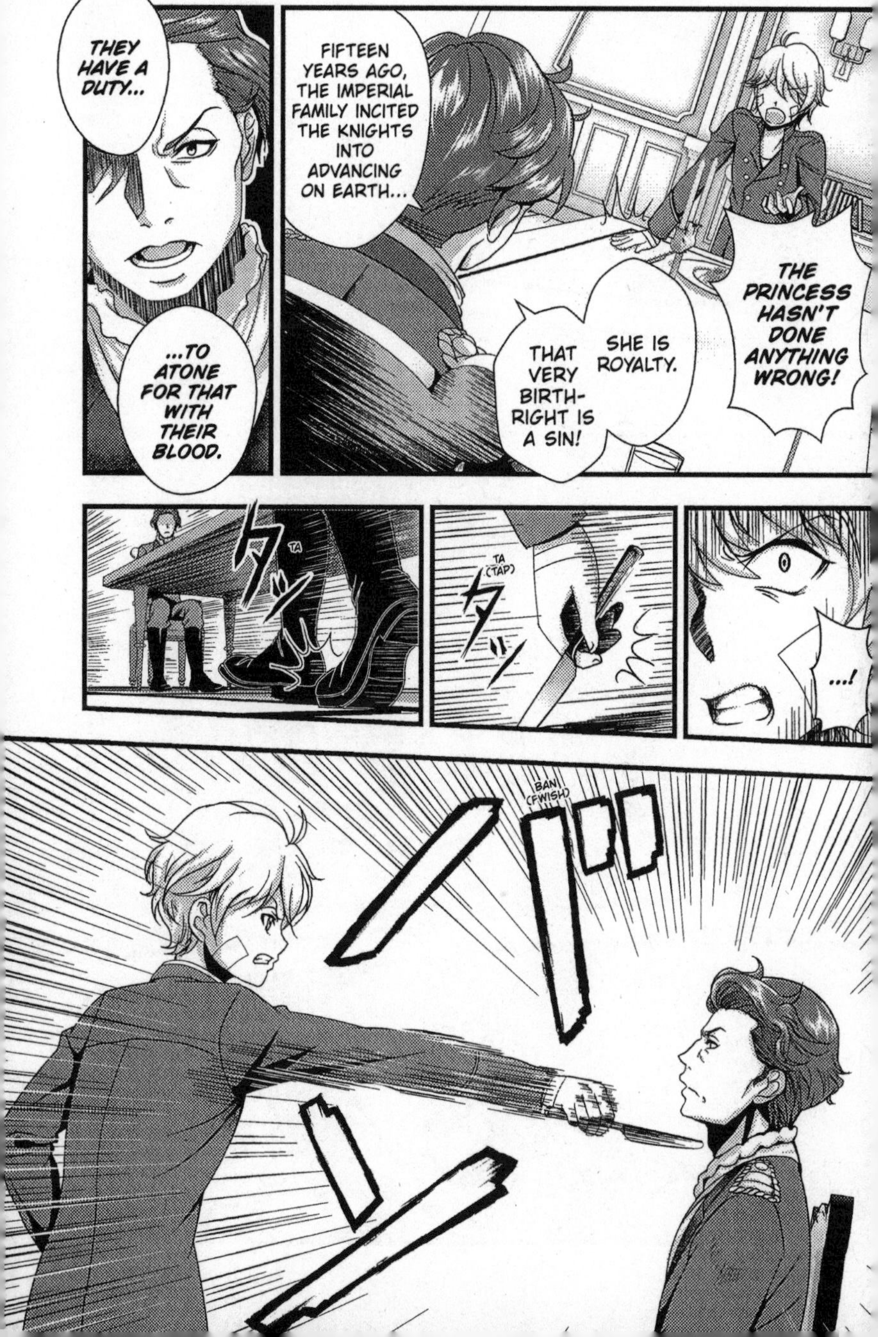
THE PRINCESS HASN'T DONE ANYTHING WRONG!
SHE IS ROYALTY.
THAT VERY BIRTH-RIGHT IS A SIN!
FIFTEEN YEARS AGO, THE IMPERIAL FAMILY INCITED THE KNIGHTS INTO ADVANCING ON EARTH...
THEY HAVE A DUTY...
...TO ATONE FOR THAT WITH THEIR BLOOD.
...!
TA (TAP)
TA
BAN (FWISH)

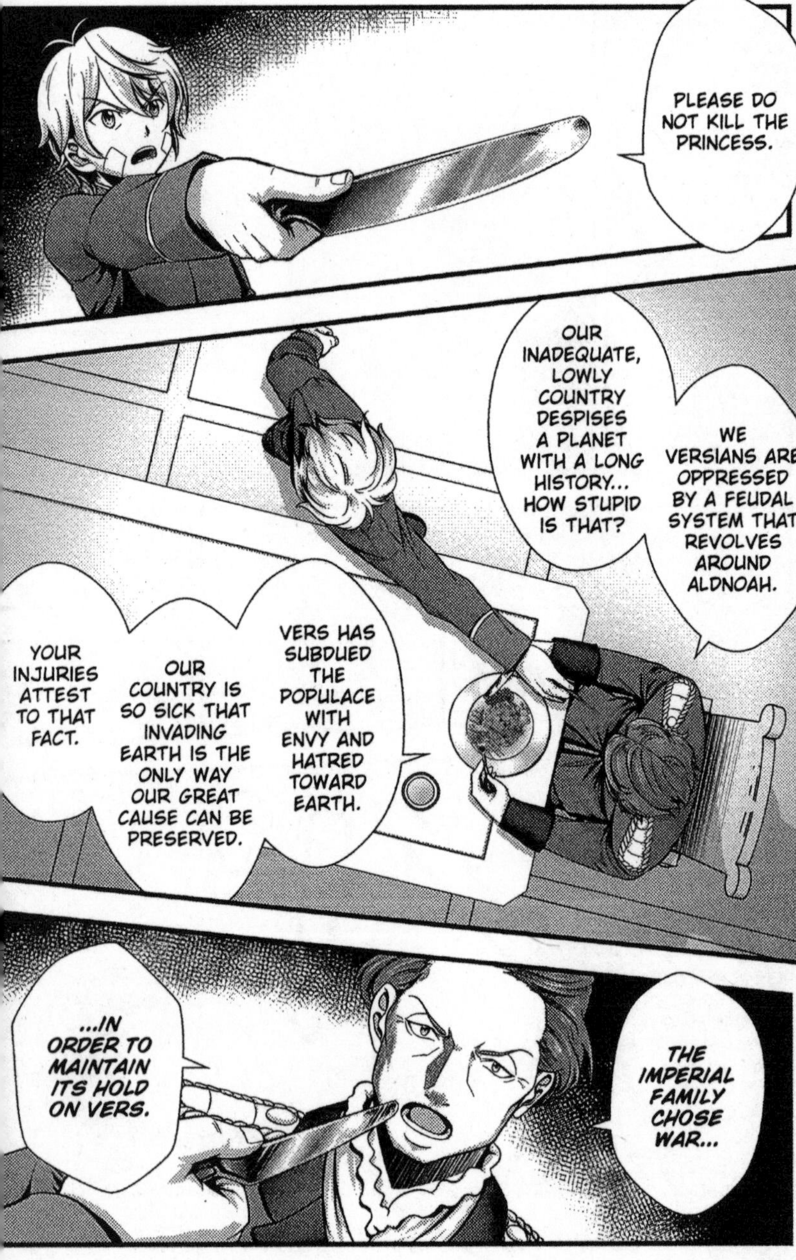
PLEASE DO NOT KILL THE PRINCESS.
WE VERSIANS ARE OPPRESSED BY A FEUDAL SYSTEM THAT REVOLVES AROUND ALDNOAH.
OUR INADEQUATE, LOWLY COUNTRY DESPISES A PLANET WITH A LONG HISTORY... HOW STUPID IS THAT?
VERS HAS SUBDUED THE POPULACE WITH ENVY AND HATRED TOWARD EARTH.
OUR COUNTRY IS SO SICK THAT INVADING EARTH IS THE ONLY WAY OUR GREAT CAUSE CAN BE PRESERVED.
YOUR INJURIES ATTEST TO THAT FACT.
THE IMPERIAL FAMILY CHOSE WAR...
...IN ORDER TO MAINTAIN ITS HOLD ON VERS.

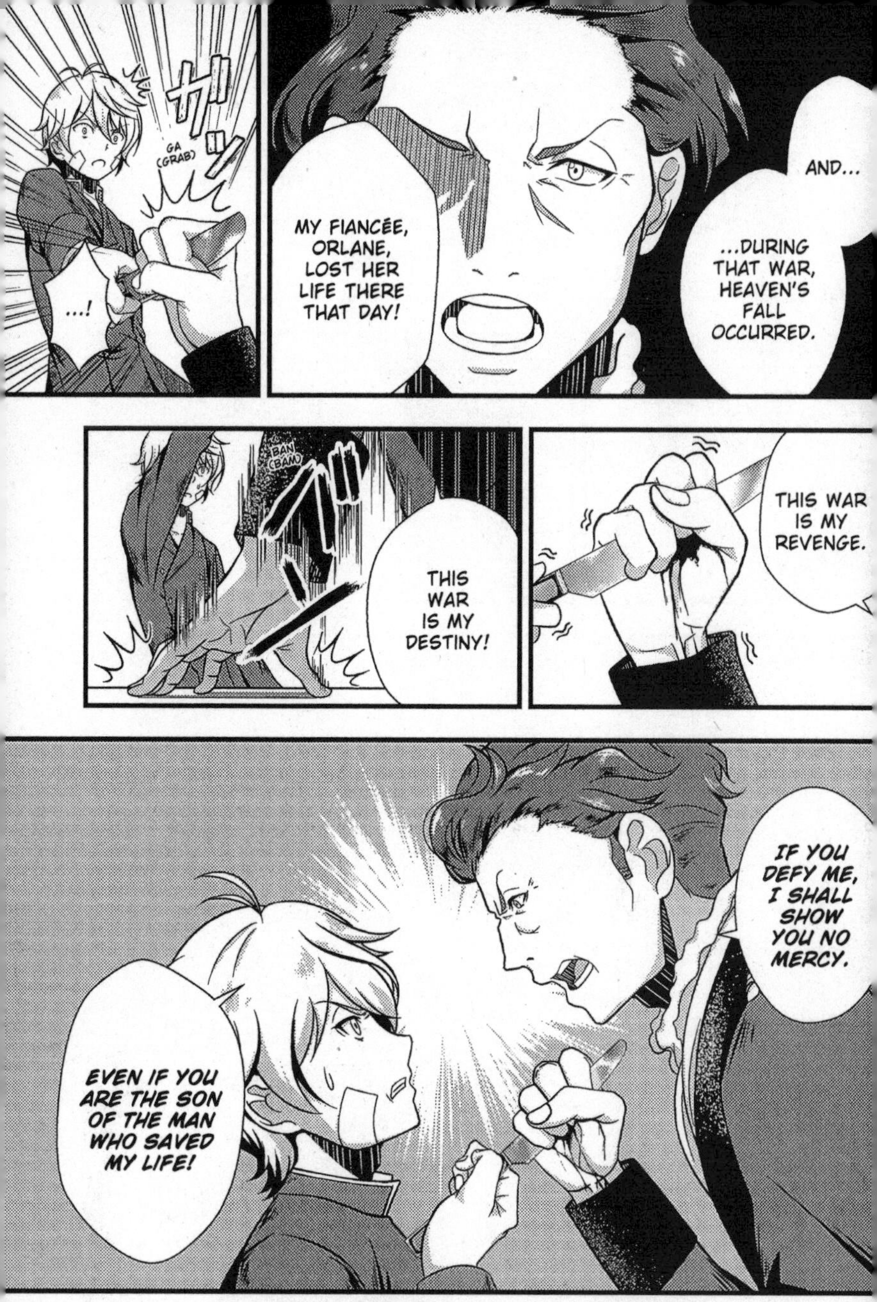
AND...
...DURING THAT WAR, HEAVEN'S FALL OCCURRED.
MY FIANCÉE, ORLANE, LOST HER LIFE THERE THAT DAY!
GA (GRAB)
...!
THIS WAR IS MY REVENGE.
BAN (BAM)
THIS WAR IS MY DESTINY!
IF YOU DEFY ME, I SHALL SHOW YOU NO MERCY.
EVEN IF YOU ARE THE SON OF THE MAN WHO SAVED MY LIFE!

[redacted]

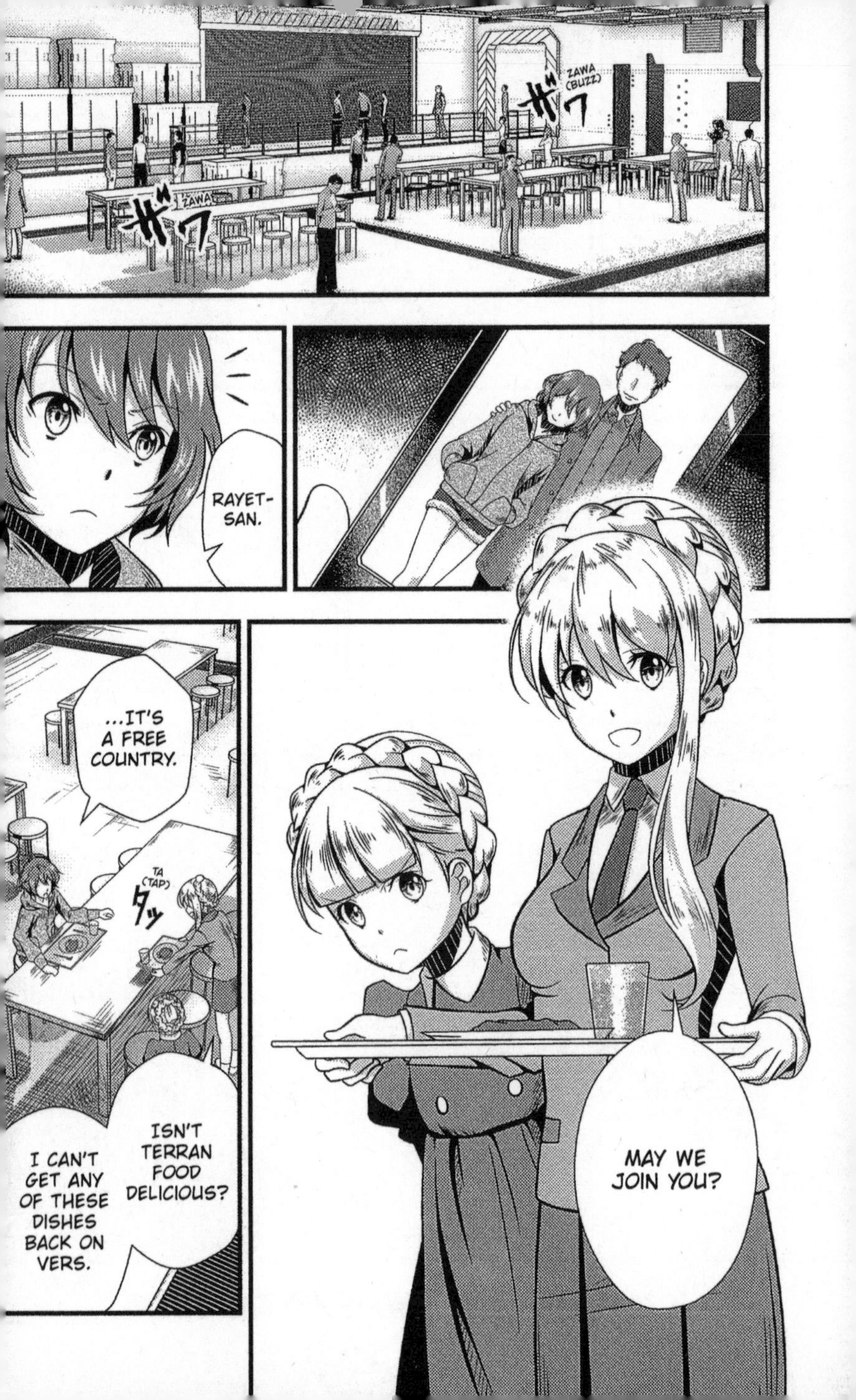
ZAWA (BUZZ)
ZAWA
RAYET-SAN.
MAY WE JOIN YOU?
...IT'S A FREE COUNTRY.
TA (TAP)
ISN'T TERRAN FOOD DELICIOUS?
I CAN'T GET ANY OF THESE DISHES BACK ON VERS.

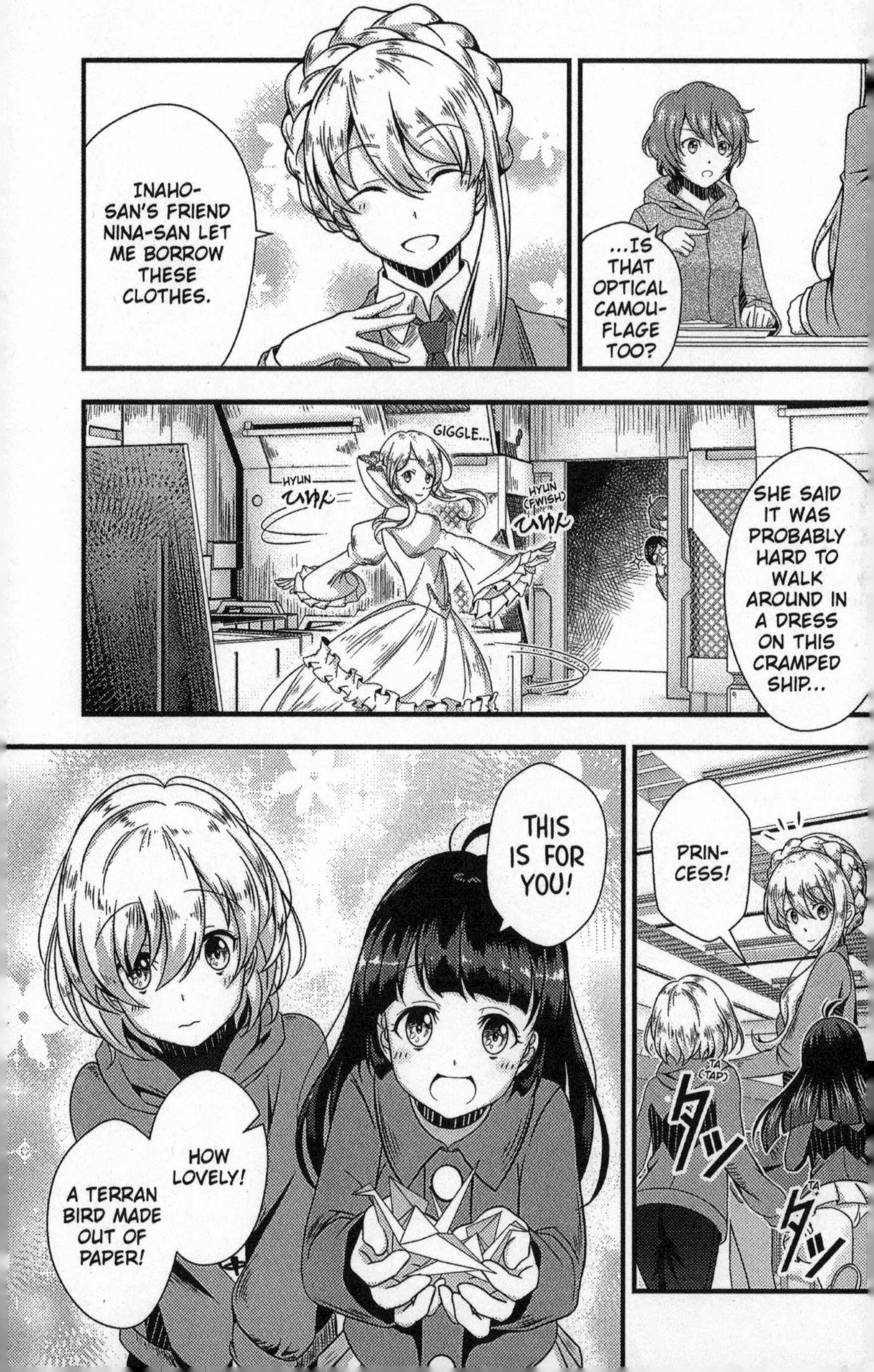
...IS THAT OPTICAL CAMOUFLAGE TOO?
INAHO-SAN'S FRIEND NINA-SAN LET ME BORROW THESE CLOTHES.
SHE SAID IT WAS PROBABLY HARD TO WALK AROUND IN A DRESS ON THIS CRAMPED SHIP...
GIGGLE...
HYUN (FWISH) ひゅん
HYUN ひゅん
PRIN-CESS!
TA TAP タッ
TA タッ
THIS IS FOR YOU!
HOW LOVELY!
A TERRAN BIRD MADE OUT OF PAPER!

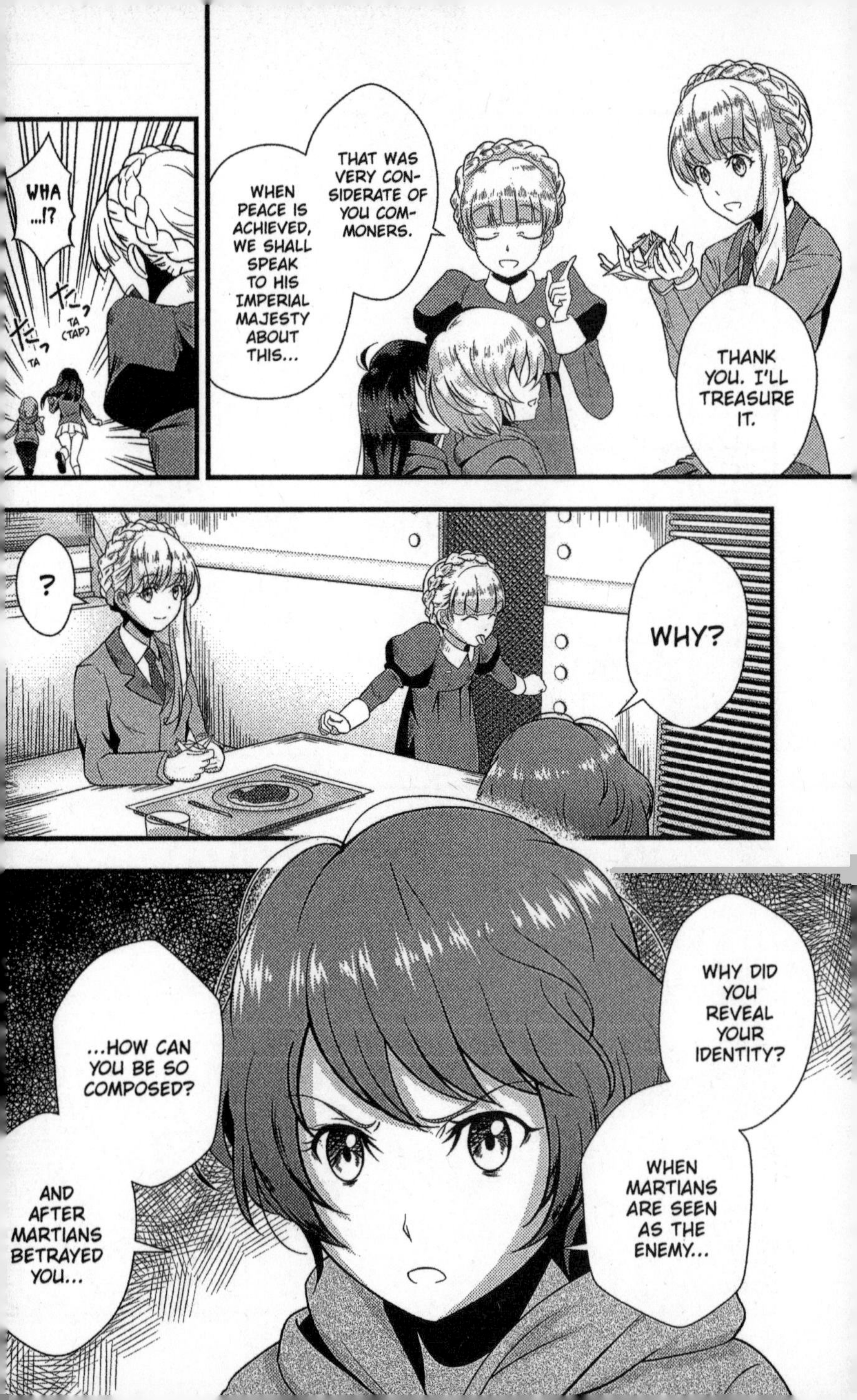
THANK YOU. I'LL TREASURE IT.
THAT WAS VERY CONSIDERATE OF YOU COMMONERS.
WHEN PEACE IS ACHIEVED, WE SHALL SPEAK TO HIS IMPERIAL MAJESTY ABOUT THIS...
WHA ...!?
TA (TAP)
TA
WHY?
?
WHY DID YOU REVEAL YOUR IDENTITY?
WHEN MARTIANS ARE SEEN AS THE ENEMY...
...HOW CAN YOU BE SO COMPOSED?
AND AFTER MARTIANS BETRAYED YOU...

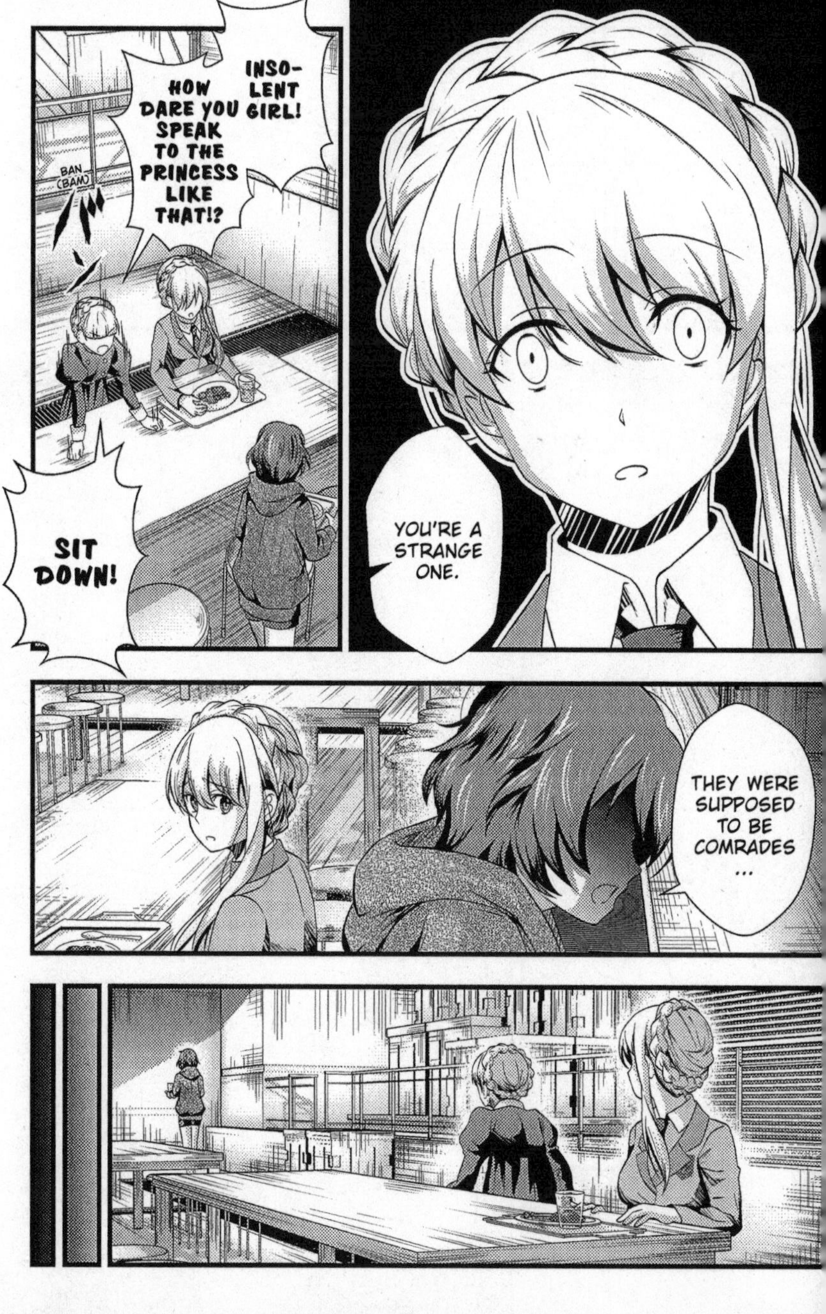
YOU'RE A STRANGE ONE.
INSO-LENT GIRL!
HOW DARE YOU SPEAK TO THE PRINCESS LIKE THAT!?
BAN (BAM)
SIT DOWN!
THEY WERE SUPPOSED TO BE COMRADES ...

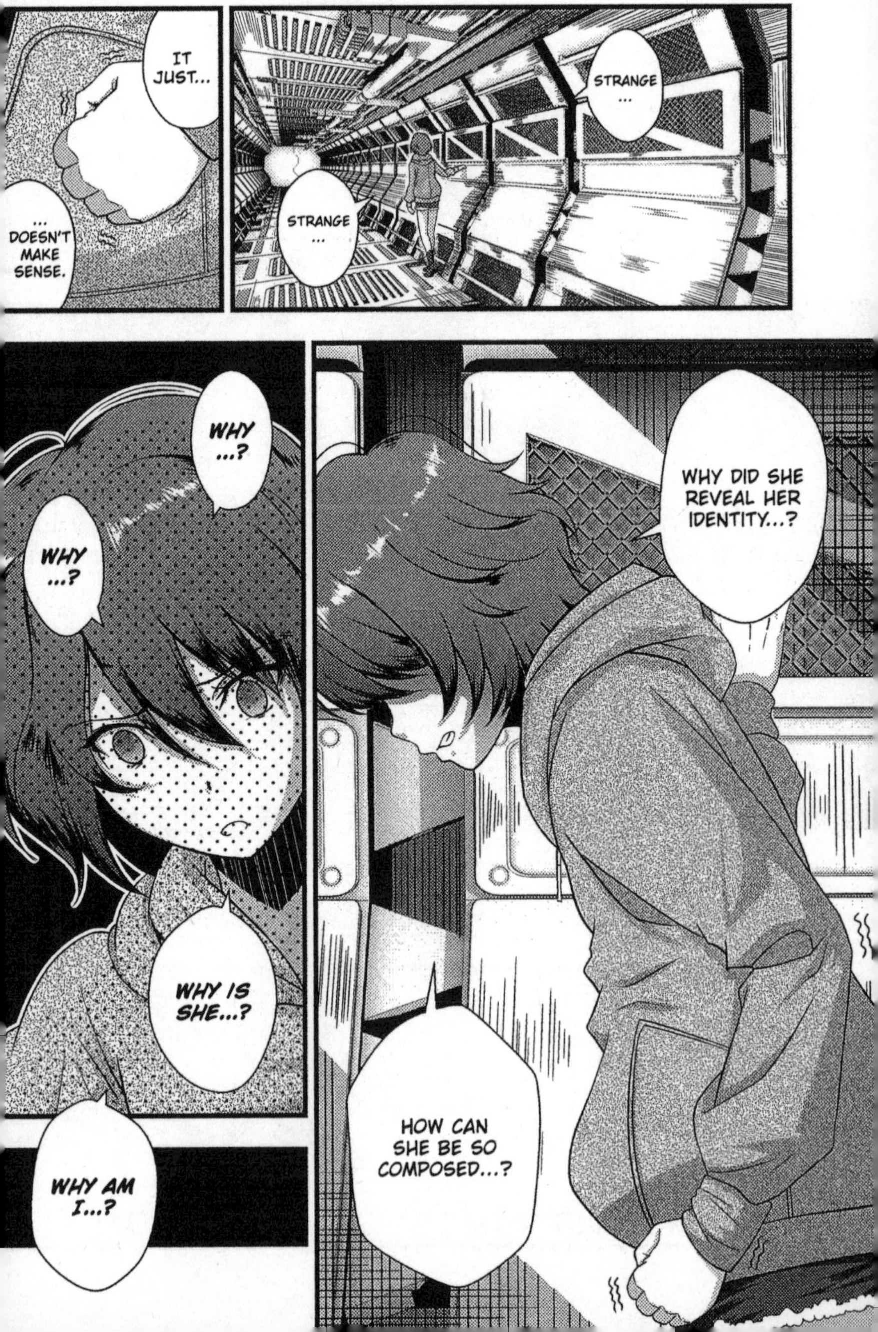
STRANGE...
STRANGE...
IT JUST...
...DOESN'T MAKE SENSE.
WHY DID SHE REVEAL HER IDENTITY...?
HOW CAN SHE BE SO COMPOSED...?
WHY...?
WHY...?
WHY IS SHE...?
WHY AM I...?

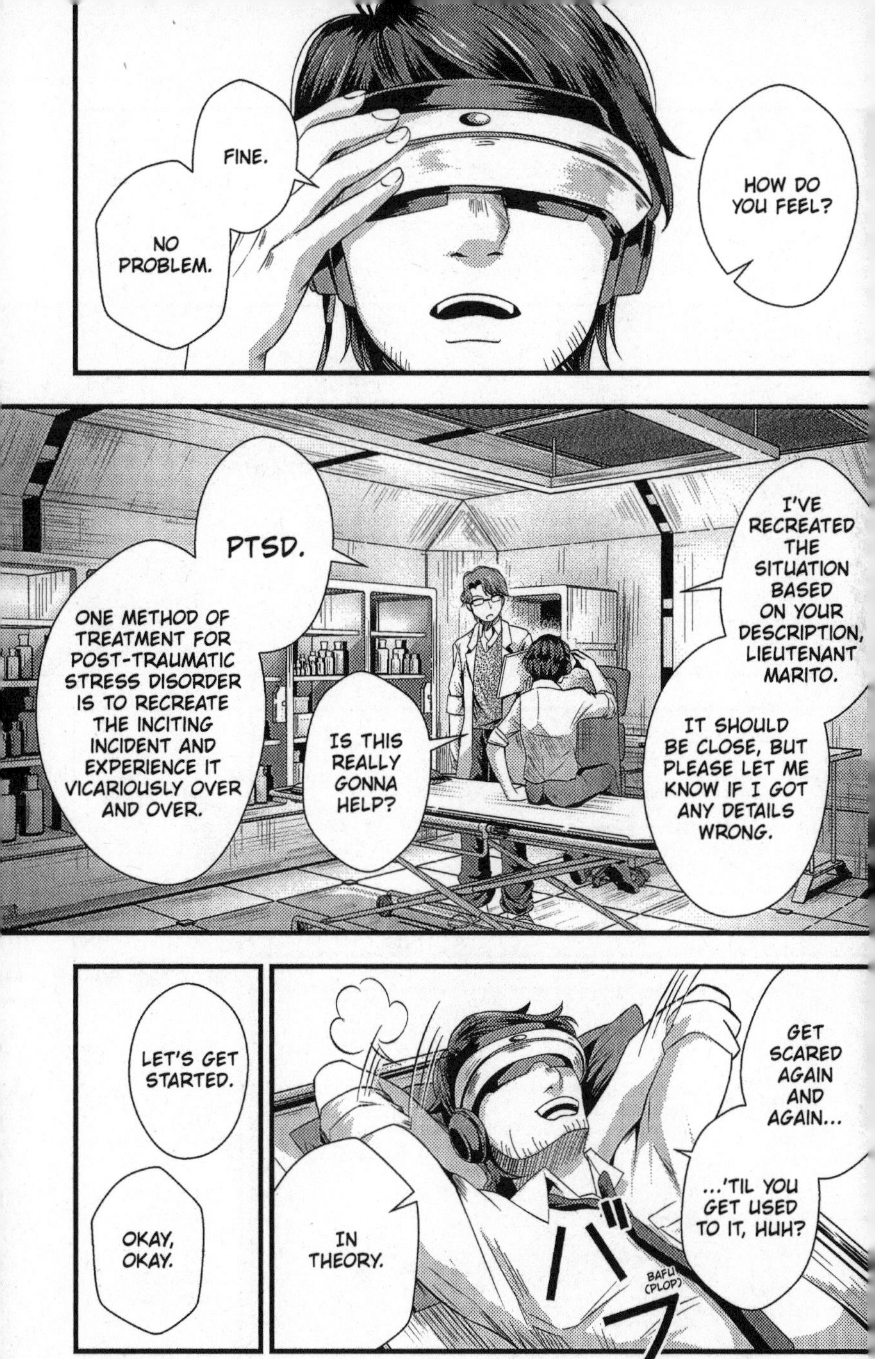
HOW DO YOU FEEL?
FINE.
NO PROBLEM.
I'VE RECREATED THE SITUATION BASED ON YOUR DESCRIPTION, LIEUTENANT MARITO.
IT SHOULD BE CLOSE, BUT PLEASE LET ME KNOW IF I GOT ANY DETAILS WRONG.
IS THIS REALLY GONNA HELP?
PTSD.
ONE METHOD OF TREATMENT FOR POST-TRAUMATIC STRESS DISORDER IS TO RECREATE THE INCITING INCIDENT AND EXPERIENCE IT VICARIOUSLY OVER AND OVER.
GET SCARED AGAIN AND AGAIN...
...'TIL YOU GET USED TO IT, HUH?
BAFU (PLOP)
IN THEORY.
LET'S GET STARTED.
OKAY, OKAY.

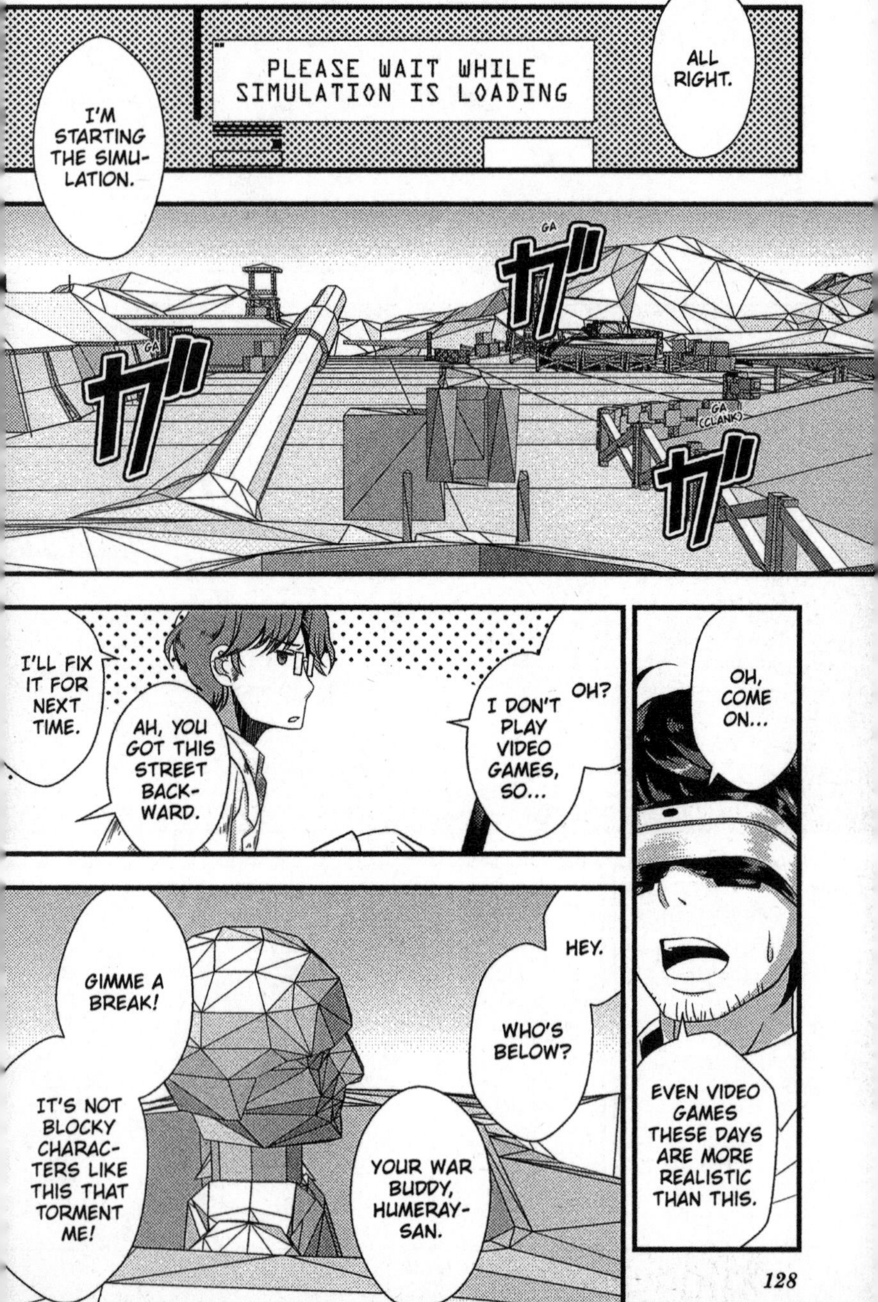
ALL RIGHT.
PLEASE WAIT WHILE SIMULATION IS LOADING
I'M STARTING THE SIMULATION.
GA
GA (CLANK)
GA
OH, COME ON...
EVEN VIDEO GAMES THESE DAYS ARE MORE REALISTIC THAN THIS.
OH?
I DON'T PLAY VIDEO GAMES, SO...
AH, YOU GOT THIS STREET BACKWARD.
I'LL FIX IT FOR NEXT TIME.
HEY.
WHO'S BELOW?
YOUR WAR BUDDY, HUMERAY-SAN.
GIMME A BREAK!
IT'S NOT BLOCKY CHARACTERS LIKE THIS THAT TORMENT ME!

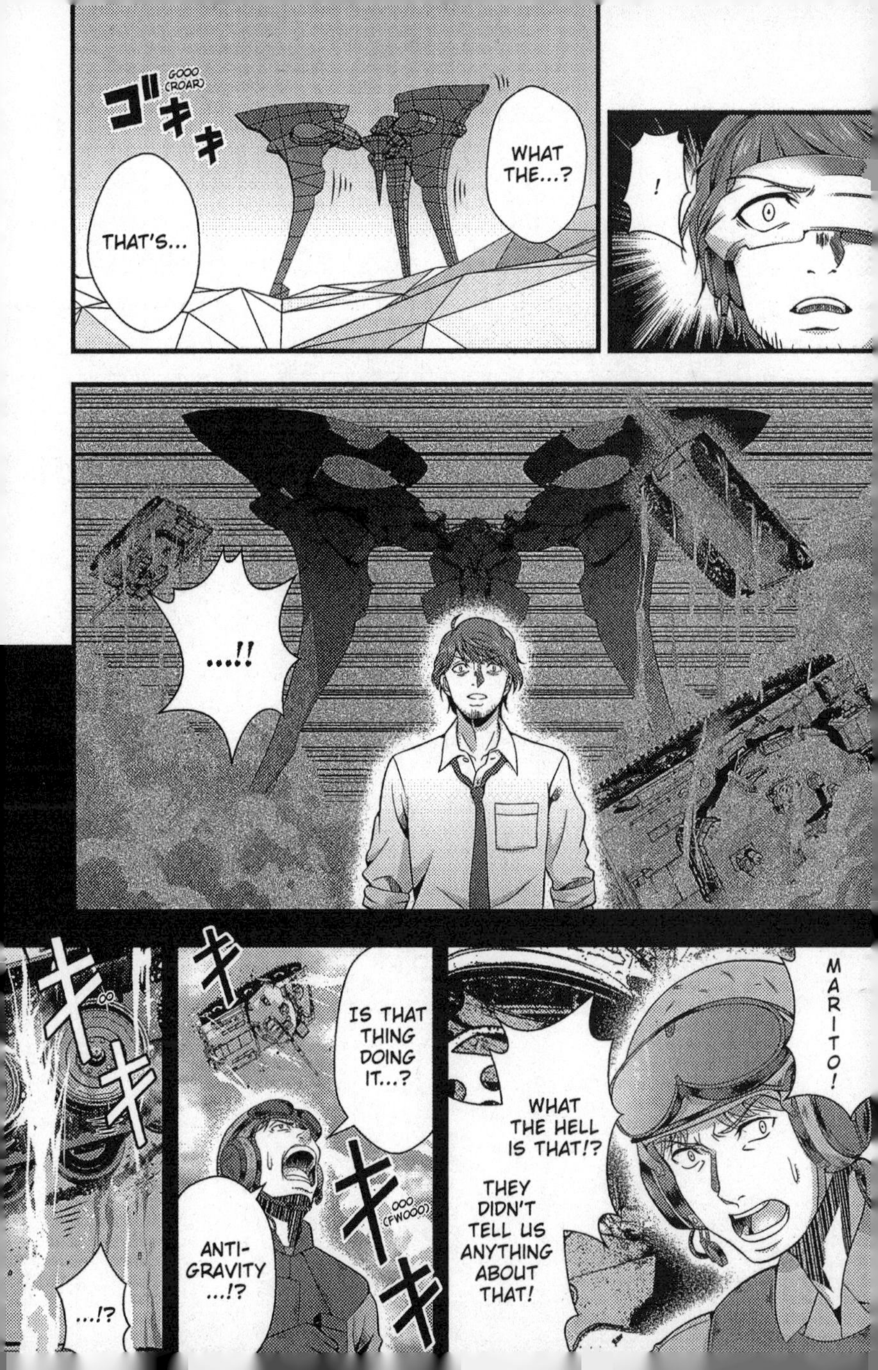
!
WHAT THE...?
GOOO (ROAR)
THAT'S...
...!!
MARITO!
WHAT THE HELL IS THAT!?
THEY DIDN'T TELL US ANYTHING ABOUT THAT!
IS THAT THING DOING IT...?
OOO (FWOOO)
ANTI-GRAVITY...!?
...!?

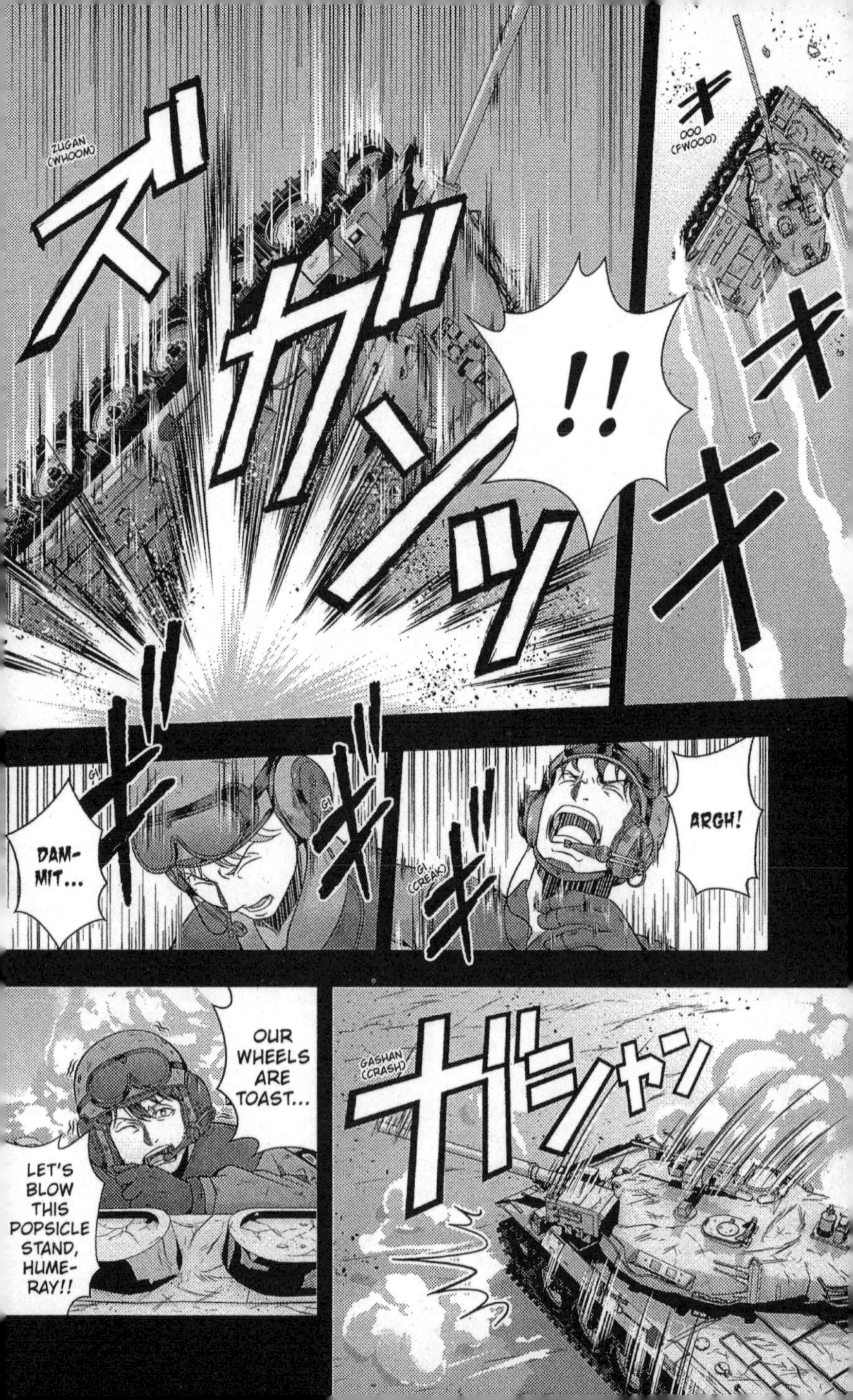
OOO (FWOOO)
!!
ZUGAN (WHOOM)
ARGH!
GI (CREAK)
GI
GI
DAM-MIT...
GASHAN (CRASH)
OUR WHEELS ARE TOAST...
LET'S BLOW THIS POPSICLE STAND, HUME-RAY!!

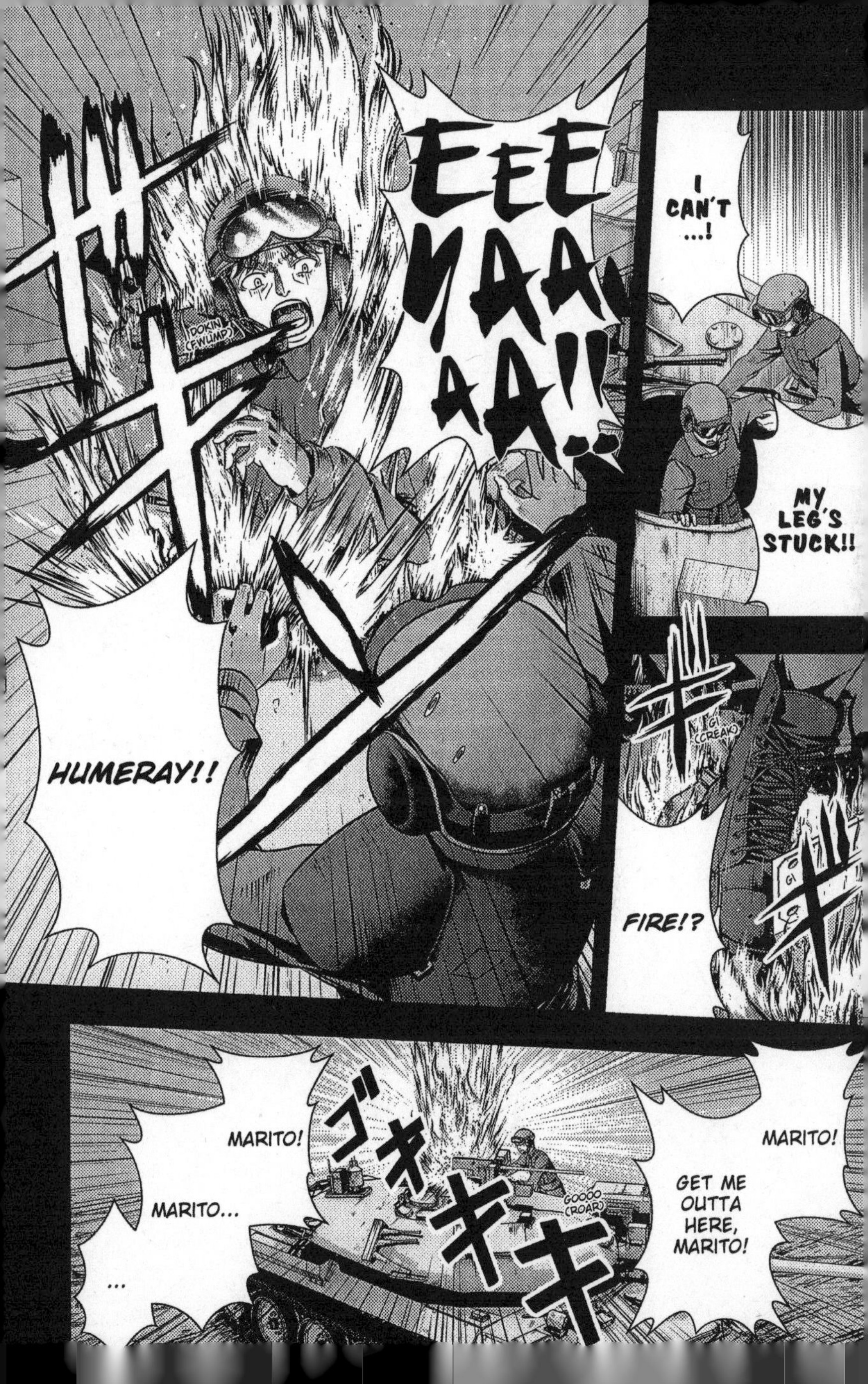
I CAN'T ...!
MY LEG'S STUCK!!
GI (CREAK)
FIRE!?
EEEYAAAAA!!
DOKIN (FWUMP)
HUMERAY!!
MARITO!
GET ME OUTTA HERE, MARITO!
GOOOO (ROAR)
ゴキキキ
MARITO!
MARITO...
...

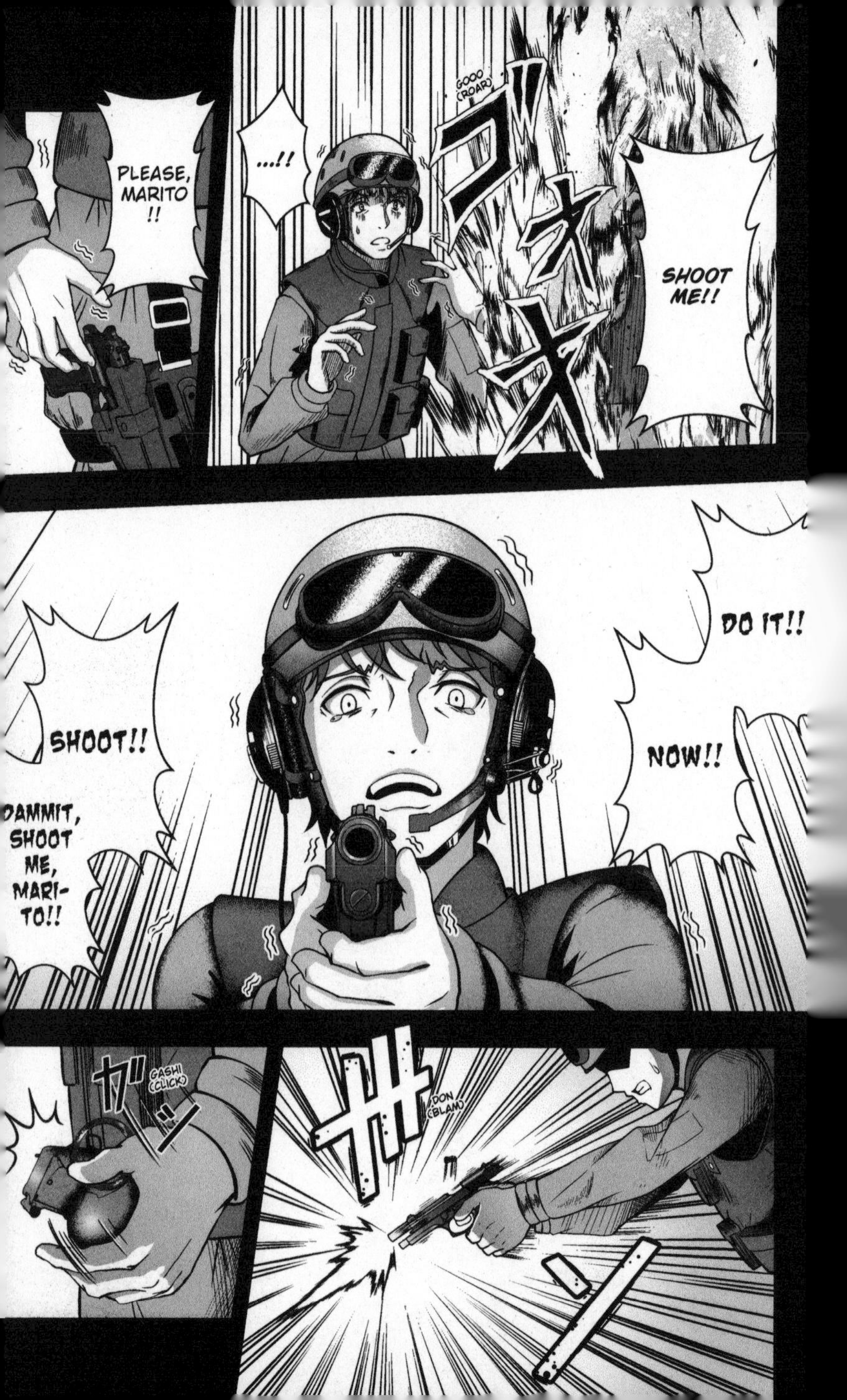
GOOO (ROAR)
SHOOT ME!!
...!!
PLEASE, MARITO !!
DO IT!!
NOW!!
SHOOT!!
DAMMIT, SHOOT ME, MARI-TO!!
DON (BLAM)
GASHI (CLICK)

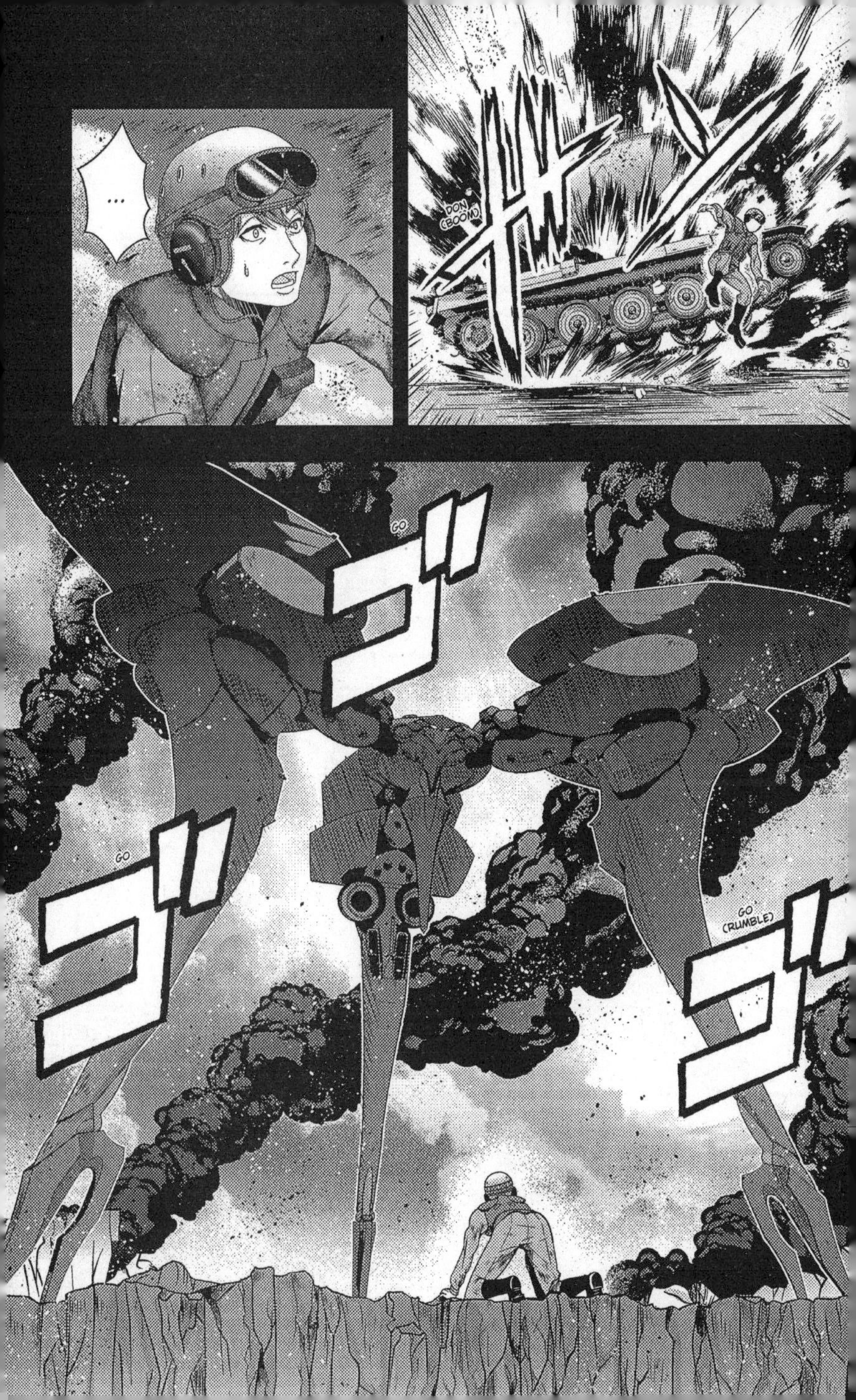
DON (BOOM)
...
GO
GO (RUMBLE)
GO

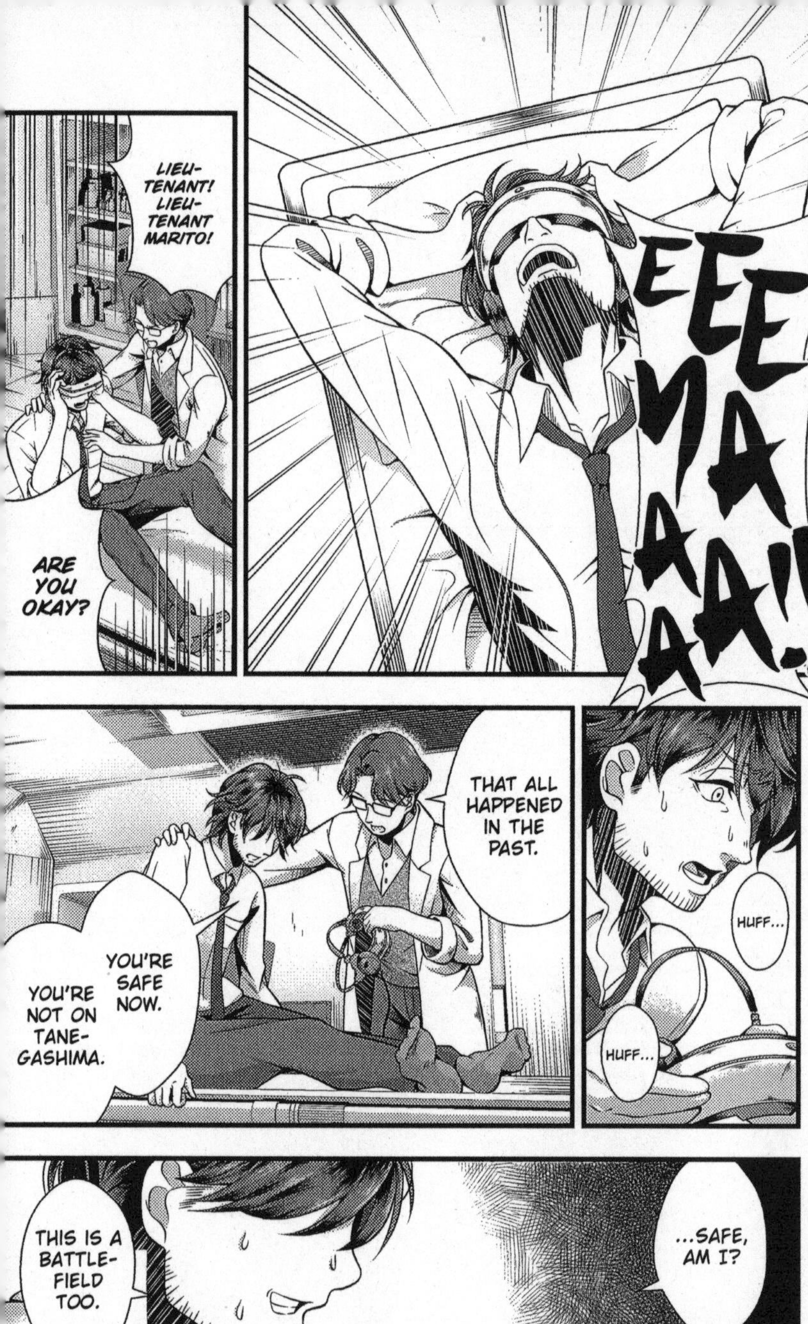
EEENAAAA!!
LIEU-TENANT! LIEU-TENANT MARITO!
ARE YOU OKAY?
HUFF...
HUFF...
THAT ALL HAPPENED IN THE PAST.
YOU'RE SAFE NOW.
YOU'RE NOT ON TANE-GASHIMA.
...SAFE, AM I?
THIS IS A BATTLE-FIELD TOO.

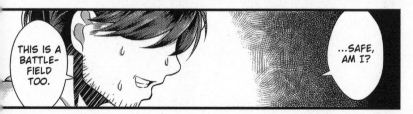

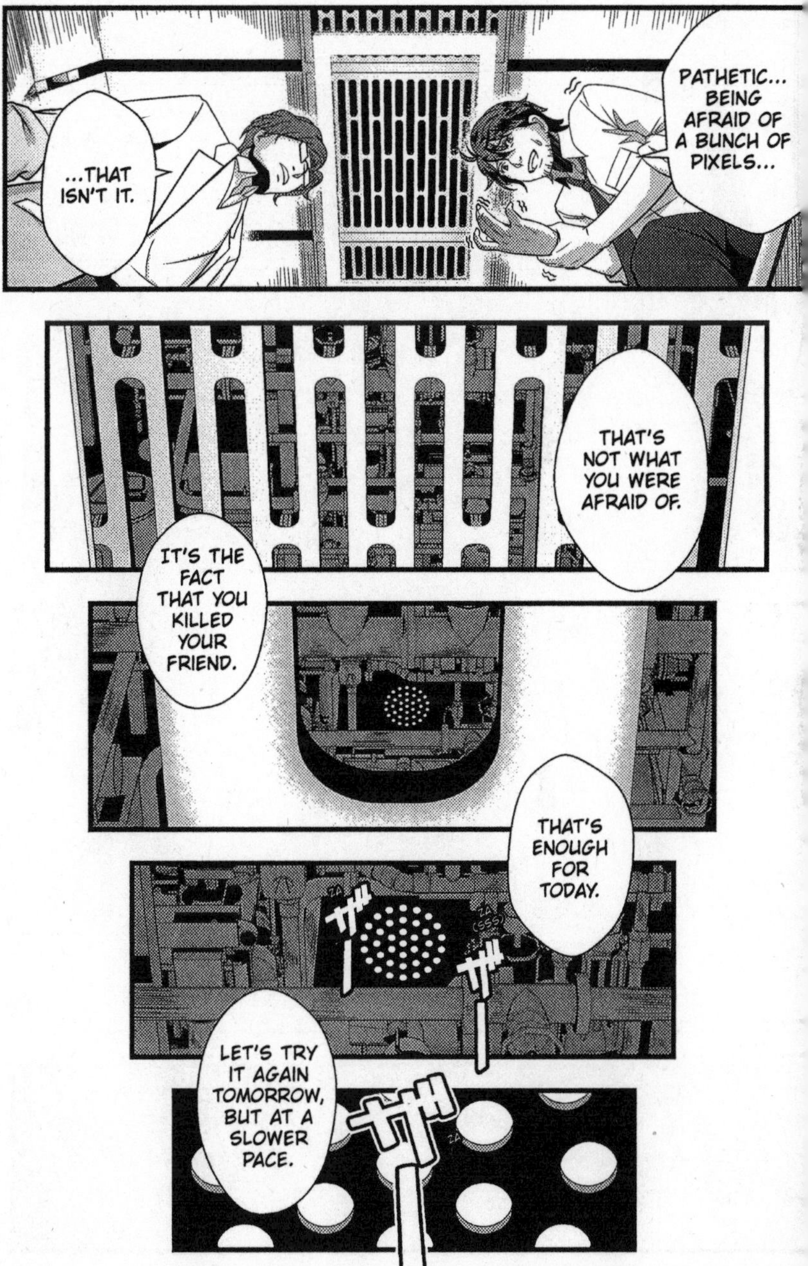
PATHETIC... BEING AFRAID OF A BUNCH OF PIXELS...
...THAT ISN'T IT.
THAT'S NOT WHAT YOU WERE AFRAID OF.
IT'S THE FACT THAT YOU KILLED YOUR FRIEND.
THAT'S ENOUGH FOR TODAY.
ZA
ZA (SSS)
LET'S TRY IT AGAIN TOMORROW, BUT AT A SLOWER PACE.

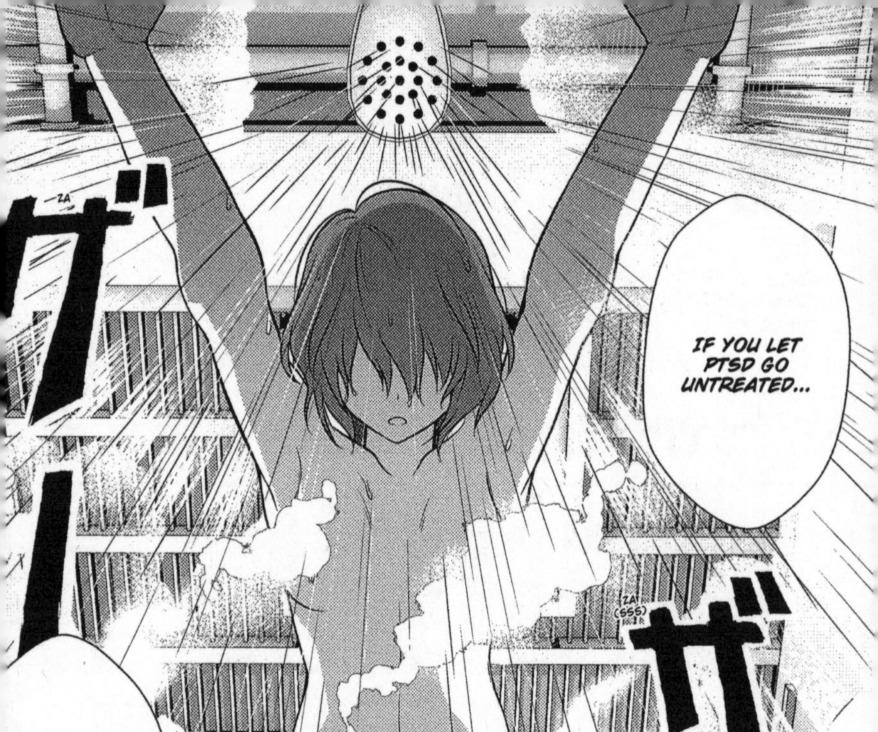
IF YOU LET PTSD GO UNTREATED...
ZA (SSS)
ZA
...THERE COULD BE SERIOUS CONSEQUENCES DOWN THE LINE.
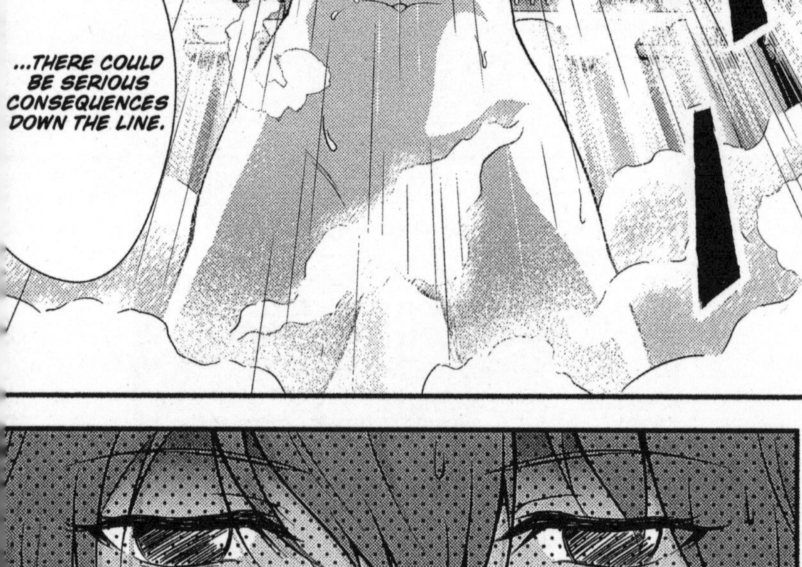

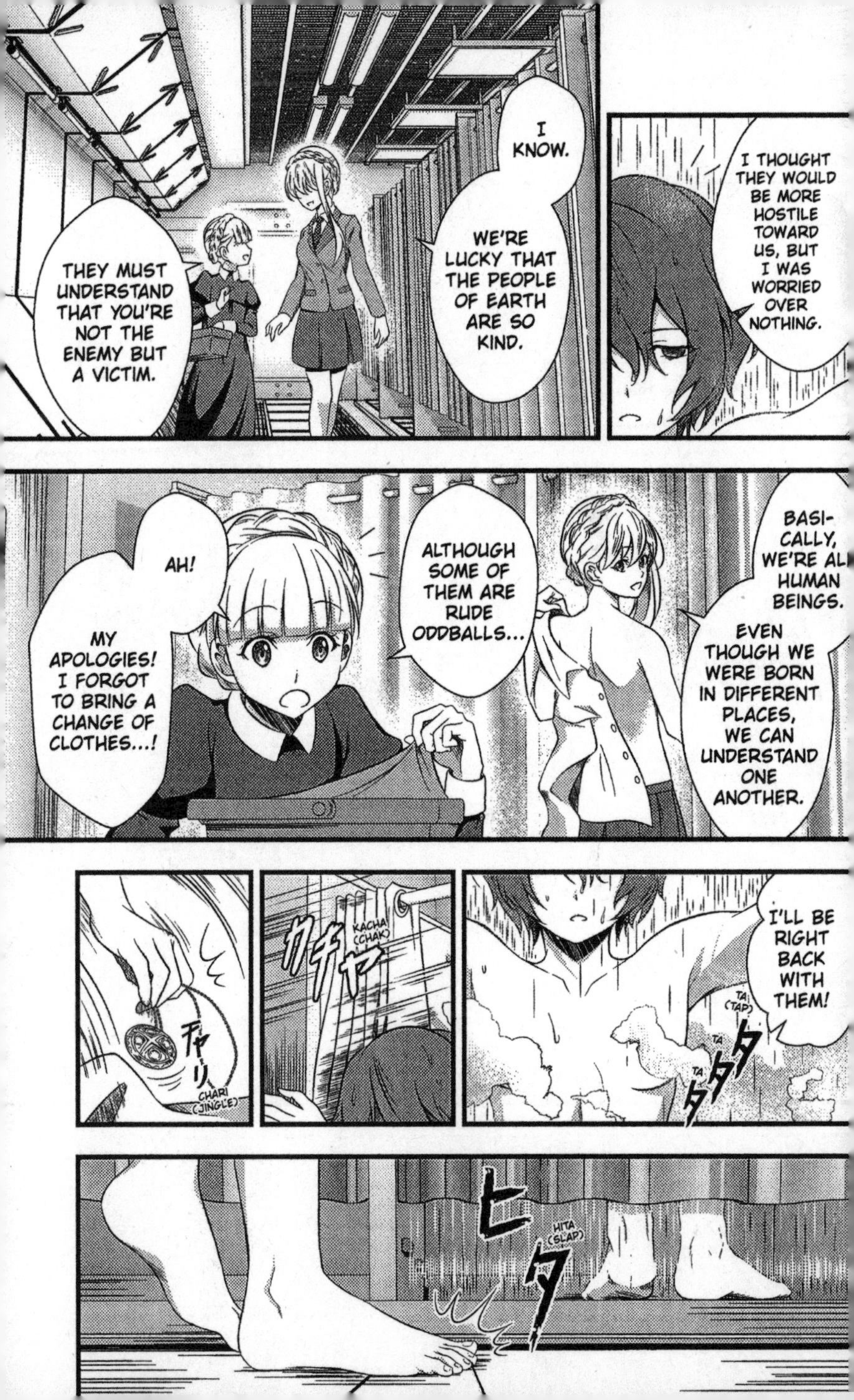
I THOUGHT THEY WOULD BE MORE HOSTILE TOWARD US, BUT I WAS WORRIED OVER NOTHING.
I KNOW.
WE'RE LUCKY THAT THE PEOPLE OF EARTH ARE SO KIND.
THEY MUST UNDERSTAND THAT YOU'RE NOT THE ENEMY BUT A VICTIM.
BASI-CALLY, WE'RE AL HUMAN BEINGS.
EVEN THOUGH WE WERE BORN IN DIFFERENT PLACES, WE CAN UNDERSTAND ONE ANOTHER.
ALTHOUGH SOME OF THEM ARE RUDE ODDBALLS...
AH!
MY APOLOGIES! I FORGOT TO BRING A CHANGE OF CLOTHES...!
I'LL BE RIGHT BACK WITH THEM!
タタタ
TA (TAP) TA TA
カチャ
KACHA (CHAK)
チャリ
CHARI (JINGLE)
ヒタ
HITA (SLAP)

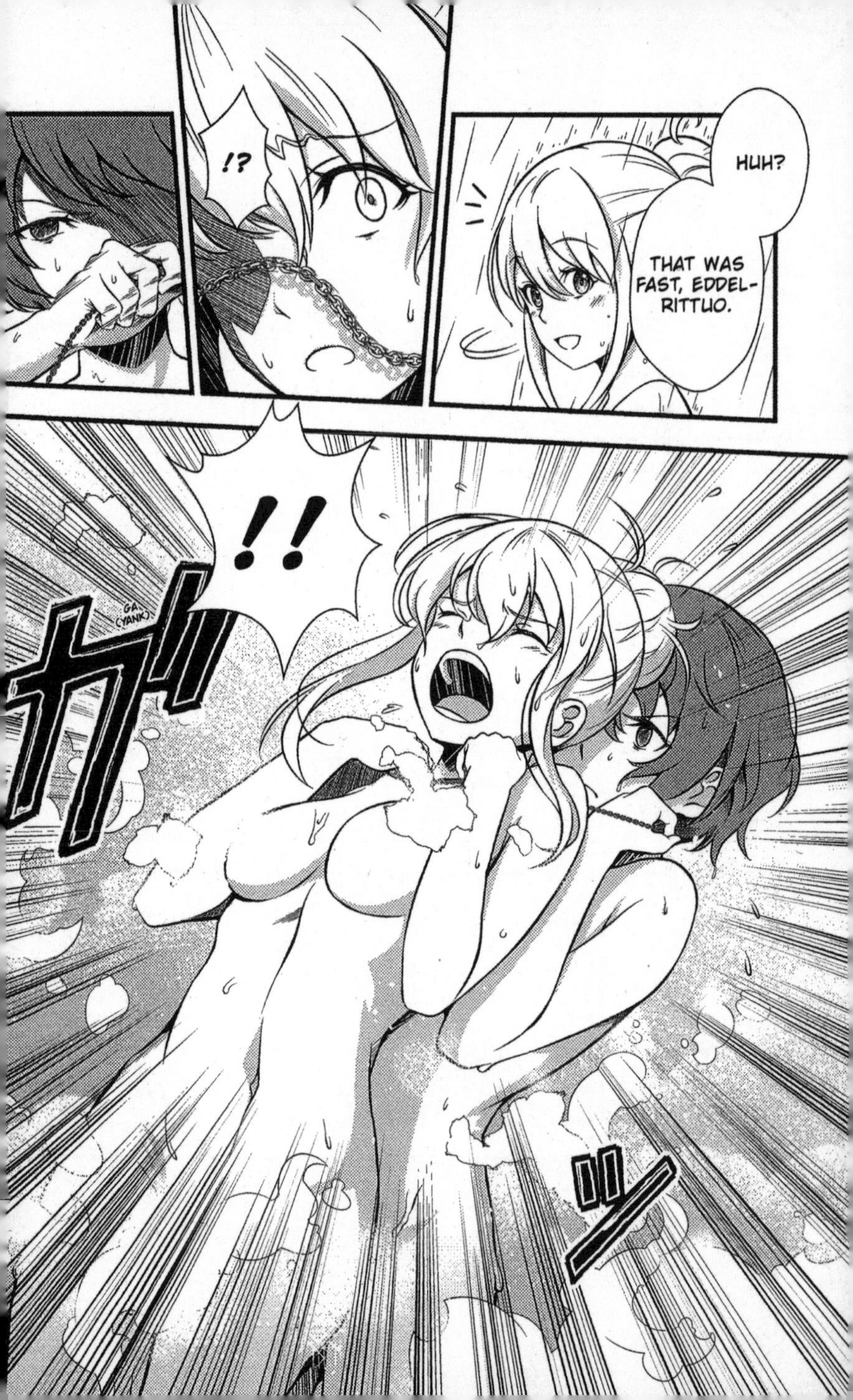
HUH?
THAT WAS FAST, EDDEL-RITTUO.
!?
!!
GA (YANK)

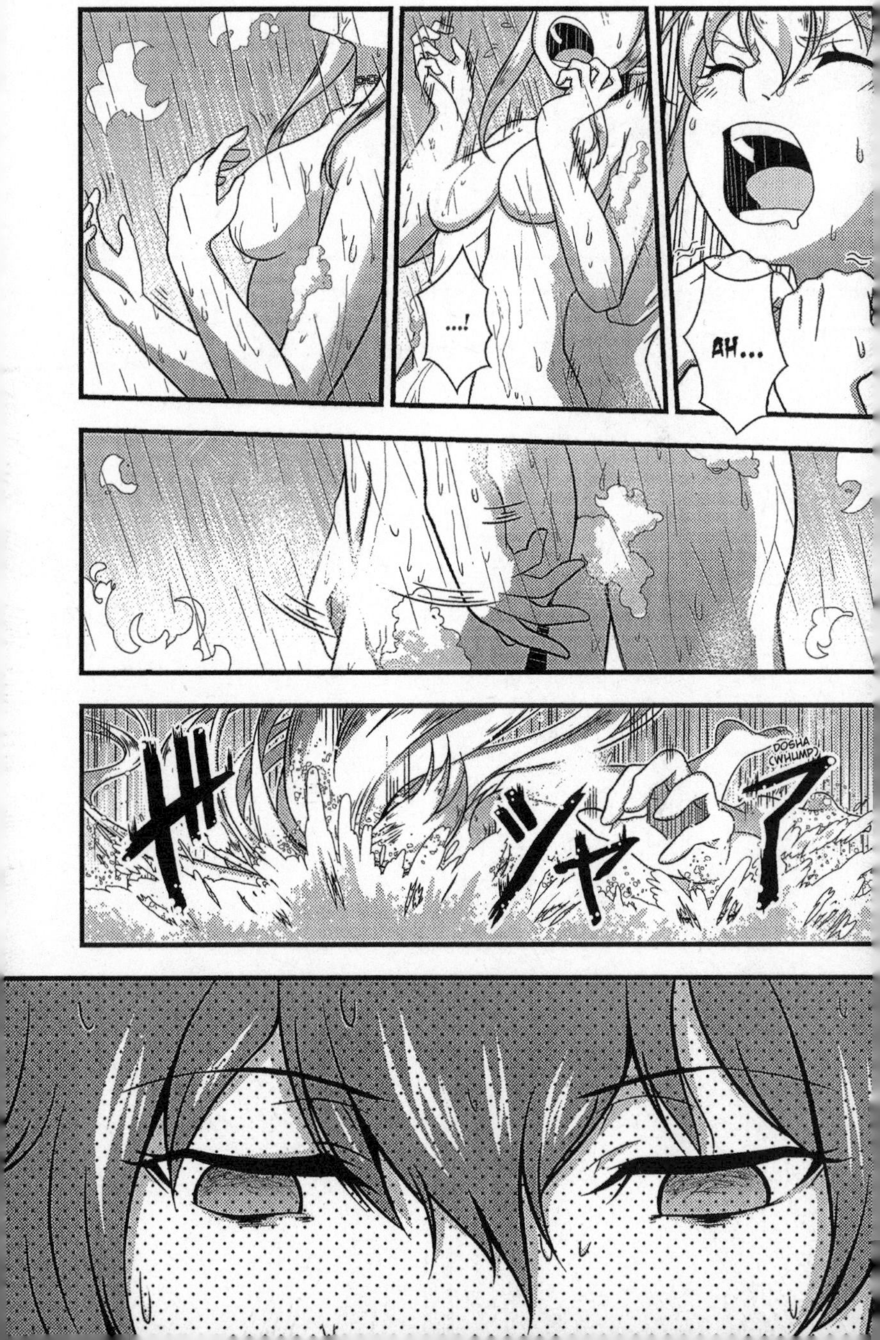
AH...
...!
DOSHA (WHUMP)

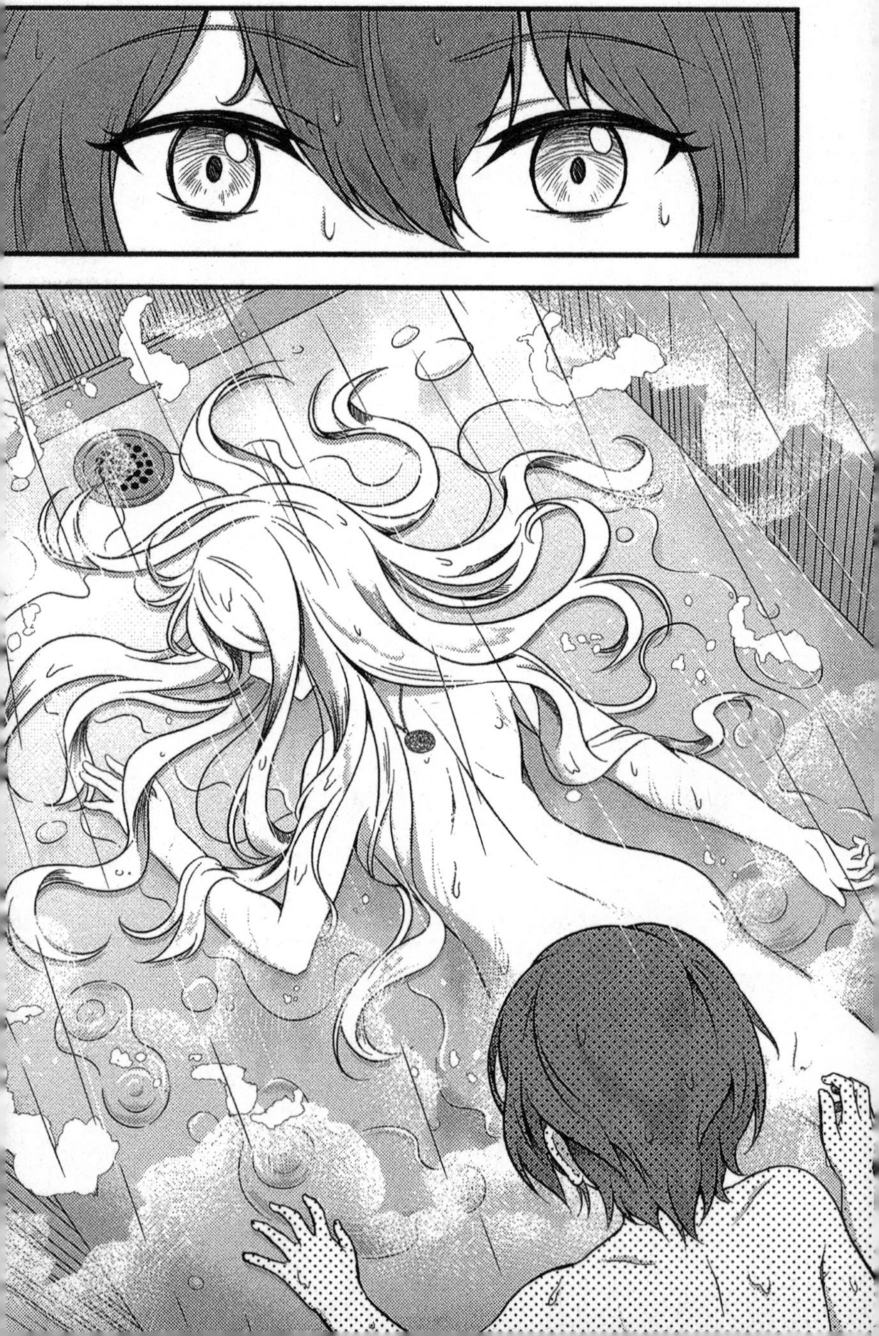

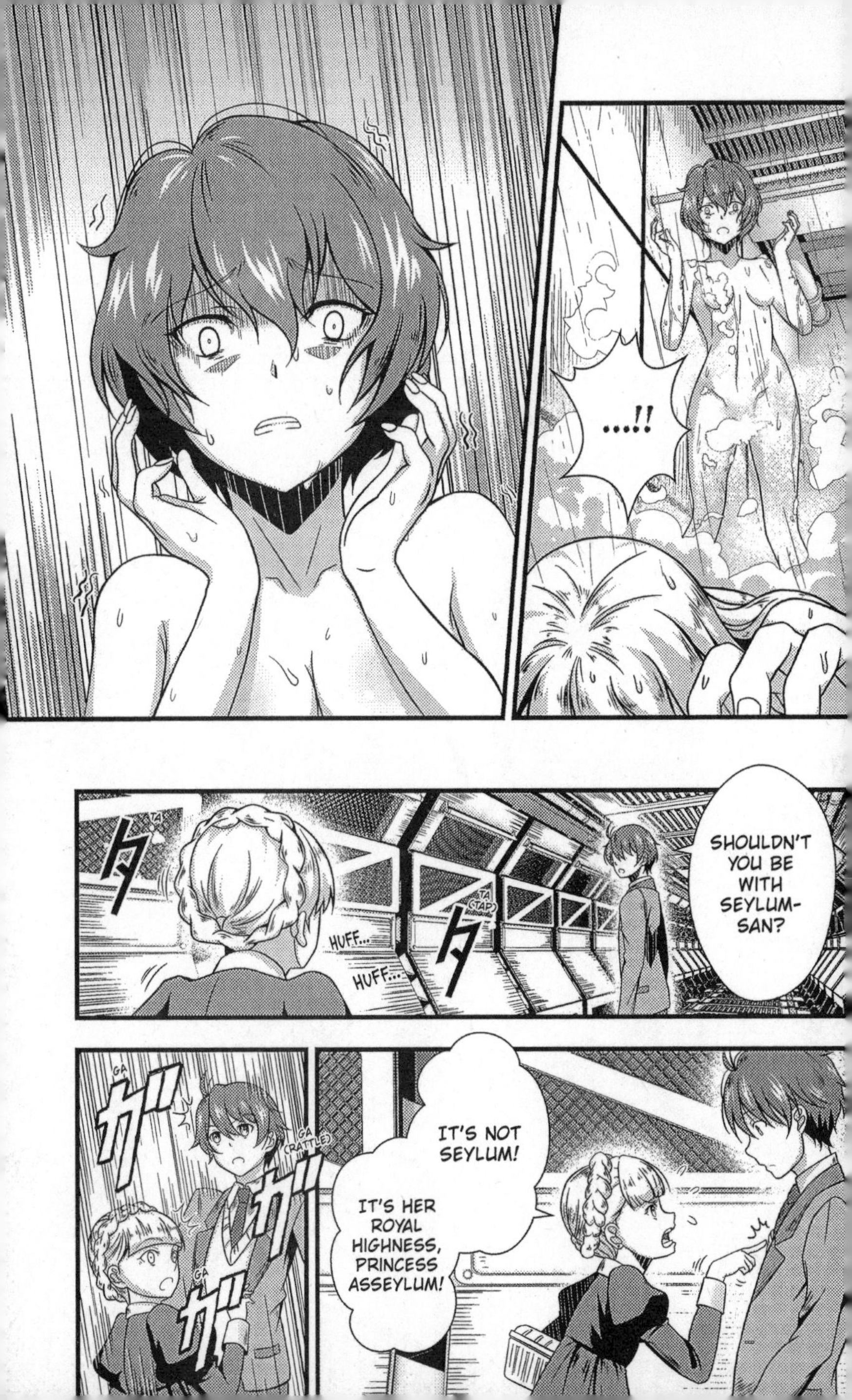
...!!
SHOULDN'T YOU BE WITH SEYLUM-SAN?
TA (TAP)
HUFF...
HUFF...
TA
IT'S NOT SEYLUM!
IT'S HER ROYAL HIGHNESS, PRINCESS ASSEYLUM!
GA (RATTLE)
GA
GA

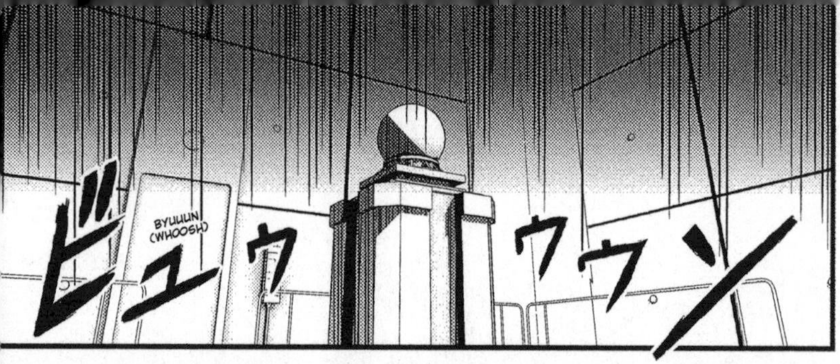
ビュウウウン
BYUUUN (WHOOSH)
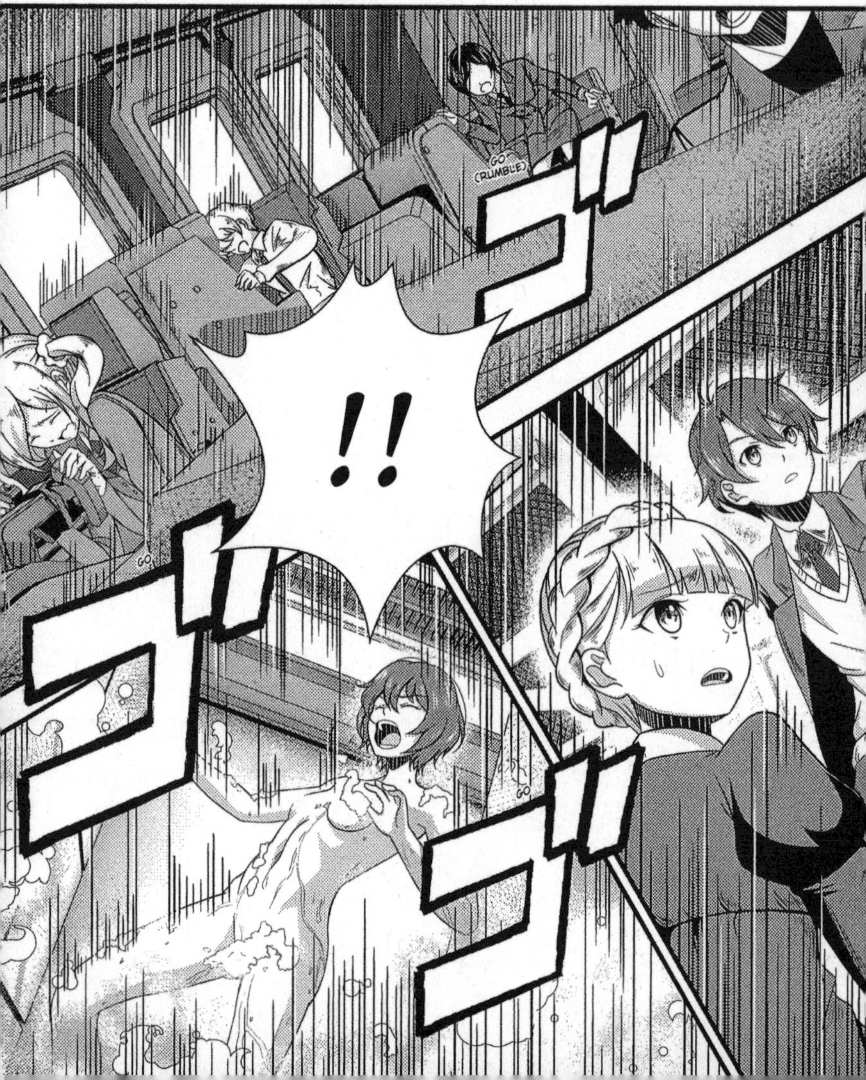
ゴゴゴ
GO (RUMBLE)
!!
GO
GO

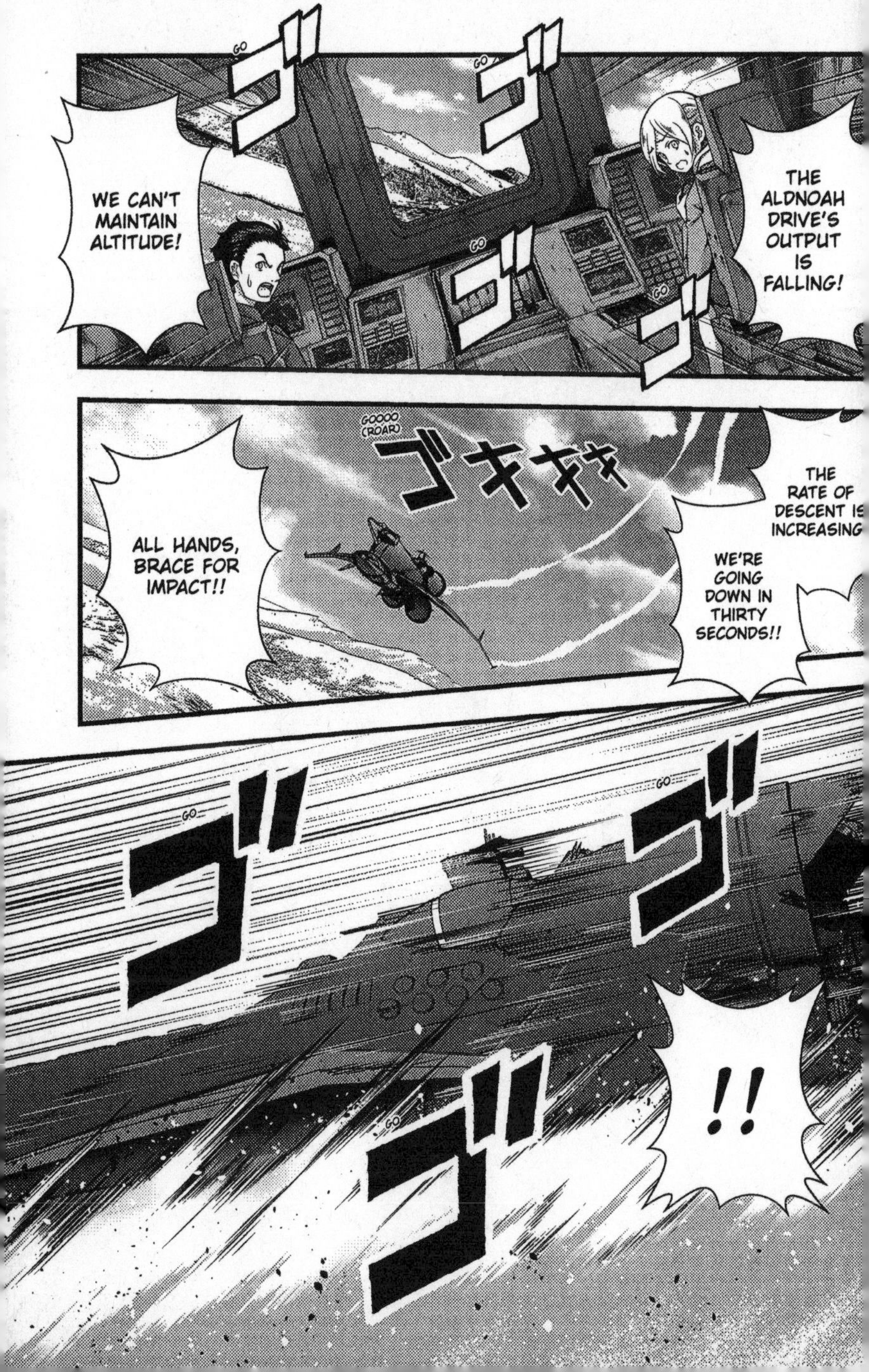
GO
GO
GO
GO
THE ALDNOAH DRIVE'S OUTPUT IS FALLING!
WE CAN'T MAINTAIN ALTITUDE!
THE RATE OF DESCENT IS INCREASING
WE'RE GOING DOWN IN THIRTY SECONDS!!
GOOOO (ROAR)
ALL HANDS, BRACE FOR IMPACT!!
GO
GO
!!
GO

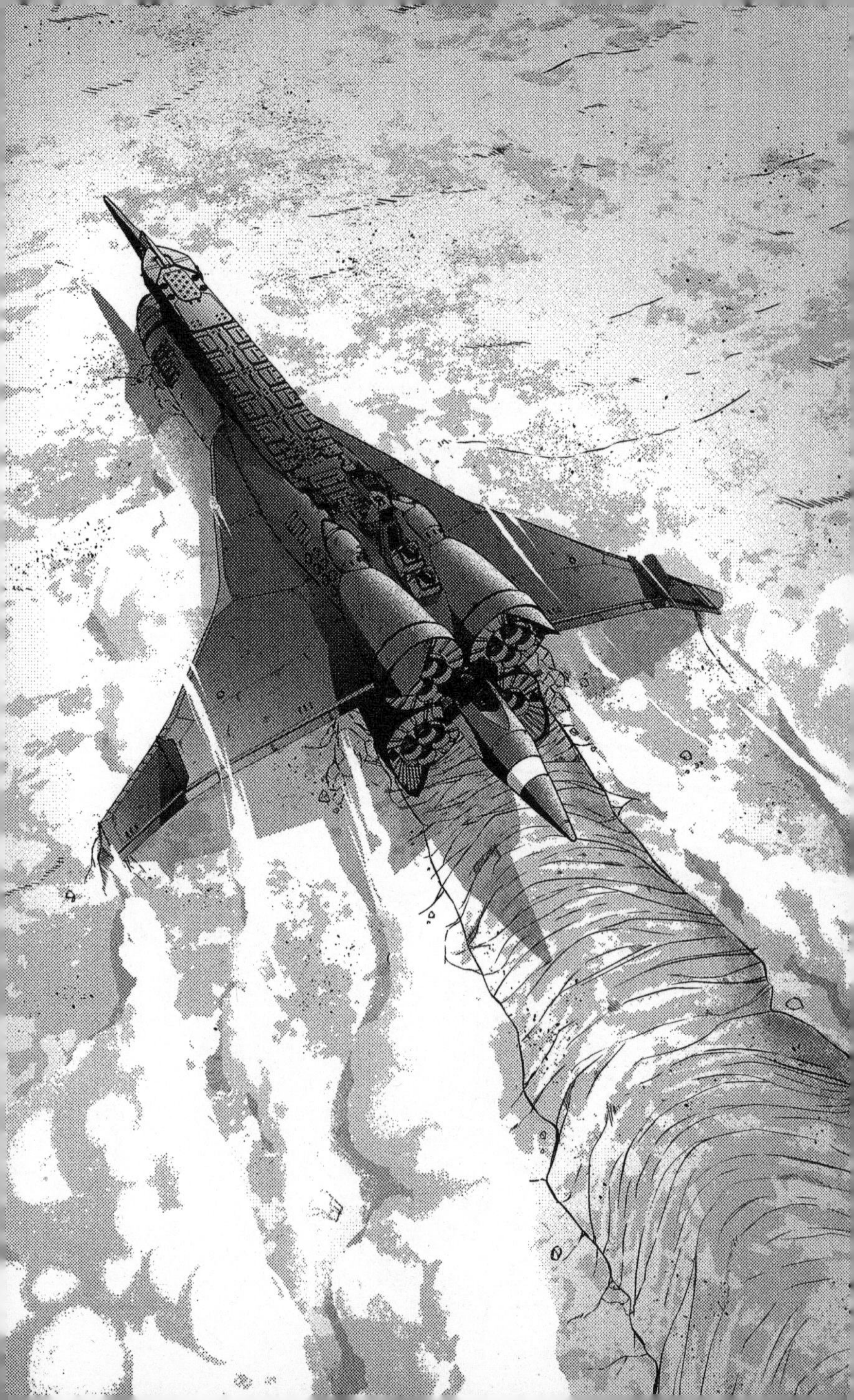

# ΛLDNOΛH
## .ZERO

To be continued in Volume 4!

# ALDNOAH.ZERO
## SEASON ONE ❸

OLYMPUS KNIGHTS
PINAKES

Translation: Sheldon Drzka

Lettering: Brndn Blakeslee

ALDNOAH.ZERO Vol. 3
© Olympus Knights/Aniplex · Project AZ. All rights reserved.
First published in Japan in 2015 by HOUBUNSHA CO., LTD., Tokyo. English translation rights in United States, Canada, and United Kingdom arranged with HOUBUNSHA CO., LTD. through Tuttle-Mori Agency, Inc., Tokyo.

Translation © 2016 by Hachette Book Group, Inc.

Yen Press
Hachette Book Group
1290 Avenue of the Americas
New York, NY 10104

www.hachettebookgroup.com
www.yenpress.com

Yen Press is an imprint of Hachette Book Group, Inc.
The Yen Press name and logo are trademarks of Hachette Book Group, Inc.

Library of Congress Control Number: 2016930996

First Yen Press Edition: May 2016

ISBN: 978-0-316-30982-0

10 9 8 7 6 5 4 3 2 1

BVG

Printed in the United States of America